Economics of Economy Pricing

Marin Muzhani

Series in Economics

VERNON PRESS

www.vernonpress.com

In the Americas:
Vernon Press
1000 N West Street, Suite 1200,
Wilmington, Delaware 19801
United States

In the rest of the world:
Vernon Press
C/Sancti Espiritu 17,
Malaga, 29006
Spain

Series in Economics

Library of Congress Control Number: 2023936060

ISBN: 978-1-64889-670-5

Cover design by Vernon Press using elements designed by kjpargeter / Freepik.

Table of Contents

List of Figures

List of Tables

Introduction

The economies of the western countries in the twenty-first century have already moved to a new level of mass production and technological progress as never seen before, at least not following a traditional Keynesian economy, thanks in part to globalization, advanced technologies, new organization management methods, and innovative supply chain strategies. A new phenomenon that has caught the attention of researchers and analysts is that a relatively large number of mass-produced commodities and services in western economies is somehow sold at discount price rather than the regular price at a much higher frequency than was ever seen before in a pre-pandemic world.

In a globalized world, the economies of advanced countries have entered a new phase called the "Economy Pricing System," where most of the mass commodities are sold at a discount price during certain periods of the year, called 'sales events,' due to decreased production costs thanks to enormous technological progress, implementation of advanced ERP systems in many medium and large corporations, high capital mobility, huge improvements in transportation and infrastructure, innovative global supply chain management and low commercial barriers. An increasing number of push and pull demand/supply strategies used for different mass-produced commodities have helped many economies stay on the economy pricing phase.

The proposed innovative book is indented to introduce new ideas and theories by challenging the current modern foundations of micro and macroeconomics theories. In fact, the challenges at the microeconomic level are more focused on the standard theory of the firm and profitability in all its aspects, such as cost function, production possibility frontier, isocost lines, marginalism, etc., and at a macroeconomic level, the challenges are more directed to inflation theory, monetary policy, interest rate theory, the role of the central bank, the IS-LM model, the aggregate demand and aggregate supply curves, and the new role of sovereign government debt.

Most of the industrialized countries, in addition to low prices, have had record low inflation (except for the global pandemic years of 2020-2023 and the war in Ukraine of 2022-2023), low-interest rates (especially after the 2008 financial crisis), low growth rates and record low unemployment rates. The decline of interest rates close to zero level during the 2008 global financial crisis and afterward, creating the perfect conditions for cheap money for the mass of borrowers, has "sealed the fate" of the economies of industrialized countries to reach a phase that we normally call the "economy pricing system" or simple "economy pricing" characterized by low inflation, low-interest rates, low growth rates, low unemployment rate, mass production and demand-push strategies into customers for a large assortment of non-premium products.

By looking at the microeconomic level, we have that competitive firms use different pricing and marketing strategies to offer customers a variety of multi-products classified as premium and non-premium. The introduction of premium and non-premium commodities concept is the core of the economy pricing, which make the firm survive in a very competitive environment. A viable multiproduct firm producing both premium and non-premium commodities will charge a higher price for premium products sold to consumers with a less elastic demand (market niche) and offer discounts for non-premium products to the majority of customers whose demand is more elastic during different sales events all year around. A characteristic of economy pricing is that by using the push-demand-to-customers strategy, reaching the maximum profit is not the firm's main objective. The firm's main objective is to hold the market share by reaching the desired sales target, which does not always equal maximizing profit for every unit sold. It guarantees a net monetary position (NMP) greater than one and a reasonable desired profit which is a key parameter for many firms operating in economy pricing.

The introduction of production capacity utilization for a given firm is another microeconomic metric of the economy pricing system. Lower capacity utilization for firms selling non-premium products is viewed as a bad sign of the economy's health. Instead, higher capacity utilization selling substantial volumes of non-premium products above the trend rate is a leading indicator of a healthy economy pricing system. For a manufacturer, the higher the unutilized production capacity, the higher the number of sales promotions offered on non-premium products and, eventually, premium goods to break even and start making a coherent profit.

The marginalist approach analysis says that a necessary condition for profit to be maximized is when the firm sets its quantity so that the difference between the firm's marginal revenue and its cost equals zero or when marginal revenue equals its marginal cost. However, the new *competitive pricing approach* based on the economy pricing system puts a different perspective on a multi-product firm that manufactures and sells a combination of premium and non-premium products to help reach a positive net monetary position (NMP) and hit the desired target profit as required by management.

At the macroeconomic level, it's interesting to analyze how monetary policy is managed in an economy pricing system dominated by low inflation, low-interest rates, and low unemployment rates. This economy is also characterized by competition, where firms bring to different market categories of premium and non-premium products to stay competitive and control costs through global supply chain management. A fascinating topic to discuss is how monetary policy works when inflation, interest rates, and unemployment rates are kept low in an economy characterized by a high level of competition in different sectors. There is also a relationship between monetary policy and low-interest rates. The low inflation is the result of competitive prices, which is mostly determined by globally managing the supply chain, which allows companies to be able to cut excess cost and deliver products to final consumers much faster and cheaper (with the exception of the global supply chain disruption during pandemic years of 2020-23).

Another area to be analyzed at the macroeconomic level is central bank independence. Due to the low-interest rate environment in the last two decades, the monetary tools used by Central Bank to operate during the financial crisis have been reduced further. Therefore, it is suggested to have a more transparent process controlled by administrative orders between treasury departments and central banks. The main idea is to reduce the independent role of the central bank and eliminate central banks' ties to large financial corporations. The new process of administrative orders between the treasury department and central banks is supposed to allow voters and stakeholders to exercise greater control over central banks' monetary policies in different countries by allowing central banks to collaborate with governments under the control of a democratic and transparent process.

The aggregate demand in an economy pricing system is another subject taken into consideration in this book. Based on our analysis and using a different concept, we'll try to explain how the global aggregate demand for an economy should be split between the aggregate demand for the private sector, public sector, and import-export sector. The interesting point is that on one side, the aggregate demand in the private sector could be measured as the total demand for all finished goods, premium and non-premium, manufactured and commercialized in different sectors of the economy. On the other side, for the aggregate supply in the private sector, we need to consider a new concept that takes into consideration the aggregate production capacity utilization of firms offering premium and non-premium products in different sectors.

This book provides a detailed analysis of the economic implications of the business strategy known as economy pricing by insightfully and efficiently connecting important concepts in business administration, finance, and economics.

The new Economy Pricing System theories introduced in this volume are written to challenge microeconomics and macroeconomics foundations and update their theories in a new economic reality of the twenty-first century dominated by low-interest rates, low inflation rates, low growth rates, and low unemployment rates. The main scope of this book is to analyze how the micro and macroeconomic events are interconnected in a globalized economy pricing system. The global COVID-19 pandemic and the war in Ukraine during 2020-2023 have disrupted the global chain supply and sharply increased the price of commodities and inflation. However, the principles and concepts of an economy pricing system remain pretty much the same in the long run, where the economies of industrialized countries converge to the trend of having low-interest rates, low inflation, low growth rates, and low unemployment rates.

Structure of the book

The introduction part of this work motivates the study and brings out some definitions and objectives of economy pricing. The book is composed of two parts and six chapters, three chapters for each part. The first three chapters in part one discuss the microeconomics of the economy pricing system, and the last three chapters in part two focus on the macroeconomics of economy pricing.

Chapter One outlines economy pricing, competition, pricing strategies, mass production, and economies of scale. The chapter will start by discussing the microeconomics of the pricing strategies in economy pricing. Economy pricing is extensively used in supermarkets and superstores, especially in the retail food business for groceries, and is based on the idea that a high anchor price being reduced by an impressive discount price would create a high perceived value to push consumers to buy as much as they can afford. This will lead to the new microeconomic model of the Three-levels of demand-push and Cost Approach in economy pricing.

Chapter Two considers the firm's theory in an economy pricing system. This chapter will discuss the concept of production and cost from an economy pricing perspective. By using the volume-based analysis, there is the introduction of a New Theory of the Firm in Product-Mix Profitability. This chapter will introduce the microeconomics techniques of a new Competitive Production Function Model and Behavioral Relationships approach based on economy pricing. A firm can use different levels of technologies to produce output by using a variety of input vectors, which different sets of production functions can summarize. This will lead to the introduction of a new cost function model in the Competitive Product-Mix associated with the Isocost lines approach.

Chapter Three talks about how the pricing strategy is influenced by several factors that might be beyond the firm's control. Here will be discussed how a firm adopting price discrimination strategies can reach different objectives. From an organization's perspective, price discrimination can offer many advantages based on the size of the company. An interesting argument will be to explore the revolutionary path from marginalism to competitive pricing by introducing the *Price Competition Approach* to explain *Marginal Cost Approach.*

Chapter Four considers how inflation, interest rates, and unemployment rates work at the macro level in an economy pricing system dominated by competition and characterized by different categories of non-premium products in almost all sectors of the economy. This chapter will explain how inflation is determined and what are the causes of inflation.

Chapter Five treats how monetary policy works when inflation, interest rates, and unemployment rates are kept low in an economy pricing characterized by a high level of competition between firms. The chapter will discuss the relationship between money growth and inflation. It will consider the *Quantity Theory of Money* (QTM) and the optimum quantity of money as proposed by Friedman in the 1960s and how this theory has evolved in the last decades.

Chapter Six discusses public debt and fiscal policy. There is a debate about whether a government uses its debt-raising capacity cautiously, which depends on its ability to render the borrowed money into economic growth without raising inflation. The growth in government spending and debt has been seen by some economists as a welcome policy to stimulate growth and finance infrastructures thanks to the borrowing costs that have been at historic lows since the global financial crisis of 2008. This chapter will talk about some criticism of aggregate demand and curve supply and introduce a new approach to aggregate demand and aggregate supply based on economy pricing concepts.

PART I:
The Microeconomics of Economy Pricing System

Chapter 1
Competition and Pricing Strategies

Introduction

This chapter will outline economy pricing, competition, pricing strategies, mass production, and economies of scale. The chapter will start off by discussing the pricing strategies in economy pricing. Economy pricing is extensively used in supermarkets and superstores, especially in the retail food business for groceries, and is based on the idea that a high anchor price being reduced by a special discount would create a high perceived value to push a consumer to buy as much as they can effortlessly.

Later in the chapter, we will discuss the importance of the *Net Monetary Position (NMP)* concept for a firm operating in an economy pricing environment. Further, we will discuss current ratios and the cost approach in economy pricing. We will see how a firm will maximize the value of the company by maximizing the Net Monetary Position during a fiscal period by using a combination of different pricing strategies for its premium and non-premium products.

This chapter will discuss in more detail the Push versus Pull strategies widely used in marketing, logistics, and supply chain management. The difference between push and pull terms used in marketing lies in how the companies approach different categories of consumers to sell their products. Later we will try to explain the three-levels of push demand where large discount superstores use the strategy of putting considerable pressure on their suppliers to keep the price down so they can give more discounts to final customers to remain competitive and have a stable net monetary position.

Another topic will be the mass-production and economies of scale. The economies of scale used in mass production reduce the average costs attributable to production as volume increases. The firms seeking to become dominant and competitive in the market are continuously looking for product improvement and achieve economies of scale

Economy Pricing and Pricing Strategies

Generally speaking, economy pricing' in economics is a method of pricing in which a low price is assigned to a product with decreased production cost. It is a valuation technique that assigns a low price to selected products during a certain period. Economy pricing is extensively used in supermarkets and superstores, especially in the retail food business for groceries such as canned, dairy, produced, and frozen goods sold under generic food brands where marketing and production costs to bring these products to selling points (supermarkets) have been kept to a minimum.

Economy pricing is based on the idea that a high price being reduced by an impressive discount price would create a sense of urgency and high perceived value to push a consumer to purchase. Modern economy pricing is a dynamic mixture of supermarkets, hypermarkets, superstores, membership marts, and convenience stores. Of these, the most important is the supermarket, introduced in the 1930s in North America. The supermarkets have grown from limited-size stores to very large-sized stores that offer consumers everything from food, non-food, garments for all ages and genders, small appliances, electronics, furniture, big appliances, and different kind of services such as coffee shops, pharmacies, photography, fast foods, etc. inside their retail center.

The supermarkets and hypermarkets offer thousands of items for sale. In 1965, the standard North American supermarket would offer between 4000 to 6000 items for sale, and in the 1990s, most of the new supermarket openings would offer between 15 000 to 18 000 items for sale. Two decades later, in the twenty-first century, the new supermarkets would offer between 25 000 to 30 000 items for sale supplied by giant distribution centers. The dominant position of supermarkets was challenged by the introduction of hypermarkets and membership marts that deal in a large assortment of food and non-food items, frequently in a warehouse store format. Most of the stream of food and non-food products flowing to supermarkets is manufactured by large industrial firms with highly sophisticated marketing strategies.

The main strategy of supermarkets has been to be price competitive, although they do so in different ways and to different degrees. The pricing pattern in a supermarket is also determined by a selection of promotional strategies and discount coupons offered by food and non-food manufacturers designed to pull the flow of products through supermarkets. The growth of supermarkets in size and the diversification to warehouse-store-format strategy results from vast expansion in the sale of foods, non-foods, and durable commodities. The "crossover" connecting foods, non-foods, and durable commodities in the activities of superstores being opened nowadays by discount chains has increased all categories of sales, giving consumers a lower price while increasing margins and profits for supermarkets.

Superstores use at least three types of general pricing strategies to attract customers. The first strategy is classic profit maximization, where supermarkets ignore market share for a certain product or group of products and try to work out a price that maximizes their profit. In this theory, this price occurs where MR=MC (marginal revenue= marginal cost). The second strategy, called sales maximization, consists of maximizing sales while trying to make a normal profit. This strategy works well if the selling price equals the average cost. The third strategy is to gain market share, where firms have a target to increase market share that could involve setting prices as low as they can afford, barely covering the variable and fixed costs, eventually leading to a price war.

There are several pricing strategies to attract customers and, at the same to, maximize profit. Some of them are listed as follows:

- **Premium pricing**. It is a pricing strategy when a company decides to make a commodity more expensive than the rest of its other products to try and give the impression that it is better quality, e.g., fashion labels, etc.
- **Loss Leaders**. This strategy involves setting a low price on some products to lure customers into the store. Hopefully, they will also buy other, more expensive goods (the firm is not allowed to sell goods below cost as it is illegal in many Western countries).
- **Price Discrimination** is a strategy that encompasses charging a different price to a different group of consumers to take advantage of different elasticities of demand.
- **Reference Pricing Strategy** consists of setting an artificially high price to be able to offer discounts on earlier advertised prices later to lure customers into buying the product.
- **Price matching** is another strategy that promises customers to match any price cuts by your competitors. This price policy will discourage competitors from cutting prices because the response will be immediate. It will also discourage price wars and give the impression of being competitive.
- **Retail Price Mechanism** (RPM) strategy is a pricing strategy in which manufacturers set a minimum price for retailers, and then retailers can adjust their price consequently (e.g., netbook agreement).
- **Psychological pricing strategy** is a strategy that consists of setting the price at important psychological levels to generate a purchase. For example, selling goods at $99.99 to make them appear cheaper could trigger the customer's desire to buy the good, thinking it's less than $100.0.

- **Premium decoy pricing strategy**, where a firm sets the price of one's commodity intentionally high to encourage demand for a lower price. For example, in the furniture industry, a company may bring out top-of-the-range furniture or mattress, which is very expensive and high quality, to make the general brand more attractive and affordable.
- **A bundle pricing strategy** is when a firm gives special offers to customers, such as buying one and getting the second item at a 50% discount or buying two items and getting the third one for free.
- **Price skimming** is another pricing strategy when a firm charges a higher price when a new product is released because it has a substantial competitive advantage. By charging a higher price, the company takes advantage of those consumers with inelastic demand. But the higher price will attract new competitors into the market, and as a consequence, the price certainly falls due to increased supply. The reduced price will attract those customers with more price elastic demand, and the product will become a mass-consuming commodity manufactured by different suppliers.
- **Penetration pricing** is a very used pricing strategy to attract customers. The price charged for products and services is set low to help establish market share. Once this objective is achieved, the price increases and the product will have a better profit margin. For example, satellite or cable companies offer introductory offers to new customers for a few months at a low price, then increase the price after the offer has expired.
- **Optional pricing** is an alternative pricing strategy to attract customers. It consists of increasing the price when the customer starts to add extras. For example, when a firm sells new mobile phones, it will add an extra service, such as an internet package, and increase the price of the mobile device.
- **Dynamic pricing** is another pricing strategy very effective in attracting customers. Here, the prices are regularly updated in response to fluctuating market conditions. For example, if an airline receives high demand for certain routes, it will increase the price of these routes and keep the price low for other low-demand flights, maximizing the revenue from high-demand flights.

Other pricing strategies help consolidate the market share, listed as follows:

- **Limit pricing** occurs when a monopoly sets a price lower than profit maximization to discourage new entries in the market. It allows the company to make a substantial profit while keeping the price low enough to dissuade new firms from entering the market.

- **Predatory pricing** happens when a firm puts the selling price below the marginal cost to force the rivals out of business. Predatory pricing is illegal in North America, but big corporations can use cross-subsidies. Cross subsidies occur when a big corporation uses the profits from one area to subsidize a price in another area and sell the product very competitively, keeping rival companies off the market.

A few pricing strategies used in economics and business management literature help determine the price. At least four of them are the most used ones:

- The first one is called *Average Cost Pricing,* which consists of the firm setting the price equal to the average cost plus a certain profit margin.
- *Mark-up pricing,* a firm sets the price of its products/services equal to the marginal cost of production plus the profit margin a firm wants to make on each sale.
- *In profit maximization,* a firm sets the price and quantity, so the marginal revenue of the product is equal to its marginal cost.
- *Market-based pricing,* firms set a price depending on supply and demand. For example, suppose the musical show companies use market-based pricing. In that case, they will increase the ticket price if thirty percent of tickets are sold out, suggesting the price is below the equilibrium.

Regarding the importance of elasticity, it is essential to know that if demand for certain products is highly elastic, then cutting prices should increase revenue. Meanwhile, increasing prices will lead to a fall in revenue. When the demand is inelastic, a price increase will lead to increased profits.

The firm type and business determine the optimal pricing strategy. If a firm produces a premium brand only, reducing the price would be considered not wise, as it will lose the brand image unless the price is reduced only during certain sales events. For other firms that produce mass consumption goods, they might offer competitive pricing through strategies such as penetration pricing as they can gain market share. In addition, during special sales events, these firms can offer further discounts, so they get well positioned in the market.

What are sales events? A sales event or promotion is an occasion, which is normally brief, for buying at specially reduced prices. There are sales held to reduce inventory or planned sales during the year, such as weekends or long weekends that help sell or "push" commodities at reduced prices into customers. The sales event differs from the Penetration Pricing strategy as it is a planned and short promotion lasting a few days with a remarkable amount of advertising. In addition to these planned sales, there are regular sales events such as Black Friday, Boxing Day, Christmas, Year-end, Long-weekend Labor Day, etc.

In an economy pricing system, everything gets sold at a discounted price: from food, clothes, shoes, bags, bicycles, computers, TVs, cellphones, fridges, dishwashers, washing machines, furniture, mattresses, sofas to cars, trucks, gold rings, gold jewelry, even business jets, and passenger planes.

Premium and Non-Premium Products in a Competitive Economy

In an economy pricing system dominated by competitive markets in different sectors, we will talk a lot about premium and non-premium products. Therefore, in this section, we will try to explain the difference between these two categories of products. Premium products are those high-quality products that have an emotional resonance with consumers, which are related primarily to self-esteem and perceptions/status. Buying premium products make consumers feel good and confident and shows other people that they have good taste, have knowledge of the product, and are (eventually) successful. A premium product can also command a price higher than other products and its competitors in the long run. The term premium could also refer to a segment of a company's brands that transmit an imaginary perception value in the upper mid-to-high price range. This marketing strategy is planned to exploit the propensity of consumers to think that expensive items enjoy an exceptional reputation or represent exceptional quality and distinction.

Price alone does not make a brand achieve premium status. It is mostly the high manufactured quality, durability and robustness, quality design, brand experience, packaging, customer service, and all the expectations that achieve a high price point set. If the brand is designed to meet or exceed consumer expectations for a certain period, then the brand generates premium equity. The general definition of brand equity is that a firm creates a value premium generated from a product with a recognizable name compared to a generic equivalent. Companies use different strategies to create brand equity for their products by making them unique, easily recognizable, and superior in quality and reliability. It is also true that premium equity does not come easily for every brand. Normally, the premium equity will come because of years of research and product development, making hard choices, and investing substantial capital. For a brand to reach, premium equity means to refuse to compromise on quality, high manufacturing standards, and design when competitors have surrendered to lowering their standards.

The logic of bringing premium brands into the market is that they are designed to bear an imprint of exclusively or rarity, especially in the mass markets, and distinguish them from general products. Targeted customer groups can be average or high income which are premium-aware and is not looking for bargains or saving money on products. Their high disposable income helps them pay top money for premium brands to own them fully. Quite often, established companies in the market will invent different brands (or sub-brands) to differentiate their product lines into a premium brand and a general or non-premium brand (e.g., Toyota with their premium Lexus brand).

The premium brand has at least three basic components based on customers' preferences and their effect on an organization: consumer perception, negative or positive effects, and the resulting value. In the consumer perception component, the customer interacts with the brand by having both knowledge and experience with it and its products. A consumer's perception of the premium brand directly results in either positive or negative effects. If the premium-brand equity positively affects customers, the organization, its products, and its financials will benefit by increasing the company's profit. Generally speaking, a premium brand should always have positive effects on customers as it attaches a level of quality to a brand, which customers perceive as being worth more than other products made by competitors, so they are willing to pay more.

The organization will suffer from low revenue and profit if the premium-brand equity negatively affects customers. In addition, the negative effects on customers will convert a premium brand to a non-premium brand which will be sold at a lower price bringing in less revenue and profit to the company. However, suppose a company converts an ex-premium-brand to a non-premium and starts mass-producing it, targeting a lower price range that most low-income customers can afford to buy. In that case, a combination of high sales volumes and lower production costs due to mass production will increase revenue and profit margins. Also, moving to a new sub-brand will allow a company to move into a new category of products, claim a new segment, or target a new audience. Hence, a company can tailor its products to meet the needs of a specific set of consumers and launch itself into a new market.

In a competitive economy, numerous companies produce and sell various products with vertically differentiated brands at different price points. For example, in the automotive market, premium brands such as Cadillac, Lincoln (Limousine), Buick, and Mercedes, place themselves above non-premium brands such as Kia, Hyundai, or Skoda. Vertical brand differentiation can be seen in several marketing decision areas, such as price, channel, and product design. Premium brands are regularly higher priced, retailed through more exclusive channels, and better designed than non-premium brands.

Non-premium brands are normally referred to as those products that highlight other elements and characteristics, such as price discounts, affordability, and reliability, which tend to be more important for value-conscious consumers and are offered at different low and medium price ranges. They are also offered at different discounts during sales events all year around, from Black Friday to Christmas, Boxing Day to New Year, and from Easter weekend to Labor Day long weekend, etc.

Different ranges of product pricing, quality ratings, and market share may impact the utility and attitude of consumers toward non-premium products versus premium products. Product characteristics are important to determine the suitability between what has been advertised and the product's real qualities, influencing the prospect of persuading knowledge and the persuasiveness of advertising for non-premium products.

Price and quality ratings can help consumers create their utility 'function' and influence how consumers perceive the quality of a product. Based on common knowledge of the non-premium product, consumers use price to assess the product's overall quality when objective quality is difficult to assess. In addition, consumers use online product reviews, brand names, physical appearance, advertising signals, and retailer reputation as indications of product quality to assess the quality of non-premium products. There is a large amount of literature on research and marketing on how consumers deal with product quality. Quite a few marketing research papers, such as Dawar and Parker, 1994; Kirmani and Rao, 2000; Milgron and Roberts 1986, Basuroy, Chatterjee, and Ravid, 2003; Floyd, Freling R., Alhoqail, Cho, and Freling T., 2014; etc., explain in detail how consumers have different methods and ways to assess the objective quality of different categories of non-premium products. Higher price and high-quality rating products, such as premium products, are more accessible for consumers with higher incomes; hence, these products can better communicate social status and prestige. Lower price and medium-low or unknown quality ratings products, such as non-premium products, are more affordable for consumers with lower-medium incomes, thus better communicating a more common-general social status in the society and no prestige. Premium and non-premium products have different properties that differentiate them from each other, as listed below:

Category of Premium Products – properties	**Category of non-premium products – properties**
Produced in limited quantities. High manufactured quality, high durability and robustness, high-quality design with unique features. Exceed government standards in all aspects.	Mass-production volumes, standard durability, and standard design. No special features. Meet regular or minimum government standards.
High brand experience, exclusive packaging, and professional customer service.	Regular or standard experience. Standard packaging and regular customer service.
Much higher price than non-premium products	Much lower prices than premium products and Price discounts
Emotional resonance with consumers relates primarily to self-esteem and perceptions/status. Communicate social status and prestige.	No emotional tone, no self-esteem and no prestige. Common-general social status
Unique brand name and well-known to the public.	Generic brands or no name. Some are known, and some are not known to the public.
No discounts offered, or rarely offered discounts during sales events.	Discounts offered continuously, especially during sales events.
Produced for high-income earners consumption.	Produced for low-income and middle-income mass-consumption.
Very profitable products due to much less competition and niche market.	Less profitable products due to high competition and open market with low barriers.
Value premium equity generated from premium brand	Generic brand equivalent
Retailed through more exclusive channels.	Retailed through common channels.

Many established companies will produce a mix of both categories of brands, premium and non-premium so that they can serve both markets, the niche market and general-mass market, and have a more stable flow of revenue from all brands (including under-performing brands). For example, in the automotive industry, Ford Corporation produces both brands of vehicles, mass-production non-premium known brands such as Ford Edge, Ford Escape, Ford EcoSport, Ford Mustang, etc., and Lincoln, which is a luxury vehicle to serve a niche market. General Motors, another American leader in the automobile industry, manufactures mass-production non-premium and semi-premium known brands such as Chevrolet, Buick, and GMC, and Cadillac, a luxury premium car brand to serve a unique segment of the automotive market. The manufacturer of electric vehicles, Tesla Inc., started with a clear strategy first to produce high-price, premium low-volume vehicles, such as sports cars (like *Tesla Model X*), for which customers were less sensitive to price. This helped the company gradually bring down the cost of batteries, which allowed them later to offer low-price non-premium high-volume cars to customers sensitive to price, such as the *Tesla Model 3*, to increase the market share. This amplified the number of cars delivered to customers from 245 200 in 2018 to 1 313 581 in 2022, where

10-20% of units sold were coming from premium cars and 80-90% from non-premium cars. This helped increase the EV segment of the market share substantially for Tesla Inc. in the U.S.

Marketing Strategy of Sales Events

In marketing science, a sales event is the occasion of a sale (normally brief) for buying at specially reduced prices. Sales events are very vital to the world of marketing and business. Sales events are critical to companies' success and help customers have a better understanding of the products and services offered. The sales events process begins with careful strategic planning involving several players, such as organizers of the venue, suppliers of goods, marketing channels, and advertising strategies to attract a large number of customers. Each sales event is critical to the event's success. Every successful event is the result of assiduous and timely planning and preparation. For successful sales, the event is important to consider the target audience, the demographic or group of people participating, and the event's content.

An effective marketing method to connect with customers is event marketing. Event marketing is part of sales events and describes developing a presentation to promote a product, service, theme exhibit, display, or in-person engagement with customers. Event marketing can be designed to occur online or offline and can be hosted, participated in, or sponsored as a method of engagement. This marketing strategy is designed to give potential customers a unique interaction with the company and the company's values and perspectives.

Sales events are strategically designed to help a company in different ways, such as the brand presence or generate leads, channel value, new opportunities, promotion of different non-premium and premium products, and increase customer satisfaction, retention, and engagement. Promoting sales events raises alertness about the event and the brand we are trying to market. The sales event, in general, helps reach potential customers unfamiliar with the company and its products. In fact, new potential customers who do not own a product may decide to give them a try, particularly if they feel they are able to get a good deal during the sales event.

Based on the marketing strategy, there are different types of sales events. However, at least nine sales events for premium and non-premium products in different sectors and industries are the most common.

1-) **Product Launches**- a strategic sales event announcing a new product's launch. This event is normally used for premium products or a higher standard of non-premium products. It generates an atmosphere of excitement for the new products, and a full marketing strategy can be built around it, heavily using social media.

2-) **Pop-Up events** – a different type of sales event with a higher frequency, such as one day a week or a month, and is presented in a shop, commercial mall, or retail space to get media and social media attention while connecting with the audience in-person. The pop-up sales event can be done in concur with the product announcement or simply to promote brand awareness.

3-) **Long-weekend sales events**- a tactical sales event done every long weekend and festivities such as Thanksgiving, Black Friday, Labor Day, Independence Day, Easter, Christmas, New Year, etc., all year around, to promote mostly the massive sales of non-premium products. This type of sales event is created to push the demand for different categories of non-premium products into customers using extensive media advertising and marketing campaigns. Checking some facts on sales events, we had that in 2021, U.S. consumers spent around $8.9 billion on Black Friday alone and $5.1 billion on Thanksgiving Day alone, despite being in the middle of the COVID-19 pandemic. Based on the data from *Adobe Analytics' Digital Economy Index 2021*, direct consumer transactions online for Black Friday in 2021 had over one trillion visits to U.S. retail sites, over 100 million SKUs, and over 18 product categories.

4-) **Roadshows** – another sales event designed to connect with customers on the city roads. The companies use this type of sales event by having tours in different major cities and wishing to make their direct connections in person with the potential customers in the markets most important to them.

5-) **Fundraisers** – another excellent type of sales event that does focus on selling indirectly by marketing the brand. This type of sales event is about more than just selling the product; it is based on creating a culture in a community. Hosting a joint fundraiser like an active sporting event, a gala, or an auction with a non-profit organization helps connect well with the company's brand, both existing and potential new customers, and also increases awareness for a good cause.

6-) **Virtual Events** –alternative sales events focusing on online audiences. It is a good method to connect virtually with customers to market new and existing products. Virtual events, like webinars, live streams, etc., are a cost-effective way to connect with customers and have no geographical restraints for attendees. It gives unmatched accessibility for a general or a focused audience, especially during the pandemic years in 2020-23, which reduced the possibility of in-person sales events.

7-) **Seminar Series** – another type of sales event emphasizing education, leadership, and brand awareness. For instance, an industry expert talks about the newest topic every month or quarter to a chosen audience of current or potential clients as an exclusive offer. This type of event can also be open to the public for more brand awareness.

8-) **Boot and Training Camps** – an alternative sales event that concentrates on customers that want to learn more about the company, sector, or industry and help develop professional development. This boot camp event is supposed to occur in one or two days that can bring together experts to host sessions on industry trends, case studies, best practices, etc. This help creates an engaging experience with a particular audience that can increase brand awareness exposure.

9-) **Incentive events** – a different type of sales event focusing on incentives for an internal team in a company. This is a great way to reward employees with incentives, perks, trips, or vacations and inspire high achievers at a given company, especially those engaged in sales teams and marketing. In fact, incentivizing them to participate in an all-expenses-paid vacation to a nice destination can help motivate them to keep up the outstanding work, generating even more business.

Part of the marketing strategy of the sales events is the target costing, where the company plans for the price points, product costs, and margins that it wants to achieve for a new product that will be promoted during sales events. Some market-based pricing strategies start with a target price, the estimated price for a product or service that customers are potentially willing to pay. This estimated price is based on understanding customers' perceived value for a product or service and how competitors will price competing products or services.

Using target costing, a firm has a controlling tool for regularly monitoring a new product from the beginning during the design phase and throughout the product life cycle. The product's life-cycle cost is important to develop specified functionality and quality and ensure the desired profit. The desired profit includes setting a target cost and subtracting a desired profit margin from a competitive market price. The target cost formula could be: *Target Cost = (Selling Price) / (1+ Desired Profit %)*. The costs can be written as the sum of the variable costs, cv (y), and the fixed costs, *FC*: $c(y) = cv\ (y) + FC$. The average cost function measures the cost per unit of output and can be written as follows: $AC(y) = c(y)\ y = cv\ (y)\ y + FC\ y = AVC(y) + AFC(y)$ where $AVC(y)$ stands for average variable costs and $AFC(y)$ stands for average fixed costs.

In the short run, the only variable a firm can control to target costing is the variable cost. Fixed and capital costs are controlled in the long run. Therefore, to keep the variable cost low for a non-premium product using the target costing approach, the firm needs to redesign the product in a certain way to use lower-grade raw materials and less labor by meeting the minimum government requirement standards. Therefore, the cost function can be written as a function of engineering design (*Eng*) and lower-grade raw materials (*Raws*), ignoring the fixed costs,

FC: c(y) = cv (Eng+Raws). By controlling the engineering side and the price of raw materials through specialized supply chain management, the firm can meet the target costing requirements and have the desired profit, which are key factors for mass production and participation in large-scale sales events in a fiscal year.

Subsidies and Dealer's Incentive Programs

A subsidy could be considered a form of financial aid or support to an economic sector, a business, or individuals, usually with the purpose of helping economic and social policy. A subsidy is normally related to subsidies issued from the government which could be a direct or indirect payment to individuals, firms, or non-profit organizations in the form of a direct cash payment (such as cash grants, interest-free loans) or indirect cash payments (such as tax breaks, insurance, low-interest loans, accelerated depreciation, rent rebates) to have an economic benefit of a certain sector or industry. Government subsidies are also used to compensate for market failures and externalities and help firms and the private sector attains better economic efficiency.

There are different forms of subsidies, such as those to the producer or production and those to consumption or the consumer. Producer and production subsidies aim to ensure producers will be in a better position by supplying market price support, direct support, or payments to factors of production. A production subsidy pushes suppliers to increase the output of certain products by partially compensating the production costs. Production subsidies aim to expand the production of some products in high demand without increasing the final price to consumers.

The subsidies related to consumption and consumers help reduce the price of goods and services to consumers. A common type of consumption subsidy is when a government subsidizes the basic needs of the population in industrialized countries, such as food, water, electricity, and education, to have most of the citizens available at a reasonable and affordable price. A consumer subsidy contributes to a shift in demand as it is given directly to consumers who benefit the most. Subsidies are an important instrument of government expenditure policy. They also affect domestic resource allocation decisions, income distribution, and expenditure productivity.

What is a Dealer Incentive?

A dealer incentive is a financial tool manufacturers use to motivate dealers to sell a particular product by offering discounts. This corporate sales strategy helps reduce the cost a dealer pays to a manufacturer, increasing the dealer's profit upon the sale of items. The reduction in cost helps dealers be more competitive in the market. Dealer incentives can take different forms, such as a reduced purchase price for the dealer, a cash payment, or simply a cash incentive which could be converted into a rebate to the consumer if the incentive is passed to the customer.

The dealer incentive, which occurs between a manufacturer and a dealer, reduces the cost sustained by the dealer by improving the profit margin of the dealer. Dealer incentives are usually applied when manufacturers want to sell an inventory that is not selling well or launch a new product to lure the dealer into marketing it to customers by getting heavy incentives. The dealer incentive is not passed onto customers, as the manufacturer cannot sell directly to customers, but rather is a benefit for the dealer who facilitates the selling of the product to final customers. These incentives often allow room for consumers to negotiate, as it allows the dealer to reduce the final price to consumers (without comprising profit), which may work in the consumer's favor. At the end of the production line, the dealer incentive also benefits final consumers.

Firms use dealer incentives and manufacturers to motivate salespersons using a cash incentive paid to salespeople for selling a particular product. These incentives allow manufacturers to reduce marketing costs, increase the market share and help promote a new product in a very competitive market in economy pricing. Dealer incentives are normally used by car and motorcycle manufacturers, furniture manufacturers, electronics and appliances firms, luxury item firms, etc., which will reduce the price a dealer has to pay to the manufacturer in the hope of increasing the sales volume of that item or model. If the dealer charges the end customer the regular price with no discount but pays less to buy the item from the manufacturer, the dealer will profit more. However, if the dealer operating in a competitive market passes the cost savings on to consumers, then the dealer incentive is called a *factory-to-dealer incentive.* In economy pricing, when the sales of certain items are disappointing, then those items might be subject to dealer incentives.

Dealer incentives could also include cash payments made by a manufacturer to a dealer based on incentives earned as sales targets are met. In such cases, dealers and salespersons are motivated to sell more items to achieve better payouts from the manufacturer, which could also mean better deals for end-consumers. Manufacturers could also use a factory-to-buyer incentive to generate sales by bypassing the dealer entirely. This incentive, also known as a rebate, is normally well-publicized to drive up the demand for a particular product.

Rebates are a marketing strategy used to lure customers into keeping purchasing. Rebates differ from discounts as they are given after the sale. Rebates benefit both customers and companies highly since both parties benefit from them. Most rebates are quantified as a percentage of the transaction value; however, they can also be recognized as a fixed amount. Occasionally, rebates are prearranged as "cashback offers" for items like mobile phone contracts and other high-value items such as electronics, furniture, cars, etc., sold along with a credit agreement. Nevertheless, retailers can use rebates to gain market share by 'pushing' more consumers to purchase their products using aggressive advertising. This strategy helps increase the firm's profits and eventually establish a dominant position in the market.

Different dealer incentive programs are used as financial tools by manufacturers to motivate dealers to sell a particular product. Some of the most commonly used in different industries are Volume rebates, Co-op marketing funds, Over and Above advertising funds, and Spiff funds.

Volume Rebates: rebate incentives are generally called volume rebates or targeted rebates. The incentives are often decided in order of incremental benefit based on the volume of units sold for a particular product during a fiscal year. The manufacturer will pay the dealer a certain rebate incentive based on the number of units sold to reach a plateau as per agreement. The rebates, unlike discounts, are paid to dealers after the initial payment of goods or when goods are sold to customers. Rebate agreements will normally specify which products, locations, and types of transactions are included.

Co-op (Cooperative marketing funds) funds dealers earn through Incentive Programs by claiming reimbursement for activities supporting manufacturers' product awareness. More in general, Co-op funds help dealers manage marketing activities that increase brand awareness and drive growth sales pipeline. The co-op funds can be invested in advertising activities that promote and publicize the product and its performing qualities. The co-op advertising funds can be used for the distribution of pamphlets, handbills, stickers, promotions, and brochures placed at the point of sale, on the roads through banners and placards.

Over and Above (O&A) advertising funds are special funds where mass media promotes brands and reaches consumers. These (O&A) funds include conventional media such as television and radio advertising, print, and social media through the internet such as Facebook, Twitter, etc. This type of communication is targeted to a wider audience and is not specific to individual consumers. Over and Above (O&A) advertising tries to reach out to the mass consumers as a wide audience, which is different from Co-op advertising, which is mostly used in distributing pamphlets, handbills, stickers, promotions, brochures, etc., placed at the point of sale.

Spiff funds, called **Sales Program Incentive Funds,** belong to a category of incentive programs companies and businesses use to increase sales. The Spiffs are very often used when commodities are not selling well or if inventory items need to be sold or cleared to make room for new merchandise. There is a difference between commissions and spiffs. The spiff funds are used briefly for a limited period, while commissions are more permanent incentives and are used often. In addition, spiffs are paid to salespeople faster as one-time bonuses for selling specific merchandise. Spiffs programs are an effective method to address employee disengagement. They have been known and used for many years to incentivize employee engagement and encourage salespersons to be more active and creative in sales. Spiffs funds are specifically designed to help businesses meet sales goals in a short period of time. A well-designed Spiff fund can help sales representative meet their sales quota quickly.

Economy Pricing and the Net Monetary Position Theory

As per the definition, the marginal revenue (MR) is the change in the firm's total revenue per unit of output. More specifically, it is the additional revenue derived from selling an additional unit of output. Mathematically the marginal revenue is given as *MR = Change in total revenue / Change in total output.* The firms (or price takers) sell most or all of their units at the same price, and each firm's marginal revenue will equal the market price. In the short term, the firms or price takers will increase output until marginal revenue (price) equals marginal cost, maximizing the firm's profits.

In general, a firm will earn a profit if the marginal revenue (selling price for the price taker) is greater than or equal to the marginal cost of that unit. Profit will continue rising as long as manufacturing and selling of a unit add more revenue to the firm than cost. The modern pricing theory in microeconomics tells us that an additional unit produced will add more to cost than it adds to revenue, and the firm's profit will be reduced if the unit is produced. However, in an economy pricing system, things seem to be working differently based on a financial accounting concept called the *Net Monetary Position.*

The Net Monetary Position Theory considers a firm that produces and sells two products: high-quality premium products at a high price and low-end mass consumption non-premium products that sell at a reasonably low price. The particularity of these products is that the premium product is sold at a higher price to reach the maximum profit when the marginal profit is zero or when the marginal cost equals the marginal revenue. Meanwhile, the non-premium product sells at a price where marginal revenue is greater or equal to the marginal cost reaching maximum profit (marginal profit is zero) for 20-40 percent of the time during the year, and at a price where marginal revenue is less than marginal cost and marginal profit is negative for about 60-80 percent of the times during the year. If the marginal profit for the non-premium product is negative does not mean that a lesser quantity should be produced. On the contrary, the quantity of non-premium products continues to rise to meet the demand for selling at discounted prices. There are three scenarios in economy pricing based on the sales of two categories of products, premium and non-premium: first, premium products sold at regular price; second, non-premium products sold at regular price; third, non-premium products sold at discount price.

The first scenario is when the markup price or firm's optimal price for a premium product is when for any chosen price p, the firm expects to have a demand q= D (p). The production vector can be split into inputs z, and outputs q, and takes the form as $Y= (-z, q)$. Given a vector of input prices v, the firm's cost to produce an output q of the finished good is given as,

$$C(q; v, Y)= min \{v\, z: (-z, q) \in Y\} \tag{1.1}$$

where z is the inputs and, y is the output. The cost given in the equation above represents the minimum cost to produce a certain output q. The cost depends on the price of inputs of the materials and on the cost of direct and indirect labor and fixed cost. By ignoring parameters v and Y from cost function $C(q)$ we have a simplified form of markup price for a premium product written as,

$$max\ [P(D(Pp)) - C(D(Pp))] \tag{1.2}$$

where $P(D(Pp))$ is the price demand and $C(D(Pp))$ is the cost related to demand $D(Pp)$ for the premium product. The first-order necessary optimality condition is given as,

$$P(D'(Pp)) + D(Pp) - C'(D(Pp)D'(Pp)=0 \tag{1.3}$$

Therefore, the optimal markup rule is,

$$\frac{P-MC}{P} = \frac{1}{\psi} \tag{1.4}$$

where $MC(Pp)=C'(D(Pp))$ is the marginal cost and ψ=-$PD'(Pp)/D(Pp)$ is the own-price demand elasticity for the premium product. The elasticity of demand that characterizes the curve of the firm's customers is normally negative. The price elasticity of demand for a premium product measures the elasticity (responsiveness) of the quantity demanded to a change in its price, or more specifically, the percentage change in quantity demanded in response to a one percent change in price.

However, the optimal pricing strategy will change completely if we assume that a multi-product firm has two main products: a high-quality premium product and a mass-consumption non-premium product. The pricing strategy for this type of firm is based on reaching not the best pricing strategy for both products but rather a good net monetary position of the firm's balance sheet. The *net monetary position* is the current ratio of current assets over current liabilities (greater than one) or current assets minus current liabilities should always be positive to show the ability of the firm to cover current working capital needs with available working capital.

The second scenario is when the non-premium product sold at the regular price has a markup price, *Pnp*, given as,

$$max\ [Pnp(Dnp(Pnp)) - Cnp(Dnp(Pnp))]\ (1\text{-}\mathcal{E}) \tag{1.5}$$

where *Dnp* is the demand for a non-premium product and $(1\text{-}\mathcal{E})$ is the occurrence that the non-premium product is sold at regular price (normally at around 20-40 percent of the time), and *Cnp* is the total cost. The first-order necessary optimality condition for the non-premium product is given as,

$$[Pnp(Dnp'(Pnp)) + Dnp(P) - Cnp'(Dnp(Pnp)Dnp'(Pnp))]\ (1\text{-}\mathcal{E})=0 \tag{1.6}$$

The price per unit sold for marginal revenue is equal to the marginal cost at a probability of $(1\text{-}\mathcal{E})$ times the price of the non-premium product, written as,

$$Pnp\ (1\text{-}\mathcal{E})= Cnp'\ (Dnp) \tag{1.7}$$

The own-price demand elasticity does not apply to the non-premium product as it has already been determined to be sold at regular price, *Pnp,* when there are no promotions available, and *Pnps,* when there are promotions.

The third case scenario is when the non-premium product is sold at a discount price which has a markup price given as,

$$[(Pnps)\ (Dnps(Pnps)) - Cnp(Dnps(Pnps))]\ (1\text{-}v) \tag{1.8}$$

where (*Pnps)* is the non-premium price discounted at *s* (as a value), when the non-premium product is sold at a discounted price, and *Dnps* is the new demand, and $(1\text{-}v)$ is the probability that the non-premium product is sold at a discounted price (normally at about 60-80 % of the times during a fiscal year) and *Cnp(Dnps)* is the cost related to the new demand. If we consider the condition of maximizing profit for non-premium products sold at discounted price *S,* we get the marginal revenue equal to marginal cost plus the discount rate *S,* written as,

$$Pnps\ (1\text{-}v)= Cnp'\ (Dnps) + S \tag{1.9}$$

The above equation means that every time the firm sells a non-premium product at price *Pnps*, it loses *[Cnp' (Dnps') + S]* because it has to give up steep discounts to loyal customers during sales events to be competitive and keep the existing market share or eventually increase it. Firms producing large volumes of non-premium products will use mass-production methods and effective supply chain management, normally leading to lower per-unit costs. This helps explain why the long-run average total cost curve (LRATC) has a downward-sloping portion.

By using the total revenue/cost approach rather than the marginal approach, we have that the **first equilibrium condition** of pricing strategy for a firm operating in an economy pricing given the demand for each of the three scenarios: premium, non-premium, and non-premium discounted products is written as,

$$[P(D(P_P) - C(D(P_p)] + \left[P_{np}\left(D_{np}(P_{np})\right) - C_{np}\left(D_{np}(P_{np})\right)\right](1-\varepsilon) +$$
$$\left[(P_{nps})\left(D_{nps}(P_{nps})\right) - \left(C_{np}\left(D_{nps}(P_{nps})\right)\right)\right](1-v) = NMP(cr) > 1 \quad \text{for}$$
$$(1\text{-}\mathcal{E})\text{=}20\text{-}40\% \text{ and } (1\text{-}\nu)\text{ =}60\text{-}80\% \qquad (1.10)$$

where *P(D(Pp))* is the price demand, and *C(D(Pp))* is the cost related to demand *D(Pp)* for premium products sold at regular price, *Pnp(Dnp)(Pnp)* and *Cnp(Dnp)P(np)* are respectively price demand and cost related to the demand for non-premium product sold at regular price, *Pnps(Dnps)(Pnps)* and *Cnps(Dnps)P(nps)* are respectively price demand and cost related to the demand for non-premium product sold at discount price, *(1-Ɛ)* and *(1-ν)* are the frequency of the non-premium product sold at a regular and discounted price. *NMP* is the *Net Monetary Position* of the Balance Sheet of the firm, and *cr*, stands for current ratio. The *NMP* is normally measured by liquidity ratios such as the *current ratio* and is always supposed to be> 1 (current ratio >1) for a firm to cover current liabilities with the current assets or *quick ratio,* which excludes inventory because inventory is not always considered liquid. This comparison allows us to assess the firm's ability to meet its short-term debts.

A **second equilibrium condition** of the pricing strategy for the firm, given the demand (or the demand-push) for premium, non-premium, and non-premium discounted products, is to meet the sales target to retain the market share, which is given as competitive,

$$\text{Dp(Pp) + Dnp(Pnp) + Dnps(Pnps) = Sales Target= Market share} \qquad (1.11)$$

where *Dp, Dnp, Dnps, Pp, Pnp,* and *Pnps* are the respective demand (demand push) and price of premium, non-premium, and non-premium discounted products sold by the firm to keep the sales target and, at the same time, meet the first condition, NMP >1.

Satisfying the second condition - meeting the sales target - does not mean that a firm maximizes profit. In a normal competitive environment, a competitive firm can sell each unit of output at the market price, *p*, and its revenue is then a simple function of output, $R(y) = py$. If x is a feasible vector of inputs to produce output y, and if w is the vector of factor prices, the cost of using input x to produce output y is simply $w{\cdot}x$. This strategy yields the maximum firm's profit π given as,

$$max\ \pi = y - w{\cdot}x.\quad for\ x, y > 0\ and\ f(x) > y \qquad (1.12)$$

In an economy pricing system with a push-demand-to-customers strategy reaching the maximum profit is not the main objective of the firm. The main goal is to keep the market share by reaching the desired target output, which does not always equal maximizing profit for every unit sold. By using inputs x, and w, as a vector of factor prices, the second equilibrium condition in economy pricing using the demand function can be re-written as,

$$Dp(Pp) + Dnp(Pnp) + Dnps(Pnps) = Sales\ Target = Market\ share \neq max\ \pi + w\,x \qquad (1.13)$$

The equation above means that a multi-product firm operating in an economy pricing and competitive environment does not necessarily have to maximize the profit for each unit sold. In a combination of mix-product sales, must have an overall NMP>1 and meet the sales target.

There are chances when a competitive firm operates at a loss because of business loss or capital loss for one or more quarters or even years until the balance sheet gets 'repaired' and grows in strength to become a profitable business. Based on the accounting theory, if NMP > 1, the firm is assumed to sell all its current assets to pay for its current liabilities. Nevertheless, if NMP (current ratio) < 1, then the firm won't be able to cover the current liabilities with current assets and will operate at a loss. A current ratio of less than one may cause concern to the firm as it may not be able to pay its short debts with current assets as they fall due. However, in some industries, a current ratio of less than one may be acceptable.

Current Ratios and Cost Approach in Economy Pricing

A firm can maximize the value of the company if it maximizes the *Net Monetary Position* during each intra-period (monthly and quarterly) and the entire period (fiscal year) using a combination of different pricing strategies during sales events for its premium and non-premium products. A firm producing multi-mix products will have a combination of pricing strategies by charging a higher price for premium products sold to consumers with a less elastic demand (market niche) and by offering discounts to a majority of customers whose demand is more elastic for non-premium products during major sales events that often run in a fiscal year. This pricing strategy intended to maximize the *Net Monetary Position* is different from the price discrimination practice in which a seller charges different consumers different prices for the same product or service.

Maximizing the profit by equaling marginal revenue to marginal cost *(P=MR=MC)* for a multi-product firm is not the case, especially in an economy pricing dominated by fierce competition. Let's assume that a firm has published the following Financial Statements for three consecutive years, as shown in table 1.1 and table 1.2.

Assets/Years (all figures in 000s)	**2018**	**2017**	**2016**
Current Assets			
Cash and Cash Equivalents	$1,450	$1,210	$1,000
Financial Assets	4,580	6,187	5,456
Acc. Receivable	42,314	38,048	35,900
Inventories	24,045	22,321	21,390
Sub Total Current assets	**72,389**	**67,766**	**63.746**
Non-Current Assets			
Property, Plant, Equip.	258,733	238,236	234,500
Intangible Assets	53,700	50,000	45,000
Financial Assets	72,300	60,000	55,000
Total Assets non-current assets	**457,122**	**416,002**	**398,246**
Equity and Liabilities			
Current Liabilities			
Bank Overdraft	$2,000	$2,000	$2,000
Accounts Payable	33,556	31,653	30,578
Current Tax Payable	5,000	5,000	5,000
Finance Lease Obligations	5,563	5,563	5,563
Subtotal current liabilities	**46,119**	**44,216**	**43,141**
Non-current liabilities			
Long-term debt	80,000	80,000	80,000
Deferred tax	36,456	33,556	31,500
Provisions	27,825	18,000	17,000
Total Liabilities non-current liabilities	**190,400**	**175,772**	**171,641**
Share Capital	55,000	45,000	43,000
Retained Earnings	211,722	195,230	183,605
Total equity and liabilities	**$457,122**	**$416,002**	**$398,246**

Table 1.1 Financial Statement Analysis. Balance Sheet and Net Monetary Position

Income Statement	2018	2017	2016
Sales	$504,778	$478,465	$435,785
Cost of Goods Sold	(275,515)	(260,293)	(250,635)
Gross Profit	**$229, 263**	**$218,172**	**$185,150**
Other Income	1,010	2,150	2,550
Distribution Cost	(96,940)	(90,529)	(78,378)
Selling Expenses	(62,385)	(57,176)	(53,456)
Administrative Expenses	(34,823)	(35,735)	(29,849)
Operating Income	**$36,125**	**$36,882**	**$26,017**
Investment Income	4,211	3,350	3,050
Finance Cost	(17,236)	(19,534)	(11,530)
Income Before Tax	**23,100**	**20,698**	**17,537**
Tax Expense	(6,608)	(9,073)	(5,261)
Net Income	**$16,492**	**$11,625**	**$12,276**

Table 1.2 Sample of Income Statement

The Net Monetary Position is the capability to cover the current liabilities with the current assets measured by liquidity ratios such as *Current Ratio= Current Assets/Current Liabilities >1.*

Current Ratio year 2016 = $63,746/$43.141 = 1.48,

Current Ratio Year 2017 = $67,766/$44,216=1.53,

Current Ratio Year 2018 = $72,389/$46,199=1.57.

The current ratio of the firm, whose balance sheet is shown in Table 1.1, has demonstrated, from the year 2016 to the year 2018, improvement in the ability to cover the current working capital needs with the available working capital. It has a steady increase from 1.48 to 1.57. Quick Ratio, instead, is another liquidity ratio used to analyze the capability of the company to cover all current liabilities with its quick assets, excluding inventory. It is given as Quick Ratio= (Current Assets- Inventory)/Current Liabilities

Quick Ratio year 2016 = 0.982

Quick Ratio year 2017 = 1.027

Quick Ratio year 2018 = 1.048

The quick ratio shows that the firm sample above is barely able to cover all current liabilities with quick assets when the value of inventory is eliminated; still, it has improved from 2016 to 2018, which shows the same trend as the current ratio. It also means that the firm needs to keep inventory at minimum levels to increase its quick assets and have a better quick ratio that translates to further discounts on its non-premium products. Some firms involved in heavy engineering may not be able to turn inventory, much of which may be work-in-progress, into cash at short notice to pay debts that have become payable.

It's important to look at some points for liquidity ratios. It's suggested to look at the industry average first, as a low ratio may be the norm in some industries. A low ratio means the company has poor working capital management (such as non-collecting receivables fast enough to balance with paying accounts payable, etc.). On the other side, a high ratio means that large amounts of cash are sitting on the balance sheet, which does not provide enough returns to shareholders. Therefore, money needs to be invested in increasing the returns. The falling ratio, instead, may indicate that the company is facing solvency problems.

It's interesting to explain below how the cost approach works at the microeconomic level in an economy pricing system. Figure 1.1 below is a simple illustration of the cost approach for a competitive multi-product market. It demonstrates the total cost and revenue approach curves in an economy pricing where a firm increases the value of the firm by maximizing the current ratio.

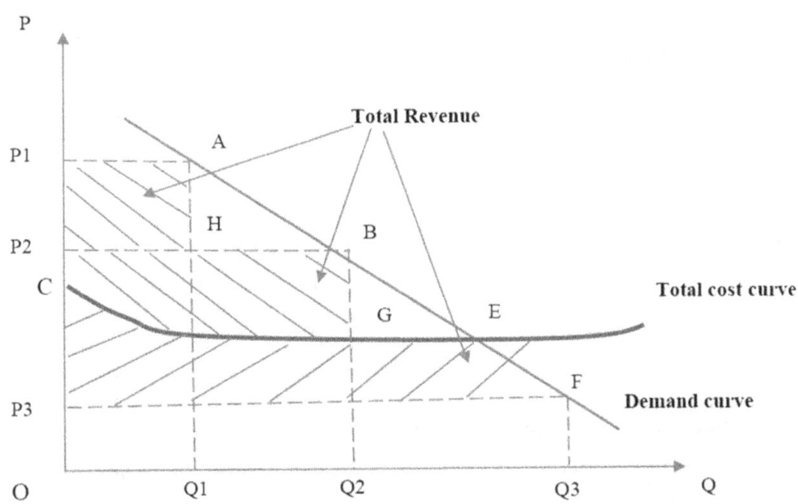

Figure 1.1 Economy Pricing: Total Revenue and Cost Approach

Figure 1.1 indicates the two main products produced by the firm: premium and non-premium. The premium product is sold at a higher price *P1*, and the non-premium product is sold at a regular price *P2* for 30-40 percent of the time and at discounted price *P3* for at least 60-70 percent of the time during a fiscal year. *The firm's Net Monetary Position (NMP)* is given by selling the premium and non-premium products at prices P1 and P2, respectively, over its total cost curve, making a substantial profit, which is given by adding the profitable areas P1P2HA+ P2BGC. These two areas combined are larger than the loss resulting from selling non-premium products at discount price P3 located under its total cost curve, given by area CP3EF.

Net Monetary Position = Current Ratio = profit areas (P1P2HA + P2BGC) > loss area CP3EF.

The discount price *P3* is located under the total cost curve, which means that the *P3* price for each non-premium unit sold can cover variable costs (manufacturing + selling and administrative) and only a part of fixed costs (such as fixed manufacturing cost but not fixed administration and selling cost). The firm assumed operating in an economy pricing does not maximize the profit for each of its products, but rather it has a current ratio greater than one or NMP>1 in its balance sheet. The sales strategy of keeping low prices for non-premium products will reduce revenue at a sustainable cost per unit; however, it will keep stable the market share and realize a desirable cash flow money during a given fiscal period.

Figure 1.2 displays the relationship between the NMP curve as a function of the quantity of the two products (premium and non-premium) produced by three firms in a given industry. The three firms are assumed to cover roughly 80-90 percent of the market of premium and non-premium products produced and sold in that industry.

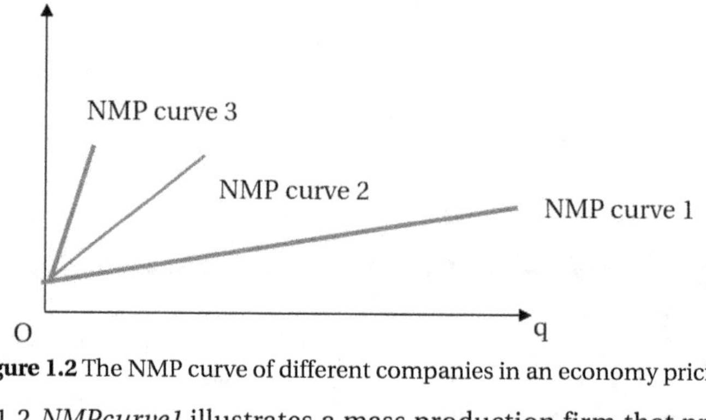

Figure 1.2 The NMP curve of different companies in an economy pricing

Figure 1.2 *NMPcurve1* illustrates a mass production firm that produces a relatively small quantity of premium products and a quite large quantity of non-premium products. This firm covers a big segment of the market (around 55-65 percent). *NMPcurve2* represents another firm that produces a medium quantity of premium products and a small quantity of non-premium products. This firm covers roughly 10-15 percent of the market. *NMPcurve3* indicates the case when a firm produces only premium products in small quantities and dominates approximately 5-10 percent of the market. The slope of *NMPcurve1* is lower than the slope of *NMPcurve2* and *NMPcurve3* as it reaches a low NMP with a reasonable current ratio and lower net income. The *NMPcurve2* and *NMPcurve3* curves have better current ratios reaching higher margin profits per each unit sold, producing relatively small quantities of non-premium products, and focusing on manufacturing high-quality premium products for a niche market.

We assume that the market of the industry above is dominated by only three firms, where each of them can produce only two products, premium and non-premium, and a low entry barrier. If a new firm wants to enter the market of both products, it must take into consideration the reaction of the existing firms that operate in this competitive market. The existing three firms may reduce further the price of their premium and non-premium products within the legal limit (no predatory pricing but by increasing the number of events that offer bargain prices), resulting in a lower NMP curve and lower net income forcing the new entrant to operate eventually at negative NMP curve or at a loss as illustrated in fig. 1.3.

Figure 1.3 shows how the three existing firms reduce their premium and non-premium products price further, lowering their NMP curves from Co to C1, C2, and C3, respectively (increasing the number of products sold) and forcing the new entrant to sell less and operate at current ratio <1. The current ratio will get worse in NMP4 (NMP-curve4 will hit more negative territories), and the new entrant firm will be forced out of business and file for bankruptcy. Nevertheless, suppose the new entrant can increase production capacity by reorganizing its resources and reducing total cost. In that case, it will result in an improved current ratio and a positive NMP curve, helping the firm with curve C4 to stay in business.

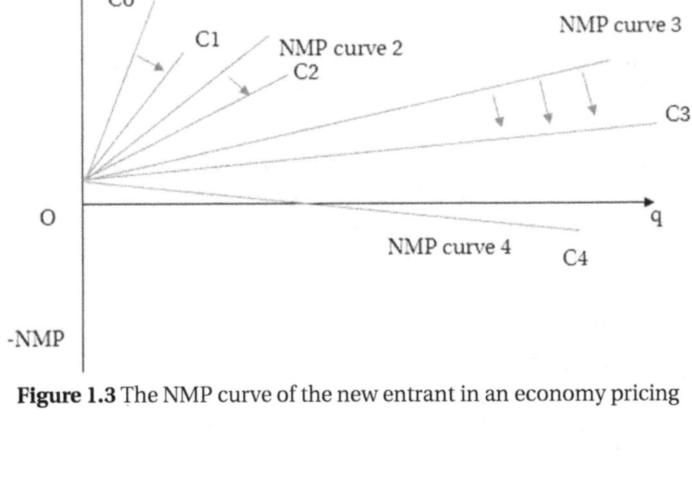

Figure 1.3 The NMP curve of the new entrant in an economy pricing

Suppose the three firms above operate in a high entry-barrier industry where licensing, patents, and high capital investments are needed. In that case, a new entrant will be able to access this industry only if it is able to put enough funds and resources to obtain necessary licensing, patents, etc. This will make the new entrant barely able to cover the current liabilities (current ratio $\approx$ 1). The new entrant may also operate at a current ratio <1 or at a loss for a few fiscal periods unless it is able to obtain other financial resources such as government funds (especially if it operates domestically or internationally in strategic sectors such as automobile, telecommunications, and aerospace industry) or other funds in the form of tax credits or from private investors that believe in the success of the new company and are willing to invest capitals on it despite the fact that the firm operates at a loss. The main concern of most firms operating in economy pricing is not maximizing the profit for each product sold but rather having a strong balance sheet based on multi-product-mix profitability and a positive net monetary position with a current ratio >1 to be competitive.

Push vs. Pull Strategies in Economy Pricing

The terms push and pull used in business terminology have been coined for the first time in logistics and supply chain management but are also widely used in marketing. The difference between push and pull terms used in marketing lies in how the companies approach different categories of consumers to sell their products. In a push marketing strategy, firms promote products by pushing them onto consumers. On the other hand, in a pull marketing strategy, the companies try to establish a loyal following and draw consumers to the products, especially if the products are of high-end premium (such as Porsche and Ferrari in the sports car industry) where there is no longer need of advertising as consumers know the products and come to them.

Push Marketing

Push marketing is often considered a promotional strategy as companies try to take their products directly to customers. The most common sales approach companies use to sell their products includes selling goods directly to customers via company showrooms and negotiating with retailers to sell their products or set up point-of-sale displays. It's common in business for retailers to receive special sales incentives and promotions from companies that want to sell their products in exchange for increased visibility in their stores. This works well in economy pricing, where companies pay coop advertising, promotions, and volume rebate incentives to the retailers, mostly during sales events, especially for their non-premium products, to push them to that category of customers that are looking for discounted prices. This strategy will help companies reach their volume sales target for their non-premium products.

The most common examples of push marketing tactics can be seen in department stores that sell appliances, computers, TVs, furniture, mattresses, or fragrance lines. The manufacturing brand of these products will often offer sales incentives, mostly for non-premium products and occasionally for premium products, to the department stores to push their products onto customers. The push marketing strategy is based on attracting customers through sales incentives and "pushing" them to buy the products. The purpose of this tactic is simple as many customers, being introduced to these products at the store is their first experience, wouldn't know to ask for them if they didn't know they existed.

Pull Marketing

Pull marketing operates in the opposite direction of push marketing. It uses the opposite approach to get customers to come to you rather than going to them; therefore, the term pull is where marketers attempt to pull customers in. Pull marketing is normally used by companies that want to create brand loyalty to high-quality premium products so customers can return. Meanwhile, push marketing is more concerned with the mass production of a high volume of non-premium products with short-term sales. The common sales techniques used for "pull" marketing are media promotions for premium products, advertised sales promotions, word-of-mouth referrals, etc. Pull marketing involves a considerable amount of advertising dollars to be spent on making brand products of a recognizable household name so customers are pulled in to buy them.

Push strategy puts the product in front of the customer so the customer is aware of the existence of the product. Push strategies use trade shows, showrooms, and mass advertising to attract a large number of customers to buy discounted products. Retailers normally try to stock non-premium products that will be sold at a discounted price and create a supply chain to facilitate distribution. A pull strategy instead motivates customers to actively look for a specific premium product when a manufacturer has a strong and visible brand.

Push-Type, Pull-Type, and Supply Chain Management

On the production side, "push-type" means that the firm must produce or *Make-to-Stock*, in which the production is not based on actual demand but on demand planning or forecast. Demand planning is the method of forecasting the demand for a product or service to increase the efficiency and satisfaction of customers. On the other hand, the term "pull-type" is considered as *Make-*

to-Order, in which the production and capacity utilization is based on actual demand. In a large manufacturing company, the supply chain management (SCM) can carry out processes halfway between push-type and pull-type or a combination of both based on the number of premium and non-premium products produced and delivered to the market.

Thanks to the evolution of information technology, supply chain management can shift the production and sales business model from "Push-Type" to "Pull-Type." Pull-type supply chain management is based on the actual demand, such as the *Just-in-Time* (JIT) and *Continuous Replenishment Program* (CRP), and the inventory is kept at a minimum, as the products can be supplied with short lead times. On the other hand, the push-type continues to supply and push the products to customers regardless of whether there is actual demand or no. Push-type supply chain management is mostly used in those mass production industries where non-premium products are manufactured and commercialized in large quantities and sold at discounted prices. On the other side, pull-type is used to manufacture high-quality premium products when there is an actual demand.

Demand Pull-Inflation and Cost Push-Inflation

The demand Pull-Inflation will materialize if the aggregate demand goes up quicker than the aggregate supply. In monetary terms, inflation will occur if aggregate demand for products and services outpaces the aggregate supply due to monetary and real factors. An example of demand-pull inflation due to monetary factors is when major inflation is caused by monetary supply expansion, especially during a financial crisis. Meanwhile, an example of demand-pull inflation due to real factors is when the inflation is caused by real factors in the economy, such as an increase in government spending not covered by tax revenue, an increase in investments in the private sector due to favorable market conditions, decrease in savings and increase in spending, increase in exports, and decrease in imports.

Cost push-inflation, differently from demand pull-inflation, is caused by the increase in the general price level caused by the rise in prices of the factors of production, based on the shortage of inputs, labor force, and capital or supply chain disruptions as in the case of a global pandemic caused by COVID-19 virus during 2020-2023 or the war in Ukraine in 2022. The total output will decrease as the inputs used to produce outputs are getting more expensive due to the shortage of raw materials. The three types of cost-push inflation consist of the following:

a) Wage-push inflation, when stakeholders and groups of the society, like labor unions, exercise their monopoly power to demand higher wages, eventually above the competitive level, which can be translated into an increase in the cost of production.

b) Profit-push inflation, when the monopoly power is used by businesses operating in the monopolistic and oligopolistic market to increase their profit margin by simply raising the price of goods and services. This kind of inflation does not happen in an economy pricing where most of the firms operate in a competitive market 'ruled' by promotions and discounted prices.

c) Supply shock inflation, when inflation arises because of an unexpected fall in the supply of necessary consumer goods or inputs used in industries and supply chain disruptions (wars, pandemics, political unrest, etc.).

There are differences between demand-pull and cost-push inflation that consist of a few factors. Demand-pull inflation is caused by the fast rise of aggregate demand and the lag of aggregate supply to following the aggregate demand. Other factors contributing to demand-pull inflation are the increase in money supply, government spending, and foreign exchange rate. Cost-push inflation instead is triggered by the rise in the price of inputs due to a shortage of production or by monopolistic groups in society. The demand-pull inflation is managed by policy recommendations associated with monetary and fiscal tools, especially during high unemployment. On the other hand, the policy recommendations on cost push-inflation are related to the administrative control of price increases and stabilizing policies to keep unemployment at an acceptable level. It is believed that demand-pull inflation compared to demand-push-inflation is the leading factor for high inflation in the economy.

In economy pricing, the conditions are completely different from non-economy pricing. Inflation is at low levels as the aggregate demand does not grow at a fast rate, and the aggregate supply always matches the aggregate demand due to high and fierce competition in many industries and sectors. Government spending is available but not as fast as it is required, as the government must identify the projects to invest money and government spending does not grow fast enough to cause demand pull-inflation.

In an economy's pricing, cost-push inflation is not triggered by the rise of the price of inputs, as there is no rise in the cost of inputs. This is due to market and push-type supply chain management that is mostly used in mass production industries where non-premium products are manufactured and commercialized in large volumes, so they can fill the market and push the products onto customers. If the costs of inputs were not offered at a competitive price for non-premium products, the manufacturing firms would not be able to reach the necessary utilization capacity to meet the net monetary position condition.

Therefore, the cost-push inflation factor for inputs must be reduced by using alternative supply chain strategies that offer competitive inputs or by the use of product upgrades in outsourcing part of the production to reduce cost and stay competitive.

Three Levels of the Demand-Push Promotion Model

Large discount superstores like Walmart, Costco, and Amazon, or discount outlets, put considerable pressure on their suppliers to keep the price down so they can give more discounts to final customers and have more return liberal policies for their loyal customers to remain competitive. This section will be focused on a new microeconomic model called the *Three-levels of Demand Push-Promotion model*, where each level of the supply chain of the final product is designed to push the demand onto the final customer.

Suppose a discount superstore sells a non-premium product (unit) denominated as *Un* at a discount price rather than at a regular price during several sale events in a given fiscal year. And here, we have the first level of demand push; the superstore pushes its products (mostly non-premium) onto customers using different marketing tactics and strategies. The discount price denominated as *P(Us)np* of one unit of product *Un* the superstore sells to final customers is given as a function of profit margin denominated as *Pa*, direct + indirect labor denominated as *L*, variable, and fixed overhead costs denominated as *VOH+FOH*, selling and administrative cost denominated as *A*, and lastly *Pm*, which represents the price the superstore buys the units from the manufacturer. The relationship, including all these variables, is given as a linear function to sell one unit of product *Un* to final customers at discount price *P(Us)np* and can be written as,

$$P(Us)np = Pa + L + VOH + FOH + A + Pm \text{ for } P(u)np < Pnp \quad (1.11)$$

where *Pnp* is the regular price of the non-premium product, which is always higher than the discount price *P(u)np* during sales events.

The second level of demand-push promotion happens when giant superstores like Walmart, Costco, and Amazon ask their suppliers, which are the manufacturers of non-premium units denominated as *Un*, to reduce their selling price during sales events to push the superstore demand to the final customer at the designed discounted price range. The manufacturers agree to reduce their prices if the superstores agree to buy the unit *Un* in large batches or volumes. Hence, the price of one unit of non-premium product *Unp*, manufactured by the manufacturer and sold to the superstore is given as,

$$PU(m)np = PMm + Lm + VOHm + FOHm + Am + P(r)npQr \quad (1.12)$$

where *PMm, Lm, VOHm, FOHm,* and *Am* are, respectively, the profit margin, direct+ indirect labor, variable and fixed overhead, selling and administrative cost of the manufacturer to produce one unit of *Un* and lastly, *P(r)npQr* represents the price the manufacturer buys raw materials *(Pr)np* times *Qr* which is the number of raw materials from the mining industry to produce one non-premium unit *Unp.* The fixed overhead of a manufacturing company (*FOHm*) that is part of the unit cost of *Unp* includes capital charges and investment in new machines (cost of leasing, repairs), etc. If the superstore agrees to buy large volumes of the unit, *Un,* then the volume of non-premium product *Un* sold at a discount price by the manufacturer, *Vlmun,* is always higher than the regular volume *Vmun* sold at regular price, *Vlmun> Vmun.*

The third level of demand-push promotion occurs when the manufacturers ask their suppliers of the raw materials or intermediate subassemblies to reduce the price of the raw materials used to produce the non-premium products so that they can support the sales event of the superstore. The mining firms or the producers of the raw materials will accept to reduce the price of their raw materials if the manufacturer buys them in large volumes. Therefore, we have that *Pr*Qr* represents the price of raw materials and quantities used in production to produce the unit *Un.* For the mining company, the selling price of all raw materials, *P(r)np,* sold to the manufacture to produce the non-premium unit *Un,* that will be sold to the superstore is given as,

$$P(r)np = Vlrun\ (PMr + Lr + VOHr + FOHr + Ar + Pl)\ \text{if}\ Vlrun > Vrun \tag{1.13}$$

where *PMr, Lr, VOHr, FOHr,* and *Ar* are, respectively, the profit margin, direct+ indirect labor, variable and fixed overhead, and selling and administrative cost of the extraction of the mining company. *Pl,* instead, is the price to buy land to extract minerals, including the mining rights or loyalties, and *Vlrun* is the large volume of raw materials sold at a discount, and *Vrun* is the volume of raw materials sold at a regular price.

Putting together equations (1.11), (1.12), and (1.13), we get a new equation that indicates the final price of the non-premium product, *Un,* sold to the final customer in the superstore based on three levels of discounts or demand-push written as,

$$PU_{(s)np} = [P_a + L + VOH + FOH + A] + [PM_m + L_m + VOH_m + FOH_m + A_m] + Vl_{run}[PM_r + L_r + VOH_r + FOH_r + A_r + \boldsymbol{PI}] \tag{1.14}$$

where *Pm,* which represents the price the superstore buys the units from the manufacturer, is equal to the second factor in square brackets, $Pm = [PM_m + L_m + VOH_m + FOH_m + A_m]$ and *P(r)np* which represents the price of raw materials for the mining company sold to the manufacturer to produce the non-premium good, is given by the third factor in square brackets, $P(r)_{np} = Vl_{run}[PM_r + L_r + VOH_r + FOH_r + A_r + \boldsymbol{PI}]$. The final sale price *PU(s)np* of non-premium product sold to the final customer is a combination of three discounted prices from the discount superstore, manufacturer, and raw-material supplier. The simplified form of three levels of demand-push for the superstore that sells the non-premium product at discount price *P(u)np* can be denoted as below,

$$P(Us)np = Pa + PUs + Pm + P(r)np \quad \text{for } P(u)np < Pnp \qquad (1.15)$$

where, $PUs = L + VOH + FOH + A$, $Pm = [PM_m + L_m + VOH_m + FOH_m + A_m]$ and $P(r)_{np} = Vl_{run}[PM_r + L_r + VOH_r + FOH_r + A_r + \boldsymbol{PI}]$ and *Pa* is the profit margin of the superstore. Suppose the superstore negotiates Dealers' Incentive Programs such as Volume rebates, Co-op marketing funds, and Over and Above advertising funds with the manufacturer for specific premium and non-premium products. In that case, the profit margin of the superstore, *Pa*, will increase further as the superstore will be able to get more money back in the form of credits from the manufacturers at the end of the fiscal period. The discount price *P(u)np* of the non-premium product that includes the *Dealer's Incentive Program* can be written as,

$$P(Us)np = [Pa + ICdp] + PUs + Pm + P(r)np \qquad (1.16a)$$

or

$$P(Us)np = Pa + PUs + Pm + P(r)np - [ICdp] \qquad (1.16b)$$

where *ICdp* is the *Dealer's Incentive Program* per unit. The credits received from the manufacturer increase the profit margin, *Pa*, of the superstore for that particular non-premium product by the amount *ICdp* per unit as in (1.16a) or reduce further the discounted price per unit, *P(Us)np*, by the amount offered from Dealer's Incentive fund, *ICdp*, as in equation (1.16b), if the firm decides to be competitive by compromising part of the profit. The superstore is willing to push the demand into customers for those items that are part of the Dealer's Incentive Programs, using the money/credit received from the manufacturer invested in Co-op advertising such as the distribution of pamphlets, handbills, stickers, promotions, brochures placed at the point of sale or Over and Above (O&A) advertising such as television and radio advertising, social media advertising through the internet such as Facebook, Twitter, etc.

In the short run, at the first level of demand-push, the supply chain manager of the superstore will 'push' to reduce the cost of product *U(s)np*, so the store can sell it at a discount price by reducing the only variable he can control in the short-run, that is the price of the non-premium unit, *Pm*, purchased from the manufacturer. Other variables such as profit margin, labor, variable and fixed overheads, and selling and administrative costs are controlled by the corporate superstore management, which may get reduced in the long-run through restructuring, reorganization, investment in research and development, new technologies, mergers, etc., but not in the short-run as the firm in the short-run will try to keep a positive net monetary position (NMP>1) in the trial balance.

The same strategy we can say will work for the second level of demand-push managed by the supply manager of the manufacturer and extraction/mining company. The supply manager of the manufacturer firm will try to reduce the cost of the unit manufactured *U(m)np* by reducing the only variable he can control in the short-term, which is the price of the raw materials *Pr(np)* used to produce *U(m)np,* purchased from the extraction/mining company in large volumes during a sales event.

In the same way, at the third level of demand-push, the sales team of the extraction/mining company will reduce the price of raw material *P(r)np* sold to the manufacturer in large volumes to produce the unit *U(s)np* that will be sold to superstore if in the short-run the supply chain manager will 'push' to reduce the price of the component, *PI* in equation (1.13) which is the price to buy new land, open new mines or increase the capacity of existing mines to speed up the extraction of minerals (including mining rights or loyalties) in enough large volumes to support the sales events of the superstore for that particular non-premium product unit *U(s)np.*

Therefore, the discount price of non-premium product *U(s)np* in the short run is controlled by the price of these three core variables of the superstore supply chain given as $PU(s)np = Pm + P(r)np + PI$, where *Pm* is the price of a manufactured unit, *Pr(np)* is the price of raw materials to produce this unit, and *PI* is the price of mineral extraction including landing rights and royalties to produce the raw materials to manufacture unit *U(s)np.* In fact, the price of minerals such as crude oil, lumber, cotton, silver, cement, iron ore, aluminum, copper, lithium, cobalt, bauxite, crude leather, etc., directly affects the price of final products. We have seen how the price of raw materials can change so quickly during external shocks like wars, pandemics, etc., as happened in 2021-2022 during the COVID-19 pandemic and war in Ukraine.

In equations 1.12 through 1.14, the price of raw materials, *P(r)np,* with all its components, including the price of land, mining rights, etc., is the main variable that guarantees the discount price in an economy pricing based on the whole supply chain of the product. The extraction of raw materials is outsourced or controlled by large corporations that have their operations located in many third-world countries where the varies component of the selling price of raw material, *P(r)np,* such as direct labor, profit margin, variable, and fixed overhead, mining rights, etc., are much cheaper (at low cost) compared to industrialized countries. Otherwise, it won't be easy to support the three-level demand-push that is the base of the economy pricing of the large discount superstores.

Below we have two graphical presentations of the demand-push promotion on the supply side and then the NMP curve and the demand-push on the supply side in economy pricing.

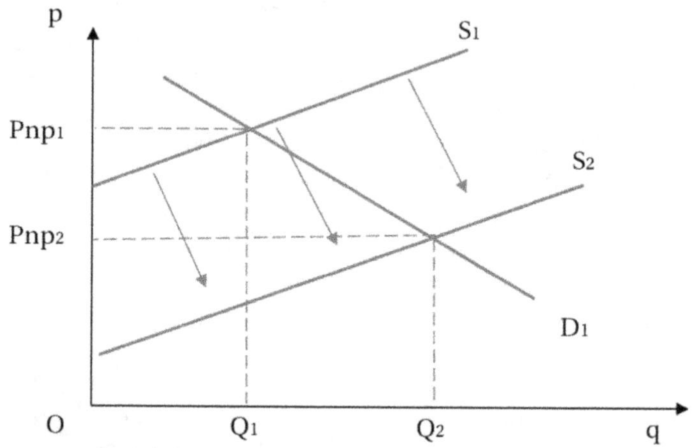

Figure 1.4 The demand-push promotion on the supply side in economy pricing of non-premium products

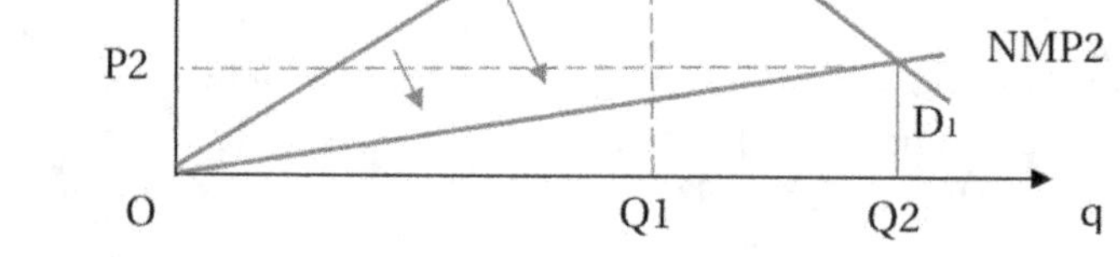

Figure 1.5 The NMP curve and the demand-push promotion on the supply side in economy pricing

Figure 1.4 above illustrates the demand-push promotion system on the supply side, which consist of using the push marketing strategy to promote non-premium products by pushing them onto consumers at discounted prices. A manufacturing company that sells non-premium products to big box superstores during sales events will reduce the price from *Pnp1* to *Pnp2* and move the supply curve from *S1* to *S2*, substantially increasing the quantity of non-premium products offered from *Q1* to *Q2*. In addition, reducing the price of non-premium products from *Pnp1* to *Pnp2* will help to reach the volume sales target that uses the push market strategy by keeping the *current ratio >1* and *NMP > 1* in the company's balance sheet.

Figure 1.5, instead, illustrates the (Net Monetary Position) NMP-p curve and the demand push-promotion system on the supply side in economy pricing. The company will be pushing the demand curve D1 onto customers to buy a non-premium product at discount price P2 (compared to regular price p1) so it can reach the volume sales target Q2 where the slope of the *NMP2* is much lower than the *NMP1* with a lower *current ratio* and lower profitability to stay competitive. If the firm does not lower the price of non-premium goods from P1 to P2 during sales events, then there is no guarantee that this firm will be competitive, as other firms may jump in to offer their own sales events and try to increase their market share. Hence, the equilibrium point to guarantee competitive pricing for the non-premium product is at the intersection of the NMP2 curve with demand curve *D1* at price level *P2* and quantity *Q2*.

The three levels of the demand-push promotion model may not work if there is a disruption in the supply chain of raw materials, subassemblies, and manufactured goods sold to superstores chains. As a matter of fact, regional wars, political unrest, pandemics, and shortage of labor force in third countries where raw materials are extracted and in developing countries where subassemblies and different components are manufactured would cause disruption to the supply chain of superstores and discount chain outlets in industrialized countries where final consumers are located. If the supply chain is strong and reliable, non-premium products will be offered at affordable prices on the discount superstores.

The three-level demand push is not guaranteed if there is a weak link in supply chain management. Even if the other links on the supply chain are strong, the strength of the supply chain depends on the weakest link. This is what happened during the COVID-19 pandemic in 2020-2022, where the price of the raw materials and subassemblies sky-rocketed not because of the shortage but due to continues lockdowns because of massive COVID-19 infections of the labor force in factories, mines, warehouses, ports, and labor shortages in a different part of the world especially in developing countries where many of these non-premium products were assembled and manufactured. The price increase of raw materials and transportation costs due to supply chain disruption and lockdowns increased the inflation rate for the first time in decades for most of the premium and non-premium products in developed countries to an average of 5-11 %. Despite this, even in the middle of the pandemic, large supermarkets and online stores were able to restock their inventories and adjust their prices to offer deep discounts for many non-premium and semi-premium products during major sales events such as Black Friday, Christmas, Boxing Day, and New Year, etc.

The three levels of the demand-push promotion model are, in a certain way, dissimilar to the *Target Costing approach,* where a company plans for the price point, product costs, and margins that it wants to achieve for a new non-premium product by specifically designing a product using lower grade materials and selling it in a very competitive market.

The three levels of the demand-push promotion system instead use the existing non-premium designed product and try to save on cost at different levels of the supply chain by pushing the suppliers to reduce the price of raw materials if the product is produced and sold in large volumes. A *target cost approach* as an alternative is the maximum total cost that can incur on a non-premium product, and a firm can still make the required profit margin from that product at a specific selling price. Target costing breaks down the target cost from product level to component level. The company's product designers and suppliers face competitive pressure to meet the target cost at the component level of the non-premium products.

In contrast to *cost-based pricing, demand-based pricing* (*demand-push*) focuses on two main things: the value to customers and the demand based on the competition. If the demand curve is elastic, then slight decreases in prices can greatly increase sales — and vice versa; a slight increase in prices can greatly reduce sales. An elastic demand curve is more prevalent in a competitive environment. If the demand curve is inelastic, prices could rise substantially, and volume would not be affected as much. For example, if the price of natural gas rises and remains cheaper than electricity, volumes would not be impacted significantly.

The Inflation Model during Sales Events

The demand for non-premium products is relatively elastic, which means that a firm can sell large quantities of non-premium products by simply lowering the price. In fact, the pricing strategy of a discount superstore consists of selling large quantities of non-premium products at a discount price during sales events compared to the quantities of non-premium products the firm would normally sell during non-sales events (regular price). Assuming a superstore has several non-premium items, *n,* that sells at discount price, *Punp,* during sales events. The revenue and volume of non-premium items sold during sales events are much higher than the revenue of the same items sold during non-sales events due to the smaller quantity sold at a higher selling price. The superstore sales revenue, *Rs,* from non-premium products is given as,

$$R_s = \sum_{i=1}^{n} P_{unp} q_u + \sum_{i=1}^{n} P_{np} q_p$$

where qu> qp and qu=cu (1.17)

where, *Punp* and *qu* are, respectively, the discount price and quantity of non-premium units *Un* sold during sales events. Meanwhile, *Pnp* and *qp* are, respectively, the regular price and quantity sold of non-premium products during non-sales events. *Cu,* is the capacity utilization of the superstore to reach a satisfactory level of revenue to meet the net monetary position condition (NMP>1). This is the first level of demand-push. In a similar way, in the second level of demand-push, we have that the manufacturer that produces non-premium products, *Un,* for the superstore during the sale events has a revenue written as,

$$R_m = \sum_{i=1}^{n} P_{munp} q_{mu} + \sum_{i=1}^{n} P_{mnp} q_{mp}$$

where qmu> qmp and qmu=cmu (1.18)

where *Rm* is the revenue for the manufacturing firm, *Pmunp* and *qmu* are respectively the discount price of units *Un* and quantity sold of non-premium products to the superstore during sales events, and *Pmnp* and *qmp* are respectively the regular price and quantity sold of non-premium products during non-sales events. In the same way, at the third level of demand-push, we can use equation (1.17) to generate the revenue of the manufacturer that extracts (in the mining industry) and produces raw materials for non–premium products, *Un,* which are needed to produce non-premium products for the superstore. Therefore, the revenue for the mining company is given as,

$$R_r = \sum_{i=1}^{n} P_{runp} q_{ru} + \sum_{i=1}^{n} P_{rnp} q_{rp}$$

where qru> qrp and qru=cru (1.19)

where again *Prunp* and *qru* are respectively the discount price of units *Un* and quantity sold of non-premium products to the superstore during sales events, and *Prnp* and *qrp* are respectively the regular price and quantity of non-premium units sold during non-sales events. Adding together equations (1.17), (1.18), and (1.19), we have that the revenue for the entire supply chain, denominated as *Rch* for the range of non-premium products, *Un,* using the three-level of demand-push is given as,

$$R_{ch} = \sum_{i=1}^{n} (P_{unp}q_u + P_{munp}q_{mu} + P_{runp}q_{ru}) +$$

$$\sum_{i-1}^{n} (P_{np}q_p + P_{mnp}q_{mp} + P_{rnp}q_{rp}) \quad (1.20)$$

The first part of the right side in equation (1.20) shows respectively the discount price of units *Un* at three levels of the supply chain and the quantity sold of non-premium products during sales events. The second part of the equation shows respectively the regular price and quantity sold of non-premium products during non-sales events. From equation (1.20), we can see that there is no cost-push inflation in an economy pricing as the price of inputs gets reduced throughout the supply chain to accommodate promotions and discounts in superstores for final customers. It is deflation for non-premium products sold at a discount price and, eventually, inflation for non-premium and premium products sold at regular prices, so the net effect of these two combined prices yields low inflation.

The consumer price index (CPI) and inflation rate for a single non-premium item sold to final customers in the superstore are given as,

CPI=(updated price / base period price) * 100= (Pnpc / Pnpb) * 100 (1.21)

$$Inflation\ rate = \left(\frac{Current\ CPI - Base\ Year\ CPI}{Base\ year\ CPI\ x\ 100}\right) * 100 = \left(\frac{P_{npc} - P_{npb}}{P_{npb}}\right) * 100 \quad (1.22)$$

where *Pnpc* and *Pnpb* are, respectively, the regular price of the non-premium products at the current period and at the beginning of the (base) period. If the price of a non-premium product between two periods is *Pnpc* > *Pnpb*, then it implies that there is inflation for the period taken into consideration. In an economy pricing system, the inflation rate should be calculated as the average of all prices, including discount prices, for a given period. In fact, the inflation rate for economy pricing, which consider the average price of a non-premium product during sales and non-sales events, is written as,

$$InflationRate = \frac{Avr \sum_{i=1}^{n}(CurrentCPI - BaseYearCPI)}{Avr \sum_{i=1}^{n} BaseYearCPI} * 100 =$$

$$\frac{Avr \sum_{i=1}^{n}(P_{npc}*q_{npc} + P_{npdc}*q_{npdc}) - (P_{npb}*q_{npb} + P_{npdb}*q_{npdb})}{Avr \sum_{i=1}^{n}(P_{npb}*q_{npp} + P_{npdb} + q_{npdb})} * 100 \quad (1.23)$$

where *Pnpc and qnpc* are respectively the price and quantity of non-premium products sold at the current period, *Pnpdc and qnpdc* are respectively the discounted price and quantity of non-premium products sold at the current period, *Pnpb* and *qnpb* are respectively the price and quantity of non-premium products at the beginning of the period which is referred to as the base-year period, and *Pnpdb* and *qnpdb* are respectively the discounted price and quantity of non-premium products at the beginning of the period which is referred to as the base-year period. In a first-case scenario, we assume that the price, *Pnpc,* of a non-premium product *Un* at a current period, let's say May 2018, is $20 at the regular price and $15 at a discount price (*Pnpdc*). The entire quantity sold during May 2018 at the regular price of $20 is 250 units (*qnpc*), and the quantity sold at the discount price of $15 is 1000 (*qnpdc)* units. These figures are compared with the base period of May 2017, during which the same non-premium product *Un* was sold at a regular price *(Pnpb* = $19.00 (240 units) and at a discount price *Pnpdb* =$15.00 (970 units). Therefore, based on equation (1.23), the inflation rate using the weighted average price during a one-month period in two different years for an average of combined sales and non-sales events for a given non-premium product can be written as,

Inflation rate=

$$\text{Weighted avr}\left[\frac{\left(\frac{(\$20*250)+(\$15*1000)}{(250+1000)}\right)-\left(\frac{(\$19*240)+(\$15*970)}{(240+970)}\right)}{\left(\frac{(\$19*240)+(\$15*970)}{(240+970)}\right)}\right]=$$

$$\frac{(16-15.79)}{15.79}=0.0133=1.33\%$$

The equation above states that the weighted average inflation rate for the non-premium product *Un* in May 2018 compared to May 2017, including the sales events, is only 1.33%, instead of 5% (regular price increase per unit from $19 in May 2017 to $20 in May 2018) thanks to the promotion programs that kept low the price of non-premium products.

In a second-case scenario, for different reasons, we assume that the superstore does not offer certain promotions for the product *Un* in the current period (May 2018) compared to last year (May 2017), and if the product is sold mostly during non-promotions events at regular price, then the weighted average inflation rate could be much higher. In fact, if the price of the non-premium product stays the same but in the current period (2018), the quantity sold during sales events changes in favor of non-sales events, then the inflation could be much higher (keeping the overall quantity sold and the price at the beginning of the period unchanged). By increasing the quantity sold during non-sales events in May 2018 from 250 units to 350 units at the regular price of $20 and reducing the quantity sold at a discount price of $15 during sales events from 1000 to 900 units, the inflation reached a much higher rate, at 3.86% as per below,

Inflation rate=

$$\text{Weighted avr}\left[\frac{\left(\frac{(\$20*350)+(\$15*900)}{(350+900)}\right)-\left(\frac{(\$19*240)+(\$15*970)}{(240+970)}\right)}{\left(\frac{(\$19*240)+(\$15*970)}{(240+970)}\right)}\right]=$$

$$\frac{(16.4-15.79)}{15.79}=0.0386=3.86\%$$

The difference in inflation rate between the first and second case scenario, based on the quantity of non-premium units sold during sales and non-sales events, using the weighted average inflation method, is around 3.86%-1.31%=2.55%. The second scenario indicates that sales events were not very successful, as the number of units sold was less than in the first scenario.

Overall, sales events are short-lived, could last for one or two days or one or two weekends, and regular sales prices instead could stay for the rest of the month. However, they have a big impact on sales. Had the weighted average price of sales and non-sales events not been used to calculate the inflation rate but rather the regular price of each period (\$20 for the current period and \$19 for the base period), the inflation of non-premium product *Un*, based on the first case scenario above could have been as follows,

$$\textit{Inflation Rate}=\left[\frac{Current\ CPI-Base\ Year\ CPI}{Base\ year\ CPI}\right]x100=$$

$$\left(\frac{\{(P_{npc})](q_{npc}+q_{npdc})\}-\{(P_{npb})(q_{npb}+q_{npdb})\}}{\{[(P_{npb})](q_{npb}+q_{npdb})\}}\right)*100=$$

$$\left[\frac{[(\$20)(250+1000)]-\{(\$19)(240+970)\}}{\{(\$19)(240+970)\}}\right]x100=8.74\%$$

By using the simple average price of the non-premium products sold during a combination of sales and non-sales events (average price of (\$20+\$15)/2=\$17.5 for the current period and average price of (\$19+\$15)/2=\$17 for base period) and by taking the total quantity of units sold during each period (quantity of 250+1000=1250 for the current period and quantity 240+970=1210 for the base period), rather than separating the quantities based on the price used to sell the non-premium product for each sales event, we have,

$$Inflation\ Rate=Avr\left[\frac{Current\ CPI-Base\ Year\ CPI}{Base\ year\ CPI}\right]x100=$$

$$\left(\frac{\{[avr(P_{npc}-P_{npdc})](q_{npc}+q_{npdc})\}-\{[avr(P_{npb}+P_{npdb})](q_{npb}+q_{npdb})\}}{\{[avr(P_{npb}+P_{npdb})](q_{npb}+q_{npdb})\}}\right)*100=$$

$$\left[\frac{\left[[avr(\frac{(\$20+\$15)}{2})](250+1000)\right]-\left\{\left[avr\left(\frac{\$19+\$15)}{2}\right)\right](240+970)\right\}}{\{[avr\left(\frac{\$19+\$15)}{2}\right)](240+970)]\}}\right]x100=6.34\%$$

The difference between the inflation rate of the regular price and the promotion price of the non-premium product during sales and non-sales events, not using the weighted inflation method but rather the simple inflation method, is around 8.74%-6.34%=2.4%. The logic behind this is that non-premium products sell at discount prices in larger volumes and have a higher weight than non-premium products that sell at regular prices at low volumes. The quantity of non-premium products and the frequency of sales events used to calculate the weighted average inflation rate is very important in determining the impact of the real inflation rate on the consumer price index.

The inflation rate in an economy's pricing can be expressed as a function of the high volume of mainly non-premium items sold during sales events. The different categories of non-premium products offered by many competitive firms in different industries are expressed as i=1...n, and the inflation rate equation takes the simple form as,

$$\text{Inflation Rate}=I = \sum_{i=1}^{n} f(Q_{nps}, S(p)_{ev}) \quad \text{for} \quad i_{NMP} > 1 \qquad (1.24)$$

where *Qnps* is the quantity in volumes of non-premium products sold at a discount price during sales events on the supply side, *S(p)ev* is the number of sales events that offer several types of discounts, *pev*, during a given fiscal year, and *iNMP>1* is the condition for a competitive firm *i* to have its *Net Monetary Position*, NMP >1. Equation 1.24 assumes that competitive firms participating in the sales events must offer large volumes of non-premium products at discount prices, pushing the demand onto customers. The higher the number of sales events of non-premium products sold during these promotion events throughout the year, the lower the inflation rate during the same period. In fact, in equation 1.24, we have that if *Qnps* and *S(p)ev* increase, the inflation rate *I* decreases, which is simply expressed as $I \downarrow= \sum_{i=1}^{n} f(\uparrow Q_{nps}, \uparrow S(p)_{ev})$.

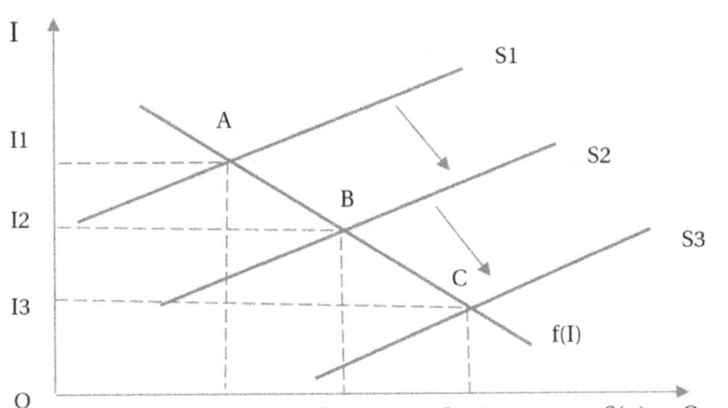

Figure 1.6 Inflation function during the sales events of non-premium products

Figure 1.6 illustrates the inflation function curve, *f(I)*, as a relationship between the inflation and sales events for non-premium goods and the quantity sold during these sales events. In addition, it demonstrates the demand-push as well on the supply side, which consists of using push marketing strategies to promote non-premium products at a discounted price.

A higher frequency of sales events will increase the volume of non-premium products sold during the year and will lower the inflation rate. As demonstrated in Figure (1.6), if the number of sales events increases from *Sev1* to *Sev2* and then to *Sev3* through supply curves S1, S2, and S3 (by increasing volumes of non-premium products offered), then the inflation rate of non-premium products during the same period will decrease from I1, to I2 and then from I2 to I3, intersecting the supply curves respectively at A, B, and C. The higher the number of sales events for non-premium products, the larger the quantity of non-premium products sold with respect to premium products, and the lower the inflation rate for this category of the consumers' products index.

Not all consumer price indices are weighted averages using weights. Consumers use items based on the CPI basket divided into major components such as housing 40.0%, food and beverage 18.0%, transport 17.0%, medical care 7%, other; 8.0%, clothing 6.0%, entertainment 4.0%, etc. By using the weighted average inflation rate during sales and non-sales events, the CPI (Consumer Price Index) basket could change based on the items that offer more discounts during certain sales events. The higher the number of sales events for the non-premium products during the year, the higher the probability that the average inflation rate will get down and reduce some components of the CPI basket, such as food, clothing, entertainment, etc., and increase the more expensive and premium components such as housing, medical care, transport, etc., based on the utility function of each customer. The frequency of sales events and consumers' disposable income will determine when the consumer is ready to move from non-premium to premium products, shifting the components of the CPI basket to more expensive premium items.

Economy pricing in industrialized countries has been characterized by a low inflation rate, especially in the last few decades (except during the pandemic 2020-2023), thanks in part to the new technological processes, continued improvements, and efficient supply chains that have helped keep low the price of raw materials and semi-assemblies used to manufacture the final products.

Suppose middle-income consumers buy items, mostly during sales events, that have a low weight in their consumption basket, such as food, beverage, clothing, furniture, electronics, entertainment, etc. In that case, they will use the extra savings to buy items that have a much higher weight in their consumption baskets, such as housing, transportation, vacation, investment in shares and bonds, or spend on more expensive premium products such as brand clothing, high-quality furniture, expensive brand electronics, expensive cars and watches, expensive vacation packages, etc.

The Role of Mass-production and Economies of Scale in Economy Pricing

The economies of scale used in mass production reduce the average costs attributable to production volume increases. The firms seeking to become dominant and competitive producers of a product or service will be looking to achieve economies of scale. A distinction can be made between internal and external economies of scale. Internal economies of scale occur when a firm reduces the cost per unit by increasing output. External economies of scale occur when an entire industry benefits from expansion, for example, through the application of new technology, the creation of improved infrastructure, a skilled labor force, or by sharing "know-how."

The opinion of economists is that producing large volumes of the same product generally reduces, at least initially, the unit cost for the following main reasons: (1) economies accompanying the use of mass-production methods, (2) higher productivity because of specialization and "learning by doing," and (3) economies of discounts, promotion, and purchasing. We'll consider these factors separately to better understand the production of large output volumes.

Mass production or economy of scale is a 'production technique' that tends to be economical when large volumes of output are planned because it involves considerable development, design, structural, and set-up costs. The production method used in mass production is designed in a certain way to reach a low marginal cost. A typical example of mass production is the production of automobiles that use molds, dies, and assembly lines production methods to reduce the per-unit cost of automobiles when the planned volume reach a large number of units, such as millions. High-volume methods are used for high rates of output that require high fixed costs causing the unit cost to be low for high volumes of production and high for low volumes of production.

Large scale-operation allows the use of less specialized labor and more multi-functional machines in production. Higher productivity comes because of specialization and "learning by doing." For example, in a typical large automotive plant, there are hundreds of different jobs requiring specialized workers trained to perform each task. In a small plant, a single worker can perform several tasks requiring longer training periods than specialized workers working in a large auto plant. Machines or robots perform many routine tasks of certain complications in big plants to eliminate human error. In small plants, introducing robots is impossible due to the small scale of production.

The employees of a firm can improve their skills as they experience "learning by doing" in their jobs. In many cases, concentrating on a narrower range of tasks can help workers develop cost-reducing techniques. Large-scale production and greater specialization can help produce more output per unit of labor. Large-volume production allows the use of specialized equipment and automation to perform repetitive tasks. Machinery and equipment cannot be used efficiently if they must switch between tasks. Increased specialization in the use of labor and capital equipment is feasible as a plant increase in size.

Economies of discounts consist of promotions, rebates, and volume discounts. In economy pricing, the suppliers of raw materials will very often charge a lower price per unit for those items if a firm buys in large quantities. When a company produces a high output volume, it needs a substantial quantity of inputs and can take advantage of the associated price discounts often offered by suppliers to reduce its per-unit costs. The larger the company, the stronger the negotiating power of the company with the suppliers of raw materials to support the economies of discounts during promotion events.

Larger firms operating at economies of scale have a cost advantage over their competitors that arises with increased product output. The firms use the cost advantage as a competitive strategy by building large plants with substantial economies of scale, using its lower cost per unit to price aggressively and increase sales volume. As a plant increases its capacity and output, the average cost per unit of output drops because the relative and capital costs decline. Suppose we have an average unit production cost made of variable and fixed costs (Production unit= variable costs + fixed costs). In that case, we can say that as output increases, the fixed cost decreases, resulting in a drop in overall costs. The residual cost reductions will come from the ability of the corporation to distribute non-manufacturing costs, such as marketing and R&D, over a larger number of outputs, further reducing the average unit cost (Amitabh and Evans, 2005).

In certain industries where the technology of production leads to large economies of scale, the long-run average total cost curve for a firm falls over the entire range of output covered by the industry demand curve. The firm that has lower per-unit costs at higher output levels will be able to charge a price lower than the average per-unit cost that prevails at much lower output levels for non-premium products. A firm with economies of scale can satisfy the market segment with other competitive rivals with economies of scale and the same lower cost per unit of non-premium products. However, the new firms trying to get into the market will not be able to charge a price low enough to compete with the established firms that already operate in economy pricing of non-premium products.

Economies of scale can easily be confused with the economic notion of returns to scale. Economies of scale refer to a firm's saving costs. Meanwhile, returns to scale indicate the relationship between inputs and outputs in a long-run production function. Returns to scale only indicates production efficiency, while economies of scale unequivocally consider costs.

As per definition, a production function has constant returns to scale if increasing all inputs by some proportion results in output increased by the same proportion: returns decrease if doubling inputs results in less than double the output, and returns increase if more than double the output. Returns to scale are represented by the degree of homogeneity of the production function. Homogeneous production functions with constant returns to scale are first-degree homogeneous. Increasing returns to scale are represented by a degree of homogeneity greater than one, and decreasing returns to scale are represented by degrees of homogeneity less than one.

Suppose a firm competes in all input markets so that the per-unit prices of all its inputs are unaffected by the volume of the inputs the firm purchases. In that case, we can say that at a particular level of output, the firm has economies of scale if it has increasing returns to scale, has diseconomies of scale if it has to decrease returns to scale, and has constant return to scale if it has neither increasing nor decreasing returns to scale.

If a firm is not competing in the input markets, but there are increasing returns to scale in some range of output levels, and the firm is large enough in some input markets that increasing its purchases of an input raises the input's per-unit cost, then the firm will have diseconomies of scale in that range of output. However, suppose the firm, through negotiations, can get volume discounts of one or more inputs. In that case, it will have economies of scale in some range of output levels even if there is a decreasing return in production in that output range. Suppliers will be willing to reduce the price of inputs (items) used by the firm only if the firm buys them in large quantities to increase output levels. In return, the firm buying discounted inputs benefit from the lower transaction costs and economies of scale that result from larger volumes to make enough savings to cover the additional costs.

The returns to scale can be explained in a better way by using multipliers. We assume to multiply the amount of each input the firm uses by the same number (multiplier) and see how output changes. The technology available to a firm is described by a production function F where the number of inputs the firm uses are given by a vector $(x1, \ldots\ldots, xn)$, where xi is the amount of input i. The production function F associates each vector of inputs an output $F(x1, \ldots\ldots xn)$. A production function F has the property of globally constant return to scale if we multiply the amount of every input by a coefficient, α, the resulting output is multiplied by $\alpha > 1$, then the production function has constant returns to scale (CRTS) which is given as,

$$F(\alpha x_1, \alpha x_2) = \alpha F(x_1, x_2) \quad \text{for all } (x_1, x_2) \tag{1.25}$$

Like above, if we multiply the amount of every input by coefficient $\alpha > 1$, the factor by which output increases is less than α, then the production function F has a *Decreasing Return to Scales* (DRTS) given as,

$$F(\alpha x_1, \alpha x_2) < \alpha F(x_1, x_2) \quad \text{for all } (x_1, x_2) \tag{1.26}$$

Lastly, if we multiply the amount of every input by the coefficient $\alpha>1$, the factor by which output increases is more than α, then the production function has *Increasing Returns to Scale* (IRTS) written as

$$F(\alpha x_1, \alpha x_2) > \alpha F(x_1, x_2) \quad \text{for all } (x_1, x_2) \tag{1.27}$$

A production function may have increasing returns to scale (IRTS) for some range of outputs, decreasing returns to scale (DRTS) over other ranges, and constant returns to scale (CRTS) in some other range of outputs. The economies of scale can be presented by a simple production function, *Y*, indicating output and multipliers. Assuming a production function given as $Y = 3K+4L$, and by increasing both K and L by *m*, we have a new production function given as,

$$Y' = 3(K*m)+4(L*m)=3*K*m+4*L*m=m(3*K+4*L)=mY \tag{1.28}$$

where $(3*K+4*L)$ has been replaced with *Y*. Since $Y'=mY$, we have that by increasing all of our inputs by the multiplier *m*; the production function has been increased exactly by *m*, bringing us to the constant returns to scale. If the production function is given as Y = 0.7 KL, then we put in our multipliers and create a new production function as,

$$Y'=0.7(K*m)(L*m) = 0.7*K*L*m^2=Y*m^2 \tag{1.29}$$

where, since $m>1$ and $m^2>m$, the new production function has increased by more than *m*, so we have increasing returns to scale. In the same way, if the production function is given as $Y = K^{0.3}L^{0.2}$, again, we put in our multipliers, *m*, and create a new production function of the form,

$$Y' = (K*m)^{0.3}(L*m)^{0.2} = K^{0.3}L^{0.2}m^{0.5} = Y*\,m^{0.5} \tag{1.30}$$

Given that $m > 1$ and $m^{0.5} < m$, our new production function (1.30) has increased by less than *m*, so it has a decreasing return to scale. If we combine all three returns to scale production functions (1.28, 1.29, and 1.30), we get a single production function that has different returns to scale in a different range of outputs; constant, increasing, and decreasing, and is given as,

$$Y' = mY + Y*m^2 + Y*\,m0.5 \tag{1.31}$$

Assuming a large multi-product company operating in economy pricing sells three products: the first product is a non-premium 1 indicated as (*np1*), the second product is a non-premium 2 indicated as (*np2*), and the third product is a premium product indicated as (*p3*). The sales of non-premium one product represent 50 percent of the total revenue, non-premium 2 represents 35 percent of the revenue, and the sales of premium product represent only 15 percent of the total revenue. This large company will have the capability to buy in bulk the raw materials used for non-premium products, so it can lower the cost per unit of the materials needed to make its final products. The company will use increasing returns to scale for non-premium one product that sells at bulk at 50% of total sales, constant returns to scale for non-premium2 that has a share of about 35% of total sales, and decreasing returns to scale for the high-end premium product that has a share of only 15% of total sales. The new production function using the three products of this multi-product company based on the range of its output is given as,

$$Y' = (0.5np1)Y^*m^2 + (0.35np2)mY + (0.15p3)Y^*\, m^{0.5} \quad (1.32)$$

The corporation above will have constant and increasing returns to scale for non-premium products (*np1* and *np2*) manufactured in large quantities by buying substantial volumes of discounted inputs from suppliers. However, for the premium product (*p3*), the firm will have decreasing returns to scale given the more expensive inputs and technical difficulties of producing a high-end premium product.

Economies of scale in an economy pricing arise very often because of the inverse relationship between the quantity produced of non-premium products and the per-unit fixed costs. Large corporations producing large volumes of non-premium products lower the per-unit fixed costs because the costs are spread over a larger number of products. Economies of scale also reduce the variable cost per unit due to efficiencies in production, skilled management, and improving supply chain management. Manufacturing costs can drop substantially if the business doubles its output.

Larger companies can take advantage of more efficient equipment, automation, hardware, and software that allows them to produce, deliver and sell more efficiently, target its customer more effectively, and give more promotions and discounts to final consumers. Big corporations achieve technical economies of scale because they use learning-by-doing and advanced training programs, setting themselves ahead of their smaller competitors on the learning curve.

Large corporations use monopsony power as they buy so much of a product that they can negotiate a lower price than their smaller competitors. For example, big-box stores like Wal-Mart, Target, Costco, and Amazon can have lower prices because their huge buying power gives them monopsony economies of scale. In the same way, the manufacturing companies that sell to Wal-Mart, Costco, and Amazon use their buying power as direct suppliers of Wal-Mart,

Costco, and Amazon to buy inputs in large quantities at a much lower price than other competitors that are not direct suppliers of big-box stores.

Big corporations have other advantages, such as the use of financial economies of scale, where they can have cheaper access to capital. A large corporation can get funded from the stock market with *Initial Public Offering* (IPO) or issuing bonds and other forms of debt at lower interest rates due to higher credit ratings compared to smaller firms. With perfect competition in the output market, the long-run equilibrium involves large companies operating at the minimum point of their long-run average cost curves, in the borderline between economies and diseconomies of scale, as illustrated in figure 1.7.

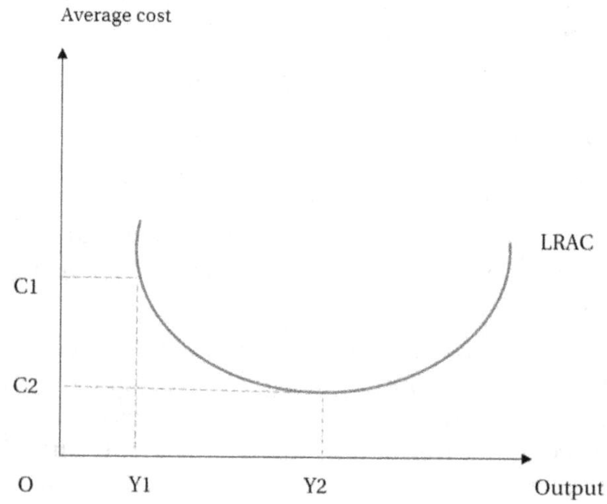

Figure 1.7 The average cost and LRAC curve in economies of scale

Figure 1.7 above demonstrates that when the volume of production increases from *Y1* to *Y2*, the average cost of each unit decreases from *C1* to *C2* in the long-run average cost given by LRAC. The economies of scale also have economies of scope. As per definition, economies of scope are when a firm can produce multiple products by using several product lines at a given output level more cheaply than a combination of different firms, each producing a single product at the same output (Kass, 1998). Economies of scale differ from economies of scope in that a company obtains a cost advantage in production by producing a complementary variety of products with a concentration on a core competency. In short, the cost of producing multiple products using the same infrastructure is smaller than the cost of producing each product separately. Economies of scope and scale are normally positively correlated and interdependent.

For example, in the bedding and sofa industry, it is common for large firms to produce their own springs before assembling a mattress or a sofa. However, the small firms operating in this industry may have to purchase springs from different suppliers at a higher price than large companies pay. The savings from producing both springs and mattresses or sofas would be an economy of scope for the large producers, although the large companies probably also have economies of scale that make it feasible to invest in spring operations in the first place.

Another example is the banking industry, where banks have economies of scope by offering a range of related financial services, such as retail banking and investment services, through a single service infrastructure (such as branches, internet websites, etc.). In this case, the cost of providing each service separately would be much higher than the costs of using a single infrastructure to provide multiple financial products.

ERP Systems and Business Efficiency

Enterprise Resource Planning (ERP) is a powerful platform that helps organizations automate and manage essential parts of their business to reach optimal performance. The ERP platform coordinates the flow of data between a company's business processes, providing a single source of valuable data across different departments and divisions of the enterprise. This complex software can integrate a company's financials, supply chain, operations, commerce, reporting, manufacturing, and human resources activities in one platform.

The ERP platform allows different departments to communicate and share information more easily with the rest of the company. ERP platform can help a corporation become more efficient by connecting production, finance, distribution, and human resources information. Many corporations employ ERP for several reasons, such as expanding in different market segments, reducing costs, and improving operations. An ERP platform allows businesses to have direct access to information required for clients, vendors, and business partners. This helps improve supplier, customer, and employee satisfaction, quicker response rates in business decisions, increased accuracy rates, and decreased associated costs as the company operates more efficiently.

After the 2000s, many ERP systems have become very important to all types of companies because they help them implement resource planning by integrating all the processes, such as purchasing inventory, production, sales, marketing, finance, reporting, business intelligence analysis, and human resources, into one single system. For large corporations, the ERP system helps collect information about the activity and state of different divisions, making this information available to operations and management, where it can be used promptly and efficiently. The EPR system helps standardize business processes to be executed efficiently and accurately. ERP system has the capability to set up alerts to inform managers of any exception that needs to be addressed promptly. Automated processes can be set up across different departments and divisions in different locations, from purchasing to inventory and production, and from accounting and finance to sales, marketing, and customer services. With an ERP system, data is entered once and then distributed and analyzed to all departments and divisions in the business. This process helps reduce time wasted on data entry and reduce error-related costs.

A standardized EPR data system delivers efficiency and visibility across departments, making the company work more efficiently and helping buyers get the right materials from suppliers and employees meet customer requirements more quickly, decreasing operating costs. By increasing organizational efficiency, ERP systems can help decrease operating costs. The proper flow of data is also valuable for management as they can make decisions faster to new opportunities and address problems before they become big issues.

There are various challenges for businesses implementing ERP systems. The main three challenges for businesses that are still hesitant about implementing the ERP are as follows:

1-) **Choosing the right ERP solution**. There is no perfect software solution for every problem in a company. However, ERP should be able to get the best of the business processes and bring them together in one integrated system that allows all departments to share the same data. This makes it important to choose the right technology for the organization.

2-) **Affording the cost of the ERP system**. Software solutions can be purchased as a total package or in modules purchased separately according to your business needs. An ERP implementation can cost between $150,000 and $850,000 for a mid-sized business to millions of dollars in a large corporation depending on the number of users and customizations required.

3-) **Integrating the new ERP system with the existing software**. An ERP software can work with the current software but also include new features and customized modules that can help business growth in the future. For example, a new ERP software can help manage the finance module, supply chain, and manufacturing side by bringing in a strong business intelligence module. Some of the common EPR systems include brands and names such as AbbaDox, SAP, Oracle, Microsoft Dynamics 365, SalesWarp, SAS, Sage, Abby, BQE Core Suite, Epicor, Syspro, etc.

Modern ERP systems are complex integrated platforms that try to resolve common challenges faced in manufacturing, such as inventory control, customer relationship management (CRM), supply chain management (SCM), capacity planning, project management, financial management, and financial reporting, job scheduling, timesheet and workforce planning, business intelligence, and reporting. The right ERP system personalized to fit business requirements will capitalize on productivity and maximize efficiency in all corporation departments. There are different ways an ERP System can improve productivity and business efficiency. Some of them are listed below:

1-) **Reduce waste across the business**: an ERP system with a perpetual inventory system can help businesses reduce material waste, maximize storage space, and anticipate and forecast seasonal demand. The ERP will help reduce material waste, productivity, and costs in different departments.

2-) **Superior Supply Chain Management**: an advanced ERP system can coordinate every stage of the supply chain by centralizing purchasing system, tracking suppliers and creditors, identifying the Pain Points (missed invoices, late deliveries), and updating the production status *On-The-Go*. This coordination saves time and money, improves customer relationships, and turns the business to benefit more from high efficiency and higher profit margins.

3-) **Real-time job tracking**: ERP systems with built-in-job-tracking functionality, the information flows in real-time, providing a complete picture of every job-in-progress in the system. In fact, this functionality helps managers and staff to anticipate any delays and alert the customer. It also can communicate to customers when the job is completed and ready to be shipped. This fast information flow helps build customer trust and makes businesses cost-effective and more profitable.

4-) **Instant quotes, invoices, and alerts**: a cutting-edge ERP system can help pull data together from quoting, costing invoicing, budgeting, banking, timesheet, and tax forecasting into one integrated to-use system. In fact, an ERP system can use functionalities such as creating quotes from anywhere, receiving alerts for overdue invoices, timesheet tools, costing sheets, tax and banking integrations, accurate financial forecasting, and reducing human errors (Johnson, 2023).

5-) **Financial forecasting and business intelligence**: an ERP allows businesses to visualize upcoming work easily and assists in optimizing capacity planning. It helps get the job done faster using the best resources eliminating unnecessary cost overruns and downtime. It empowers staff and management to anticipate problems and increase accuracy in forecasting demand by generating a high level of business intelligence reports for the management.

An ERP system can facilitate collaboration between departments, a sign of a healthy business working to optimum productivity levels. All personnel in different departments receive key information whenever they need it, keeping all areas of the business up to date with the latest demands. Business efficiency and improved productivity can be expressed as an increased function of five variables that enhance business efficiency using an ERP system. This function is given as,

$$BuE = f(Rw, SCM, Rt, Iq, FfBI) \tag{1.33}$$

where *BuE* is the increased business efficiency because of improved five variables: *Rw*- reduced waste; *SCM*- Superior Supply Chain Management; *Rt*- Real-time job tracking; *Iq*- Instant quotes, invoices, and alerts; *FfBi*-Financial Forecasting and Business Intelligence. The equation above indicates that for a business to be efficient, profitable, and competitive, it must invest in an advanced ERP that can improve all five core areas of the business. An ERP system can be expressed as a linear function written as,

$$ERPs = MvX + Bf \tag{1.34}$$

where *Mv* is the variable cost to maintain, repair, secure, and update the ERP system, and *Bf* is the fixed cost to invest in a new advanced ERP system, including the monthly fee charges. Figure 1.8 illustrates the relationship between the *ERP* and Business Efficiency curves (BuE) for two firms that use an ERP system in an economy pricing system. Firm-1 uses *ERP1,* and firm-2 uses *ERP2.*

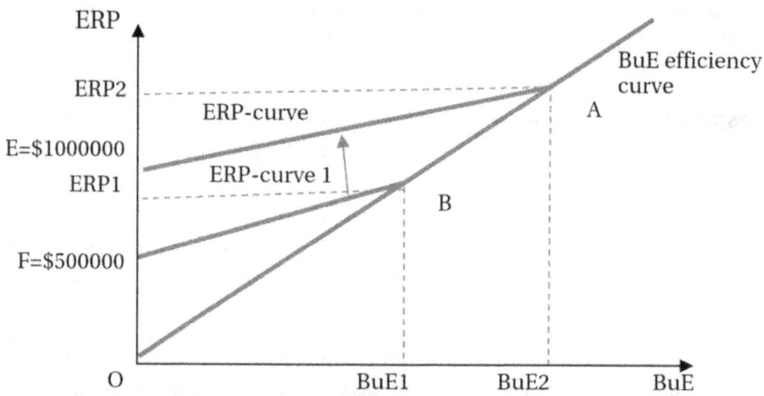

Figure 1.8 The relationship between ERP curves and business efficiency

The linear function for *firm-1,* indicated by upward-sloping *ERP-curve1* in the figure above, has a fixed investment of $500 000 in an *ERP1* system given by point F in the vertical axis and intersects the *BuE* efficiency curve at point B. At point B, the business efficiency is given by *BuE1.* However, the linear function of *firm-2,* indicated by *ERP-curve2,* has a higher fixed investment of $1 000 000 in a different *ERP2* system given by point *E.* At point A, the business efficiency for *firm-2* is superior to the business efficiency for *firm-1,* indicated by a higher point *BuE2* in the horizontal axis. This means that the five core areas of the business in *firm-2* are more efficient and productive than the five areas of business in *firm-1* due to a superior ERP system that integrates better and more efficiently all the business departments. Customers will appreciate more those firms that have products shipped faster, have better warranty coverage, and have superior customer service—this increases customers' loyalty to these firms and their products. Especially in an economy pricing system, during promotions and sales events, an integrated ERP system is crucial for firms to promote and sell non-premium products, fill the orders correctly and ship on time to customers, and process the returns swiftly and properly.

Conclusions about the Basic Microeconomics of Economy Pricing

This chapter has taken into consideration various aspects of microeconomics in economy pricing.

Economy pricing is widely used in supermarkets and superstores where marketing and production costs to bring these products to selling points have been minimal. In the last two-three decades, with the advent of the internet and online shopping, economy pricing has entered a new phase where products are not needed to be brought to the selling point but rather to big distribution centers and warehouses, bringing even further down the marketing, overheads, and production costs. The main purpose of economy pricing is that reducing the regular price to a new discounted price would create a sense of urgency and high perceived value by customers to push them to purchase discounted items.

On the supply side, the firms operating in economy pricing must adjust to the rules of discounts and promotions to survive in a competitive market. These firms must manufacture two types of products - premium and non-premium - to make them competitive and, at the same time, profitable. The firms will maximize the value of the company if their *Net Monetary Position* (NMP) during intra-periods and the entire fiscal year is greater than one by using a combination of different pricing strategies during sales events for their premium and non-premium products.

The two important strategies used in economy pricing are push-and-pull marketing strategies. The difference between push and pull strategies lies in how the companies approach different categories of consumers to sell their products. In a push-marketing strategy, the firms promote products by pushing them onto consumers. This type of strategy is used mostly for mass-produced non-premium products. Instead, in the pull-marketing strategy, the companies try to establish a loyal customer-base to follow and draw consumers to the products, especially if the products are of high-end premium.

The three-level demand-push promotion model is another effective strategy used in economy pricing by giant discount superstores to make their non-premium products competitive. In fact, at the first level, the superstore pushes the demand by pushing their discounted products (mostly non-premium) onto customers using different marketing tactics and asking manufactures to reduce the price of non-premium items for certain sales events. The second level of demand-push occurs when the manufactures of non-premium goods ask their suppliers to reduce the price of their intermediate subassemblies or raw materials to support the superstores' sales events. And the third-level demand-push follows when the producers of raw materials (or subassemblies) ask their mining sector suppliers to reduce the price of raw materials so they can have a lower cost for their subassemblies offered to the manufacturing sector of non-premium products. The system of three-level of demand-push creates significant discounts for final consumers during the sale events keeping at the same time inflation at low levels.

The mass production of non-premium products and the economies of scale are other economic phenomena in economy pricing to reduce cost and be competitive. The firms operating in economies of scale have the cost advantage over their competitors that arises with increased output of a product. They use the cost advantage as a competitive strategy by building large plants with substantial economies of scale, using its lower cost to price aggressively whenever possible and increase sales volume.

Chapter 2
Theory of the Firm in Economy Pricing

Introduction

An important aspect of microeconomics is the theory of the firm. This chapter will discuss in depth the theory of the firm in economy pricing. This discussion includes the concept of production and costs from an economy pricing perspective. The firm's cost or the cost of goods sold is the expenditure it must incur to acquire the inputs used in production to manufacture the output. A firm can use different levels of technologies to produce output by using a variety of input vectors, which the level sets of the production function can summarize.

Therefore, the firm must decide which of the possible production plans and marketing/sales strategies must be used to remain competitive in economy pricing. Suppose the firm's objective is to maximize profits from premium and non-premium products. In that case, it will necessarily choose the cost-minimizing production combination plan for premium and non-premium products to reach this goal. This objective won't guarantee that the firm will remain competitive in the long run in the market. Suppose the goal of the firm is to maximize profits of the premium products and eventually cover the cost of non-premium products. In that case, it will necessarily choose the cost-minimizing production plan for premium products and cost-covering variable costs for non-premium products, especially during the sales events, to increase sales volume and have a stable flow of revenue.

To determine the cost-minimizing production plan, the firm must take into consideration the terms at which it can purchase inputs and the use of technological possibilities in production. These conditions, in turn, depend on the situations the firm can face to reach favorable trade agreements in the input markets. Depending on the size of the firm, it may face upward-sloping supply curves for some of the inputs used in the premium products and downward-sloping supply curves for most of the inputs used in the production of non-premium products. These topics will be touched on in this chapter: capacity utilization, volume-based analysis and profitability, production possibility frontier, behavioral relationships, cost function, and isocost lines.

The Role of Capacity Utilization in Economy Pricing

Capacity utilization, by definition, is the extent to which an enterprise or, in the case of the national economy, a nation (taking into consideration all the productive sectors) uses its installed productive capacity. Capacity utilization is the connection between the industrial output manufactured with the installed equipment and the potential output that could be eventually produced with it if production capacity was fully utilized. A more technical definition of capacity utilization is about the potential output representing the maximum amount of output that can be produced in the short run by a company, industry, or country with the existing installation of capital. Capacity utilization can be measured likewise as the weighted average of the ratios of the actual output of firms to the maximum output that can be produced per unit of time with the existing stock of capital installed in a plant (Berndt and Morrison, 1981). In a few words, capacity utilization is the ratio of the actual level of output to the maximum level of output that can be produced in an existing plant without adding new equipment.

There is also a distinction between "engineering capacity," which is the maximum production over a certain interval of time, and "economic capacity," which is the desired level of output for a given plant from an economic perspective. The Federal Reserve in the U.S. calculates the output, capacity, and capacity utilization measures for each industrial sector by publishing monthly industrial production indexes. Each industry utilization rate is equal to an output index divided by a related capacity index. The Federal Reserve calculates and analyses the output, capacity, and capacity utilization figures for the U.S. economy for each industrial sector that consists of manufacturing. The capacity indexes are normally ratios that represent the concept of sustainable, practical capacity as the highest output each plant can maintain within the regular work schedule, taking into consideration normal downtime and assuming to operate the use of machinery and equipment efficiently in place (Corrado and Mattey, 1997).

Another aspect of production capacity is capacity expansion. Capacity expansion is a major strategic decision due to the capital required, the difficulty of forming accurate forecasting, and the long-term lead times and commitment. The main forecasting problems are the long-term demand, technological development, and the behavior of competitors. A firm expanding its production capacity must avoid overcapacity. Sometimes, capacity expansion is also referred to as market penetration because it involves increasing the quantity of a product pushed into an existing market. Under capacity tends to be a short-term issue, as the profit normally will attract investors to invest in adding production capacity. Overcapacity tends to be a long-term problem, as firms are more likely to compete aggressively rather than reverse their expansion and production capacity.

In an economy pricing where market competition is the rule, any plant operating in a range with short-run scale economies would reach a higher NMP (Net Monetary Position) curve for the non-premium products by increasing capacity utilization and pushing down prices as it moves along a downward sloping region of the supply curve. Therefore, in the presence of market competition or short-run increasing returns, there is a possibility of a negative correlation between capacity utilization and price changes for non-premium products. Lowering the prices of non-premium products during sales events will increase the volumes of sales orders received by manufacturing plants from retail stores, which translates into increased plant capacity utilization. Increasing returns suggest that changes in industrial output mainly reflect changes in the capacity of industry to produce. If the measured increase in capacity utilization is not accompanied by rising mark-ups of prices over wages but rather decreasing mark-up prices over wages for non-premium products, then it could be evidence in favor of short-run increasing returns.

The economic significance of capacity utilization is that if market demand grows, capacity utilization will rise, which is a sign of inflationary pressure. If demand weakens, capacity utilization will slacken off. In economy pricing, the market demand will grow mostly due to competitive factors and three levels of demand-push, which in turn help increase capacity utilization. If capacity utilization rises above 80%, it will normally trigger price inflation, but in economy pricing, the inflation usually remains low due to lower input prices. Any excess capacity means that insufficient demand exists to permit the expansion of output. In economy pricing, insufficient demand will turn to sufficient demand if promotions and discounts are offered for non-premium products, eliminating excess capacity.

Lower capacity utilization (relative to the trend capacity utilization rate) for firms selling high volumes of non-premium products is viewed as a not-good sign of the health of the economy. Instead, strong capacity utilization for non-premium products above the trend rate is considered a leading indicator of healthy economy pricing. In some cases, in a given industry, lower capacity utilization with respect to the trend capacity utilization rate is viewed as favorable for the bond market. Bondholders see strong capacity utilization as a leading indicator of higher inflation for certain types of premium and semi-premium products, which in turn, decreases the bond prices, often prompting a higher yield to compensate for the higher expected rate of inflation.

In other cases, standard literature sees the capacity utilization rate as an indicator of efficiency in the factors of production. In fact, based on this literature, many industries in developed economies suffer from some sort of excess capacity. Therefore, for the critics of market capitalism, the system is not efficient because at least 20-30 percent of additional output could be produced with the existing installed production capacity if the buying power was better distributed. However, these critics do not consider the utilization capacity in economy pricing, where most non-premium products are sold at a discounted price during promotions and sales events. The sales events increase capacity utilization and keep inflation low. A level of utilization to some extent below the maximum production capacity usually prevails, regardless of economic conditions and sales events in any type of industry.

Capacity utilization is used to assess a company's current operating efficiency. It can also be used to determine if the unit cost rises during a volume production change. For example, if firm A produces 8 000 widgets at the cost of $3.0 per unit and increases its production up to 12 000 widgets without raising costs, then the company will be running at a capacity of 66% (8 000/12 000). Therefore, capacity utilization is given as,

$$\text{Capacity utilization} = (\text{actual output}/\text{capacity}) \times 100$$

Capacity utilization tends to oscillate with the business cycles, with firms adjusting production volumes in response to changing demand and sales events. During a recession, the demand for commodities will decline sharply, giving rise to a higher rate of unemployment, wage fall, consumer confidence fades, and business investments dip to their lowest levels. The research department of the Federal Reserve has published capacity utilization figures since the early 1960s, covering several economic cycles. The highest level of capacity utilization in the U.S., approaching 90 percent, was achieved in the late 1960s and early 1970s. The deepest drop occurred in 1982 and 2009, when capacity utilization fell to 70.9 percent and 66.7 percent, respectively.

In many aspects, low-capacity utilization is considered, for some researchers, a concern to fiscal and monetary authorities. In recent years, especially in 2015 and 2016, European economies, such as Italy, Spain, and France, struggled with the effects of low-capacity utilization. During the financial crisis of 2008, some European economies, such as France and Spain, were struggling with the effects of low-capacity utilization.

Despite aggressive monetary policies consisting of keeping historically low-interest rates for a long time to stimulate the economy, the inflation used to measure the economy's health remained below target levels for extended periods, and the threat of deflation loomed. In some European countries, low-capacity utilization because of low demand for premium and non-premium products and lower number of sales events compared to North America created a higher unemployment rate compared to the U.S. and so much slack in those economies that prices were slow to adjust and react to simulative efforts. Rising production activity did not require significant capital investment by having excess capacity in these economies. Table 2.1 shows the average installed productive capacity utilization rate for different countries.

Average Utilization Rate for Installed Productive Capacity

The average utilization rate of installed productive capacity in the industry in different countries was estimated in 2003/2004 and is given as below:

- United States 79.5% (April 2008 — U.S. Federal Reserve)
- Japan 83–86% (Bank of Japan-2004)
- European Union 82% (Eurostat-2004)
- Australia 80% (National Bank estimate-2004)
- Brazil 60–80% (Statista-Brazil Statistics & Facts)
- India 70% (Indiastat.2004)
- China 60-65% (National Bureau of Statistics of China, 2004)
- Turkey 79.8% (September 2008 –Turkish Statistical Institute)
- Canada 87% (Statistics Canada-2003)

Table 2.1 Installed Production Capacity

Figure 2.1 below illustrates the production capacity utilization in economy pricing, which has a similar form of a production possibility frontier. The production capacity utilization curves in economy pricing composed of premium and non-premium products are normally drawn as bulging upwards or outwards from the origin ("concave") and can be represented as linear (straight), depending on the combination of premium and non-premium products manufactured. Based on the second equilibrium condition of the firm's pricing strategy, given in equation (1.11) - which takes into consideration the demand for premium, non-premium, and non-premium discounted products and sales target to reach a desired profit - the production capacity utilization will have to reach an average of 70-80 percent normally. Denominating by *Uc* the production capacity utilization, we have that the linear demand function that meets the production capacity utilization condition is given as,

$$Dp(Pp) + Dnp(Pnp) + Dnpd(Pnpd) = Sales\ Target = Uc \qquad (2.1)$$

where *Dp, Dnp, Dnpd, Pp, Pnp,* and *Pnpd* are the respective demand (push demand) and price of premium, non-premium, and non-premium discounted products.

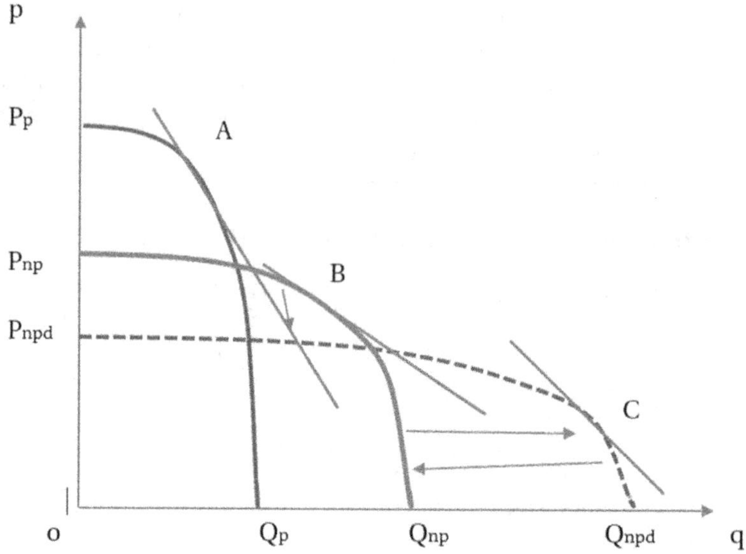

Figure 2.1 The production capacity utilization curves for premium and non-premium products in Economy Pricing

The production capacity utilization curves for premium, non-premium, and non-premium discounted are respectively depicted by curves A, B, and C in Figure 2.1. Curve A indicates premium products will have a higher selling price, *Pp*, but a lower production capacity utilization given by a lower quantity of units manufactured at *Qp* compared to the quantity of non-premium units manufactured given by *Qnp*. Curve B will have a lower selling price, *Pnp*, but a higher production capacity utilization given by a higher quantity of units manufactured at *Qnp*. And finally, curve C will have a lower selling price at a discount *Pnpd* but a much higher production capacity utilization given by a large number of units manufactured at *Qnpd*. Curve B will move to curve C during sales events of the non-premium products increasing the production capacity utilization to *Qnpd* and returning to production capacity utilization *Qnp* during the non-sales event.

The combination of the linear demand function for premium and non-premium products for a multiproduct firm manufacturing both premium and non-premium products is equal to the total production capacity utilization during a fiscal period. If the demand for premium, non-premium, and non-premium discounted products based on equation 2.1 is given respectively by 10%, 30%, and 40% (of the total industrial capacity installed), then we have that total production capacity reaches 80%, and the linear demand function can be written as,

$$Dp(Pp) + Dnp(Pnp) + Dnpd(Pnpd) = 80\% Uc \quad (2.2)$$

$$10\% + 30\% + 40\% = 80\% = Uc \quad (2.3)$$

where *Uc* is the production capacity utilization reaching an average of 80%. Equations (2.2) and (2.3) state the demand for premium and non-premium products with a total capacity utilization of (10%+30%=40%) is not enough to reach 80% of manufacturing production capacity. Therefore, the firm needs an extra production capacity utilization of 40% that needs to come from the volume of non-premium products sold at a further discount price during sales events to reach the 80% of total production capacity utilization deemed necessary to cover total variable and fixed costs and reach the sales target. A firm that has 80 percent total production capacity utilization during a fiscal period can cover total variable and fixed costs for a given output produced and reach the desired profit margin. Thus, the production capacity utilization for the firm can be written as follows,

$$80\%\ Uc = TC = (AVC + AFC) \times Output\ (Q) \quad (2.4)$$

where *TC* is the total cost for a given quantity of Output (Q), *AVC* is the total variable cost, and *TFC* is the total fixed cost. If, for some reason, the firm does not have promotions or sales events during the year, it will mean that the demand for non-premium discounted products is zero, and the production capacity utilization reaches only 40 percent, which may not be enough to cover total variable and fixed costs. The total demand composed of premium and non-premium demands, respectively expressed as *Dp(Pp)* and *Dnp(Pnp)*, is given as,

$$10\%\ Dp(Pp) + 30\% Dnp(Pnp) + 0 = 40\% Uc < (AVC + AFC) \times Output\ (Qtot\text{-}Qnpd) \quad (2.5a)$$

$$10\%\ Dp(Pp) + 30\% Dnp(Pnp) + 40\%\ Dnpd(Pnpd = 80\% Uc < (AVC + AFC) \times Output\ (Qtot\text{-}Qnpd) \quad (2.5b)$$

where *Output (Qtot-Qnpd)* is the difference between the total output of premium and non-premium products minus the output of non-premium discounted products. Therefore, an extra demand for non-premium discounted goods, *Dnpd(Pnpd)*, at 40% is needed to reach the targeted production capacity utilization and cover the total costs as indicated in equation (2.5b).

What happens if a manufacturing firm does not reach 70-80% production capacity utilization? It means that the capacity is under-utilized, and the firm is not selling enough to cover fixed costs. Fixed costs are divided by a lower level of output. The firm is barely covering the variable costs; as a result, the average fixed costs per unit of output increase, so profitability falls. This means prices might increase, increasing average costs due to falling efficiency and capacity utilization levels. The firm will be less competitive. At this stage, the firm has no choice but to lay off employees and administrative staff and eventually can face financial distress.

For a manufacturer, the higher the unutilized production capacity, the higher the promotions offered during sales events on non-premium products and, eventually, premium goods. In fact, if the unutilized production capacity is under 70-80%, the output of non-premium products (Qnp) ↑↑ must increase, and eventually, the number of premium products (Qp)↑ could increase as well, through different promotions to reach the budgeted sales target which will ensure a steady market share for its products. This strategy is given as: [***70 %Uc < (Qnp) ↑↑+Qp↑ = sales target = market size***], where both non-premium↑↑ and semi-premium ↑outputs need to be increased through price discounts and various marketing promotion strategies. Suppose the capacity utilization gets close to 70-80% or goes higher. In that case, the discounts on non-premium goods must be reduced, and the focus should be on offering non-premium products at regular prices to increase profitability. This strategy is given as ***70 %Uc > (Qnp) +Qp= sales target = market size***], where both premium and non-premium outputs are produced in enough large quantities to occupy more than 80% of the production capacity utilization, and there is no need to offer extra discounts other than regular yearly promotion events. A firm with a high-capacity utilization will have a lower cost per unit and gain an edge over its competitors.

Volume-Based Analysis and the New Theory of the Firm in Product-Mix Profitability

Volume-based analysis and profitability are part of management accounting and have its main scope to emphasize a customer focus and the requirements to remain competitive through satisfying customer needs. Activity-based costing examines the customer profitability analysis as a tool to evaluate the portfolio of customer profiles. In an economy pricing system, firms must have economies of scale to manufacture and put several products of different standards and hierarchies on the market to meet the demand for a broad category of customers, from low-end to high-end demand. A multi-product firm that sells low-end products in large quantities and high-end products in smaller quantities guarantees strategic competitiveness in the market.

There is a process called the *Product Quantity* (PQ) method that separates into segments the product mix based on the annual production volume for each product. The product quantity (PQ) method has identified two distinct segments in a typical manufacturing product mix: the products that belong to the high-mix but low-volume (HMLV) segment and products that belong to the low-mix, but high-volume (LMHV) segment. A production system designed for one segment will not be optimal for the other segment due to the product's structure.

The analysis of PQ will encourage the utilization of different production systems and value stream mapping for each segment, HMLV, and LMHV. For example, the HMLV segment, which includes high-mix, low-volume premium products, requires short production runs, while the LMHV segment, including low-mix, high-volume non-premium products, calls for long production runs, two to three shifts a day affecting several manufacturing parameters.

The number of manufacturing factors affected by the production of the premium low-volume segment (HMLV) and non-premium high-volume segment (LMHV) includes a wide range of factors, such as i) the number of different setups performed during a regular shift, ii) the regular flow of process parameters during machine operation, iii) the time required by an operator to learn specific tasks, iv) methods related to production planning, inventory control, operations, scheduling, and supply chain management, v) employee training on the un-lean processes, vi) the number of tasks assigned to each employee, vi) the level of automatization in different manufacturing sites, vii) the amount of inspection and automated process control for any task and risk.

The low-mix high-volume (LMHV) non-premium products are relatively few product numbers being produced in large quantities. These non-premium products are mass-produced in large quantities on single or multiproduct production lines. The high-mix, low-volume (HMLV) premium products are being produced in small quantities that tend to be manufactured in a process often referred to as a job-shop-layout. The PQ analysis implies that different products being produced in similar quantities will have a process and a functional layout able to manufacture the entire product mix. On the other hand, a wide variety of quantities can be grouped into two or more product segments committed to separate production areas with different layouts.

The Product Quantity analysis can be explained better if we introduce a **New Theory of the Firm in Product-Mix Profitability**. This theory considers a competitive firm that uses a multi-product mix strategy to reach its desired overall profitability, based on the case scenario illustrated in tables 2.2 through 2.6.

Table 2.2 shows a manufacturing company operating in economy pricing, called ***Manufacturing Inc.*** which produces three main products: 2 non-premium products and 1 (luxury) premium product. The total number of units manufactured in one month is 33,500 (or 402,000 units for 12 periods=1 per year), where 76% of them, or 25,500 units, are sold at a discount price, and the other 24%, or 8,000 units, are sold at regular price.

No. of products	Type of products manufactured	Full price/Unit	Discount	Price discounted/Unit	Volume (Units sold) 1 period	Revenue for 1 period	Sales as % of Sub-total sales	Sales as % of Total Sales
1)	**Non-premium 1**	$100	39%	$61.0	12000	$732000	47%	36%
2)	**Non-premium 2**	$120	32%	$81.6	9000	$734400	35%	27%
3)	**Luxury Premium**	$280	20%	$224.0	4500	$1008000	18%	13%
Sub-Total					**25500**	**$2474400**	**100%**	**76%**

Table 2.2 Manufacturing Inc. represents a volume of 76% of final sales due to discounts

No. of products	Type of products manufactured	Full price/unit	Discount	Price Discount/Unit	Volume (Units sold) 1 period	Revenue for 1 period	Sales as % of Sub-total sales	Sales as % of Total Sales
1)	Non-premium 1	$100	0%	$100	4000	$400000	50%	12%
2)	Non-premium 2	$120	0%	$120	3500	$420000	44%	10%
3)	Luxury Premium	$280	0%	$280	500	$140000	6%	1%
Sub-Total					**8000**	**$960000**	**100%**	**24%**
Grand-Total					33500	$3434400		100%

Table 2.3 *Manufacturing Inc.* represents a volume of 24% of final sales with no discounts (regular price)

Product Manufactured	Non-Premium 1	Non-Premium 1	Non-Premium 1	Non-Premium 2	Non-Premium 2	Non-Premium 2	Luxury Premium	Luxury Premium	Luxury Premium	Income Statement-1 period		Income Statement - 1 year
	1 Period	1 Period	1 Period	1 Period	1 Period	1 Period	1 Period	1 Period	1 Period	1 Period		12 periods
	Unit Price	Units sold	Sales Revenue	Unit Price	Units Sold	Sales Revenue	Unit Price	Units Sold	Sales Revenue	IS-P1	Total Units/per	IS-12 Periods
Price/Unit	$61	12000	$732000	$81.6	9000	$734400	$224	4500	$1008000	$2474400	25500	$29692800
Prod % as of total sales		47%			35%			18%			100%	
Material	$35	12000	$420000	$50	9000	$450000	$60	4500	$270000	$1140000	x P12	$13680
Direct Labor	$7	12000	$84000	$8	9000	$72000	$9	4500	$40500	$196500	X P12	$2358000
Manufacturing VOH	$5	12000	$60000	$6	9000	$54000	$7	4500	$31500	$145500	X P12	$1745000
Manufacturing FOH	$2.5	12000	$30000	$2.5	9000	$22500	$2.5	4500	$11250	$63750	X P12	$765000
Cost of Goods Sold	**$49.50**	**12000**	**$594000**	**$66.5**	**9000**	**$598500**	**$78.50**	**4500**	**$353250**	**$1545750**	**X P12**	**$18549000**
Gross profit	**$11.5**	**12000**	**$138000**	**$15.10**	**9000**	**$135900**	**$145.50**	**4500**	**$654750**	**$928650**	**X P12**	**$11143800**
Delivery Expenses	$2.1	12000	$25200	$2.1	9000	$18900	$2.1	4500	$9450	$53550	X P12	$642600
Promotion Expenses	$4.5	12000	$54000	$4.5	9000	$40500	$4.5	4500	$20250	$114750	X P12	$1377000
Prod. Improv.Exp.	$2	12000	$24000	$2.2	9000	$19800	$2.8	4500	$12600	$56400	X P12	$676800
Coop Adv. Expenses	$3	12000	$36000	$3	9000	$27000	$3	4500	$13500	$76500	X P12	$918000
Other VAR expenses	$2	12000	$24000	$2	9000	$18000	$2	4500	$9000	$51000	X P12	$612000
Tot. OP Var. Expenses	**$13.6**	**12000**	**$163200**	**$13.80**	**9000**	**$124200**	**$14.40**	**4500**	**$64800**	**$352200**	**X P12**	**$4226400**
VAR. Contrib. Margin	($2.1)	12000	($25200)	$1.3	9000	$11700	$131.10	4500	$589950	$576450	X P12	$6917400
Plant Salaries, benefits	$5	12000	$60000	$5	9000	$45000	$5	4500	$22500	$127500	X P12	$1530000
Office Sal. + benefits	$6	12000	$72000	$6	9000	$54000	$6	4500	$22500	$153000	X P12	$1836000
Tot. Operating fix Exp.	**$11**	**12000**	**$132000**	**$11**	**9000**	**$99000**	**$11**	**4500**	**$49500**	**$280500**	**X P12**	**$3366000**
Misc. Op. Expenses	$4	12000	$48000	$4	9000	$36000	$4	4500	$18000	$102000	X P12	$1224000
Income from Operations	**($17)**	**12000**	**($205200)**	**($13.70)**	**9000**	**($123300)**	**$116.10**	**4500**	**$522450**	**$193950**	**X P12**	**$2327400**
Depreciation	$3.9	12000	$46800	$3.9	9000	$35100	$3.9	4500	$17550	$99450	X P12	$1193400
Income before Tax (EBIT)	**($21)**	**12000**	**($252000)**	**($17.6)**	**9000**	**($158400)**	**$112.20**	**4500**	**$504900**	**$94500**	**X P12**	**$1134000**
Tax 30%	($6.3)	12000	$75600	($5.28)	9000	($47520)	$33.66	4500	$151470	$28350	X P12	$340200
Net Income profit/(loss)	**($14.7)**	**12000**	**($176400)**	**($12.32)**	**9000**	**($100880)**	**$78.54**	**4500**	**$353430**	**$66150**	**X P12**	**$793800**
												=2.67%

Table 2.4 Cost breakdown of the volume manufactured that represents 76% of the final sales sold at discount price

Product Manufactured	**Non-Premium 1**	**Non-Premium 1**	**Non-Premium 1**	**Non-Premium 2**	**Non-Premium 2**	**Non-Premium 2**	**Luxury Premium**	**Luxury Premium**	**Luxury Premium**	**Income Statement-1 period**		**Income Statement- 1 year**
	1 Period	**1 Period**	**1 Period**	**1 Period**	**1 Period**	**1 Period**	**1 Period**	**1 Period**	**1 Period**	**1 Period**		**12 periods**
	Unit Price	**Units sold**	**Sales Revenue**	**Unit Price**	**Units Sold**	**Sales Revenue**	**Unit Price**	**Units Sold**	**Sales Revenue**	**IS -P1**	**Total Units/period**	**IS -12 Periods**
Price/Unit	$100	4000	$400000	$120	3500	$420000	$280	500	$140000	960000	8000	$11520000
Prod % as of total sales		50%			44%			6%			100%	
Material	$35	4000	$140000	$50	3500	$175000	$60	500	$90000	$405000	x P12	$4860000
Direct Labor	$7	4000	$28000	$8	3500	$28000	$14	500	$21000	$77000	x P12	$924000
Manufacturing VOH	$5	4000	$20000	$6	3500	$21000	$7	500	$10500	$51500	x P12	$618000
Manufacturing FOH	$2.5	4000	$10000	$2.5	3500	$8750	$2.5	500	$3750	$22500	x P12	$270000
Cost of Goods Sold	**$49.50**	**4000**	**$198000**	**$66.50**	**3500**	**$232750**	**$83.50**	**500**	**$125250**	**$556000**	x P12	**$6672000**
Gross profit	**$50.50**	**4000**	**$202000**	**$53.50**	**3500**	**$187250**	**$196.50**	**500**	**$294750**	**$684000**	x P12	**$8208000**
Delivery Expenses	$2.10	4000	$8400	$2.1	3500	$7350	$2.1	500	$3150	$18900	x P12	$226800
Promotion Expenses	$4.5	4000	$18000	$4.5	3500	$15750	$4.5	500	$6750	$40500	x P12	$486000
Prod. Improv.Exp.	$2	4000	$8000	$2.2	3500	$7700	$2.8	500	$4200	$19900	x P12	$238800
Coop Adv. Expenses	$3	4000	$1200	$3	3500	$10500	$3	500	$4500	$27000	x P12	$324000
Other VAR expenses	$2	4000	$8000	$2	3500	$7000	$2	500	$3000	$18000	x P12	$216000
Tot. OP Var. Expenses	**$13.60**	**4000**	**$54400**	**$13.80**	**3500**	**$48300**	**$14.4**	**500**	**$21600**	**$124300**	x P12	**$1491600**
VAR. Contrib. Margin	$36.90	4000	$147600	$39.70	3500	$138950	$182.10	500	$273150	$559700	x P12	$6716400
Plant Salaries, benefits	$5	4000	$20000	$5	3500	$17500	$5	500	$7500	$45000	x P12	$540000
Office Sal. + benefits	$6	4000	$24000	$6	3500	$21000	$6	500	$9000	$54000	x P12	$648000
Tot. Operating fix Exp.	**$11**	**4000**	**$44000**	**$11**	**3500**	**$38500**	**$11**	**500**	**$16500**	**$99000**	x P12	**$1188000**
Misc. Op. Expenses	$4	4000	$16000	$4	3500	$14000	$4	500	$6000	$36000	x P12	$432000
Income from Operations	**$21.90**	**4000**	**$87600**	**$24.70**	**3500**	**$86450**	**$167.10**	**500**	**$250650**	**$424700**	x P12	**$5096400**
Depreciation	$3.9	4000	$15600	$3.9	3500	$13650	$3.9	500	$5850	$35100	x P12	$421200
Income before Tax (EBIT)	**$18**	**4000**	**$72000**	**$20.80**	**3500**	**$72800**	**$163.20**	**500**	**$244800**	**$389600**	x P12	**$4675200**
Tax 30%	$5.4	4000	$21600	$6.24	3500	$21840	$48.96	500	$73440	$116880	x P12	$1402560
Net Income profit/(loss)	**$12.60**	**4000**	**$50400**	**$14.56**	**3500**	**$50960**	**$114.24**	**500**	**$171360**	**$272720**	x P12	**$3272640**

Table 2.5 Cost breakdown of the volume manufactured that represents 24% of the final sales sold at no discount price

	76% of total volumes discounted (72% sales)	24% of total volumes are non-discounted (28% sales)	100% Total sales	Units	Units
	IS- 12 periods	**IS -12 Periods**	**Income Statement-12 periods= 1 year**	**Total units produced/sold – 1 period**	**Total units produced/sold – 12 periods=1 year**
Total Revenue =1 year	$29692800	$11520000	$41212800	33500	402000
Cost Breakdown					
Material	$13680000	$4860000	$18540000	33500	402000
Direct Labor	$2358000	$924000	$3282000	33500	402000
Manufacturing VOH	$1746000	$618000	$2364000	33500	402000
Manufacturing FOH	$765000	$270000	$1035000	33500	402000
Cost of Goods Sold	**$18549000**	**$6672000**	**$25221000**	**33500**	**402000**
Gross profit	**$11143800**	**$8208000**	**$19351800**	**33500**	**402000**
Delivery Expenses	$642600	$226800	$869400	33500	402000
Promotion Expenses	$1377000	$486000	$1863000	33500	402000
Prod. Improv.Exp.	$676800	$238800	$915600	33500	402000
Coop Adv. Expenses	$918000	$324000	$1242000	33500	402000
Other VAR expenses	$612000	$216000	$828000	33500	402000
Tot. OP Var. Expenses	**$4226400**	**$1491600**	**$5718000**	**33500**	**402000**
VAR. Contrib. Margin	$6917400	$6716400	$13633800	33500	402000
Plant Salaries, benefits	$1530000	$540000	$2070000	33500	402000
Office Sal. + benefits	$1836000	$648000	$2484000	33500	402000
Tot. Operating fix Exp.	**$3366000**	**$1188000**	**$4554000**	**33500**	**402000**
Misc. Op. Expenses	$1224000	$432000	$1656000	33500	402000
Income from Operations	**$2327400**	**$5096400**	**$7423800**	**33500**	**402000**
Depreciation	$1193400	$421200	$1614600	33500	402000
Income before Tax (EBIT)	**$1134000**	**$4675200**	**$5809200**	**33500**	**402000**
Tax 30%	$340200	$1402560	$1742760	33500	402000
Net Income profit/(loss)	**$793800**	**$3272640**	**$4066440**	**33500**	**402000**
	72% of sales (net income)	28% of sales (net income)	100% of sales (net income)		
		Net Income as % of sales	=9.87%		

Table 2.6 Cost breakdown of total sales (76% discounted sales, +24% regular sales =100% sales)

Income statements per unit and per unit sold in total for each of the three products produced by *Manufacturing Inc.* using *Absorption Costing Method* are given in Tables 2.4 through 2.6. All three products are profitable and have a positive net income if they are sold at regular prices (no discount) during the year, which represents around 24% of the total sales. The net income of the combined three products sold at regular price (24% of total volumes) during one single intra-period is $272,770 or $3,272,640 (for 12 periods) yearly, as per Table 2.5). The two non-premium products, 1 and 2, are sold at a loss if a discount applies during the year, with a volume of around 76% of all sales or 25,500 units out of 33,500 units per month/period or 306,000 units out of 402,000 units per year. The premium luxury product is sold at a substantial profit, making up for the losses of the two non-premium products. In fact, the net income of the combined three products sold at a discount price representing 76% of total sales volume during one single month/period is $66,150, and for 12 months representing one fiscal year, it is $793,800, as per Table 2.4.

During the sales events, the non-premium products *np1* and *np2* have losses respectively of ($176,400) and ($110,880) per period, and the luxury premium product earns a considerable profit of $353,430 for each period. The net earned income of all three products is a positive amount (profit) of approximately $66,150 for each period during the sales event. Normally, the discounted sales price of each non-premium product is $61 and $81.6, which will cover only the *Cost of Goods Sold* (COGS) portion and part of operating variable expenses, but not the operating fixed expenses and promotion/advertising expenses.

The COGSper unit for non-premium 1 (*np1*) and non-premium 2 (*np2*) products are respectively $49.50 and $66.50, and the operating variable expense for *np1* and *np2* are respectively $13.6 and $13.8, which leaves a variable contribution margin of ($2.1) for *np1* and $1.3 for *np2*. If we deduct operating fixed expenses and miscellaneous operating expenses, we get that the income from operations has a loss of ($17.10) per unit of *np1* and ($13.70) per unit of *np2*. By deducting the depreciation expenses for each product, we have a net income loss before tax (EBIT) of ($14.70) per unit of *np1* and ($12.32) per unit of *np2*. On the other hand, the premium product sales will cover all the costs even during the promotion sales events.

The case scenario above considers a multi-product company with two non-premium products and one premium product; however, in real business life, the firms operating in a competitive environment have multiple types of non-premium products that use multiple sales events during the year. As seen in the tables above, the biggest portion of the profit of these companies is during sales events where mass production of non-premium goods is sold in large quantities pushing the demand into customers. The sales events count between 60% and 80% of the total sales volume for a given year.

The firm's strategy is to sell more non-premium products to increase the volume and production capacity utilization to generate enough liquidity to invest in manufacturing premium products that sell at more profitable margins. As in the case of *Manufacturing Inc*, during promotion events, about 74 percent of the total sales volume comes from the non-premium products np1 and np2 and luxury premium products sold at discount prices. The rest of the volumes, about 24% in units or 28% of sales, comes from premium and non-premium products sold at a regular price during the entire year. There is a marketing strategy in the economy pricing system of offering continuous discounts on non-premium products to keep a stable production capacity utilization level and provide a stable flow of cash.

Let's assume that the production plan chosen by a manufacturing company consists of 4 products (2 premium and 2 non-premium). The firm to maximize its profit, should increase the quantity produced of both non-premium products *np1* and *np2*, which have a low and competitive selling price, and produce a limited quantity of premium products *p1* and *p2*, which sell at a much higher price, as shown in the equation below,

$$Y'np1+Y'np2+Y''p1+Y''p2=Y'np+Y''p=\Pi j(p) \quad (2.6)$$

where *Y'* and *Y"* are the respective outputs of non-premium and premium products and *np1, np2, p1, p2* are the respective sales prices of the non-premium1, non-premium2, premium1 and premium2 products manufactured by the firm. Non-premium product sales prices *np1* and *np2*, for simplicity, can be represented by the combined output sales price, *np*, and in the same way, the sales prices of premium products *p1* and *p2* can be represented by the combined output price, *p*. We use a constrained optimization solution for equation 2.6, where the variables are required to satisfy certain conditions for the firm to keep a steady market share of its products.

By using the Lagrangian function, we have that in 2.6, output quantities for non-premium products, defined as *Y'*, must be maximized but not their prices indicated by *np*. For the premium products, the sales prices indicated as p must be maximized. Still, not their output quantities given by *Y"* to defend the market share of the company given as *Ms*. Therefore, the non-premium and premium outputs are given as *Y'* and *Y"* respectively, and the price of the premium and non-premium products are given as *p* and *np* respectively are subject to the following conditions:

$$Y'+p \text{ subject to constraint } (Y'np+Y''p=Ms) \quad (2.7)$$

The Lagrangian function is given as,

$$L(\Pi j(p))=Y'+p-\lambda 1(Y'np+Y''p-Ms) \quad (2.8)$$

The first-order conditions require that,

$$\delta L/\delta Y'=1-\lambda 1np=0 \quad (2.9)$$

$$\delta L/\delta p=1-\lambda 1Y''=0 \quad (2.10)$$

$$Y'np+Y''p=Ms \quad (2.11)$$

Equation (2.9) and (2.10) implies that

$$\lambda_1 = \frac{1}{np} \text{ and } \lambda_1 = \frac{1}{Y''} \tag{2.12}$$

Using the *λ1* values above it implies that,

$$Y'' = np \tag{2.13}$$

Inserting the above expressions into (2.11) and rearranging yields,

$$Y' = \left[\frac{M_s}{np}\right] - p \tag{2.14}$$

Multiplying both sides above by *np*, we get the solution for *Y'* and *p* respectively as,

$$Y' = \left(\frac{M_s}{np}\right) - p \tag{2.15}$$

$$p = \left(\frac{M_s}{np}\right) - Y' \tag{2.16}$$

The solution in equation (2.15) implies that the selling price of non-premium products will have to be decreased during promotion events so the quantity of the non-premium products, *Y'*, can be increased. In the same way, equation (2.16) implies that the selling price of the premium products, *p*, must increase, and as a result, the volume of sales of premium products will decrease proportionally to guarantee the profitability of premium products to cover the lower profitability of non-premium products. Using this strategy in a very competitive market setting, the firm can defend the market share, *Ms*, despite having lower overall profitability due to a mix of non-premium and premium products.

Production Possibility Frontier in Economy Pricing

The production possibility frontier (PPF) curve is a microeconomic application shown by a graph that indicates various combinations of amounts of two commodities that an economy can produce per unit of time using a fixed amount of each production factor when a production technology available is given. The PPF curve graphically represents a production set of one commodity's maximum possible production level for any given production level of the other existing technologies available (Nicholson, 2005, 339-345).

The production possibility frontier curve is a graphical representation of a possible combination of two finished goods with constant resources, technology, and supply management operating in economy pricing. It is a graphical illustration of the maximal mix of outputs that a firm can produce to stay competitive in an economy pricing by fully using its existing resources most efficiently. The PPF curve similarly defines the production efficiency in the context of that production set, where a point in the PPF frontier represents the efficient use of the available inputs to produce commodities, and any point beneath the curve indicates inefficiency. The combination of commodities is indicated by any point in the PPF frontier where an efficient economy is supposed to operate and shows the priorities the economy has decided to commit resources, such as the production of certain commodities that are more important than others.

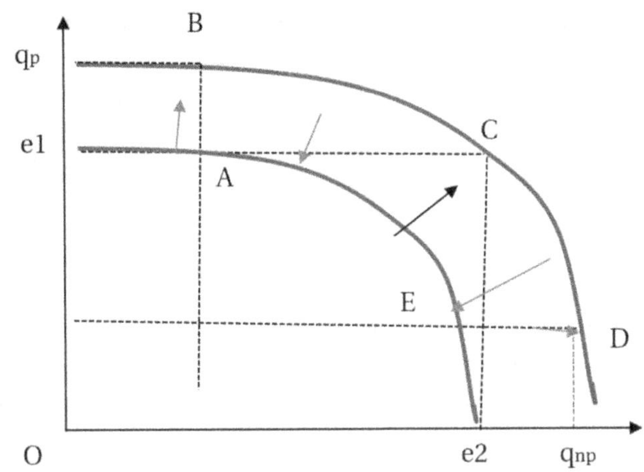

Figure 2.2 Production Possibility Frontiers for Premium and Non-Premium Products

Figure 2.2 illustrates a combination of amounts of two commodities, premium (*qp*) and non-premium (*qnp*) that an economy operating efficiently can produce per unit of time using a fixed amount of each production factor when the production technology is available. Given that the economy is efficient at this stage, it can choose between combination points in the PPF curve. Point B in the PPF curve indicates that the premium product is in high demand in the market and the company is putting most of the resources and inputs into producing the premium product, *p*. If the non-premium product, *np*, is in high demand in the market, then the company will be shifting the resources and inputs from point B in the PPF curve to the point D giving priority to the production of a non-premium product. If the demand for products *p* and *np* is equally distributed into the market, points B and D converge to point C in the PPF curve, where an equal mix of premium and the non-premium product is required.

As mentioned earlier, an economy is operating efficiently if it is operating on the PPF curve. In fact, points B, C, and D in the PPF curve in Figure 2.2 are both operating efficiently. In an economy pricing, it might happen that a firm, for different reasons related to market trends and competition factors, is not any more competitive. This means that the quantity of premium and non-premium products manufactured has dropped significantly due to the sales decline, turning to operate inefficiently. The efficient points *B, C,* and *D* will drop below the PPF curve, and the firm is said to operate inefficiently because it could reallocate resources to produce more of both goods so it can sell more of both goods in the market.

All points on the left of the PPF curve or inside the frontier, such as point *A* representing premium and point *E* representing non-premium commodities, can be manufactured but are inefficient as the company is not competitive enough to sell more quantities of them in the market, resulting in significant loss of the market share. Points A and E lie in the new inefficient curve inside the PPF frontier line called the *inefficient non-competitive* curve, *e1e2.* By redesigning or re-marketing non-premium products to offer new discounts during sales events, point E will shift into the frontier curve, eventually at the efficient point D, as it will increase the quantity of non-premium products offered in the market by shifting the resources from premium to non-premium product. Once the sales event is over, the non-premium product might be inefficient again, moving back to the left of the PPF curve, at point *E,* until the next sales event or promotion is on. Point *A,* instead, used to describe the premium product, does not move that much, especially if there are no sales events for this kind of product.

Points along the PPF curve describe the tradeoff between premium and non-premium goods; the sacrifice to produce premium versus non-premium goods is part of the opportunity cost. In general, opportunity cost in PPF is measured with the number of units of the premium goods forgone for one or more of the units of the non-premium goods and vice-versa. The opportunity cost also determines the classical shape of the PPF curve, which is based on the increasing opportunity costs with a curve concave to the origin.

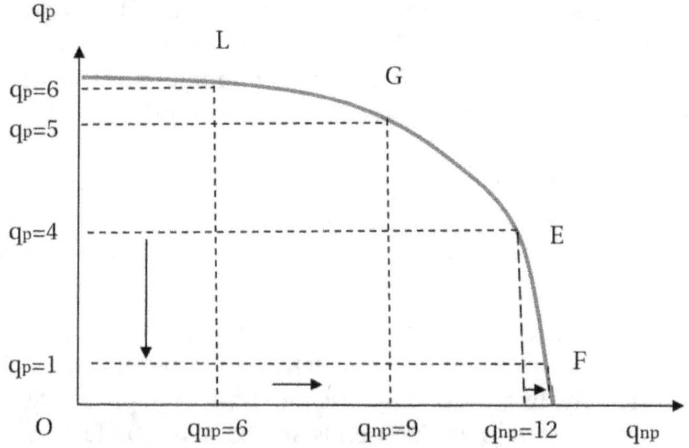

Figure 2.3 PPF curve and opportunity cost

The opportunity cost generally will differ depending on the start and end points. Figure 2.3 illustrates the relationship between the PPF curve and opportunity cost. As indicated in figure 2.3, on the right, where the non-premium product has a quantity of qnp=9, manufacturing three more units of non-premium products, increasing the production from 6 to 9, will cost the loss of 1 premium product as indicated by the movement in PPF curve from point *L* to *G*.

At point *E*, the economy is already close to its maximum potential of non-premium output, thanks to the promotions during several sales events. To manufacture six more units of non-premium products from 6 to 12, three more premium units must be sacrificed, as shown in Figure 2.3, with a movement from point *E* to *F*, where qp=1 and qnp=12. The ratio of gains to losses is usually determined by the *marginal rate of transformation,* which is the slope of the production–possibility frontier (PPF) at any given point is called the marginal rate of transformation (MRT) (Barthwal, 2007). The slope defines the rate at which the reallocation of productive resources can redirect the production of one premium unit into the production of several non-premium units during sales events.

The *marginal rate of transformation* (MRT) is also called the (marginal) "*opportunity cost*" of a commodity which is the opportunity cost of one premium unit in terms of non-premium units at the margin. The marginal opportunity cost measures how much of one premium unit is given up for one more unit of non-premium goods or vice versa during regular or promotional sales. The shape of a PPF is generally drawn as concave to the origin to represent increasing opportunity cost with increased output of a good. The increasing opportunity cost means that it is required a more specialized labor force and eventually added capital to produce the premium products compared to a less specialized labor force and less capital to manufacture the non-premium products.

In the PPF curve, the main determinants regulating the position of the PPF at any given time, especially in an economy pricing, are the state of technology, the management expertise (which are reflected in the available production functions), the supply chain management and the available quantities of factors of production such as materials, direct labor, and factory overhead. Given the state of technology, management expertise, know-how, and supply chain management, the points on or within a PPF curve are essentially possible to achieve in the short run.

It will be possible to move from a short-run to a more efficient long-run PPF curve if there are capital investments in plants and machinery and investment in new technology for use in achieving its long-term business goals and objectives. If the supply of factors of production increases and if the management expertise and supply chain management improve significantly, then the company's capacity to produce both premium and non-premium goods will increase. This leads to more potential realization, more production capacity, and economic growth. The increase is normally shown by a shift of the production-possibility frontier further to the right. All points on or within the PPF curve are part of the production set based on the combination of premium and non-premium goods that the economy pricing could potentially produce in any given sector.

New Competitive Production Function Model and Behavioral Relationships

Much of the recent literature on multiproduct companies is focused on international trade. The international trade flows are subject to multinationals and other medium-large companies that operate in a multiproduct environment. Firms that exported more than one product title in the early 2000s accounted for around 99 percent of the U.S. export. The research has shown how reductions in barriers to international trade can affect a firm's productivity and product scope. Reducing trade barriers has led to increased competition, improved management supply chain and productivity, and augmented technical and organizational skills (Bernard, Jensen, Redding, and Schott, 2007).

Increased competition normally drives firms to concentrate on competitive commodities and eventually reduce or drop the least competitive products from the selection of domestic or exported goods. Changes in product scope are frequent among multiproduct firms. Ending the production of an old and non-competitive product and starting a new product is part of the major decision in a firm's production and competition strategy. Product choices and varieties are important variables in the marketing strategies used by competitive firms with repercussions on market structure, competition, and incentive to invest in product variety and quality (Bernard, Redding, and Schott, 2010).

Many multiproduct firms use what is called *flexible manufacturing*. Flexible manufacturing is used in different industries, meaning that producers can add new products to their assortment without making substantial investments in production technology. A *flexible manufacturing system* gives manufacturing firms an advantage to swiftly change a manufacturing environment to improve process efficiency and, thus, lower production costs. A flexible manufacturing system is related to the concept of core competency, which means that a multiproduct firm can focus the production on one or a few of its goods more efficiently than the rest. (Bernard, Redding, and Schott, 2011). Standard production function normally does not accommodate the concepts of flexible manufacturing or core competency.

Production functions are usually estimated without considering the demand for the goods, but in economy pricing, output demand is the key to identifying good-specific input allocations and production functions. Competitive firms try to reach market power by using different pricing strategies where their production decisions are functions of the downward-sloping output demand curves. Functional forms and, likewise, most of the other assumptions used in production functions are familiar from empirical microeconomic literature. The production function is specified at the product level for a firm having one output and at the firm level for a firm having a multiproduct output.

A firm uses a given technology to transform inputs, also called factors of production, into outputs or finished goods which are sold to final consumers. There are three types of categories of inputs used in production: capital services, labor services, and raw materials that are consumed in making the final product. The production function for a firm that uses only labor and capital is given as Y = (K, L) and represents the set of technologically efficient production points for a given configuration of inputs, K, L, where output Y is the maximum feasible output. The neoclassical form of the production function for an output *y* can be expressed as,

$$y = (x_1, x_2, \dots, x_m) \qquad (2.17)$$

where the output y is connected to a series of factors of production $x_1, x_2, \dots, x_m$[1].

In an economy pricing system, we have the formulation of a production process for a given firm *i* (i = 1,...,n) in a given period *t* (t = 1,..., T) in which physical capital *Kit*, labor *Lit* and materials *Mit* (intermediate input) are being transformed into two main outputs, premium and non-premium, respectively identified by *Yitp* and *Yitnp* via the time-varying production function *Ft(·)* given Hicks-neutral productivity can be written as,

---

[1] The properties of the production function are normally assumed by Neoclassical economists. Let there be *m* factors of production and let vector $x = (x_1, x_2, .., x_m)$ denote a bundle of factor inputs. We shall define an *input space* as the acceptable set of inputs for an economy. Typically, any input bundle x lies in R_+^m, the non-negative of m-dimensional Euclidian space. Let y be output, which is assumed to be a single, finite number, i.e. y R. Therefore, a production function maps acceptable input bundles to output values, i.e.: R_+^m R. In general, the following assumptions are often imposed on any generic production function : R_+^m R

1-) (x) is finite, non-negative, real-valued, and single-valued for all non-negative and finite x.

2-) (0, 0, .., 0) = 0 (no inputs implies no output)

3-) If x x , then (x) (x) (monotonicity, i.e. an increase in inputs does not decrease output)

4-) is *continuous* and twice-continuously *differentiable* everywhere in the interior of the production set.

5-) The set V(y) = {x | (x) y} is a convex set (quasi-concavity of)

6-) The set V(y) is closed and non-empty for any y > 0. (Levinson-Petrin, 2003)

$$H(Yitp, Yitnp) = Ft(Kit, Lit, Mit, A) = T(A), F(Kit, Lit, Mit,) \quad (2.18)$$

where $T(A)$ is an index of the state of technology and $T(t) \geq 0$ is the type of technological progress defined as product augmenting. Labor L and capital K are substitutable across the product lines of the firm. All the factors of production are continuously divisible and exclusive across the product line, which means that they can easily be flexibly allocated across different product lines, and only a portion of a firm-level input stock can be used in one product line at a time (Eckel and Neary, 2010).

Regarding the production function, economists do not agree that decision-makers are profit maximizers. Production function parameters estimated under the profit maximization assumptions are basically "as if" production function parameters. We can think of separating the logic behind the distinctive characteristics of technological and behavioral relationships. Behavioral relationships are relationships that incorporate different technological assumptions and behavioral assumptions. Production function parameters that are estimated under duality have a strong behavioral component.

The recent production theories recognize that strict profit maximization for every product or output is unrealistic and impracticable. Behavior must adjust to uncertainty and risk. There are new models of production function related to production behavior under uncertainty. One of the challenges that happen in production is to interpret the factors that are behind the production decisions and understand what leads producers to make different choices. As a matter of fact, production choices under stringent profit maximization may be different than those under risk aversion and have limited analytic capacities. The same type of technological relationships may result in different outcomes under different behavioral assumptions.

There is a new behavioral assumption for multiproduct production function regarding the economy pricing. The multi-product production function for a firm operating in an economy pricing system must be equal to the firm's production capacity utilization (Uc) of 70-80% to meet the sales target and profit margins in the short period. Therefore, equation (2.18) can be rewritten as,

$$H(Yitp, Yitnp) = Ft(Kit, Lit, Mit, A) = T(A), F(Kit, Lit, Mit,) = Uc\ (80\%) \quad (2.19)$$

where Uc is subject to constraint $Ft(Kit, Lit, Mit, A)$. The firm operating in a competitive environment must make decisions to reach a reasonable profit by reaching the desired production capacity utilization. This is reached by the firm's first-level dynamic optimization problem, which is given as,

$$H\ (Sjtp, Sjtnp) = max\ \Pi itjt\ (Sjt) - C(Ijt) + (1/(1-\rho))\ E[V(Sjt+1, Mjt, Ljt+1, Ijt+1)] \quad (2.10)$$

where $\Pi(Sjt)$ is the static profit earned in period t, $Sjt = (Ljt, Kjt, Mjt)$ is the vector of the state variable, $C(Ijt)$ is the cost of investment, ρ is the discount rate, and Mjt, Ljt, and Ijt are respectively the combinations of the raw materials, labor, and investment used into production. It is assumed that the firm will choose to produce its goods in the next period $t+1$, indicated by $Mjt+1$. The dynamic optimization problem gives rise to policy functions, Mjt, Ljt, and Ijt. Given that the dynamic optimization problem is not resolved, it is necessary to solve only the static profit maximization problem, which is more than enough to identify the production function parameters. The static profit maximization problem lies in allocating the firm-level human resources Ljt and capital stock Kjt among the various product lines i and setting the product-specific materials $Mijt$ for each product line. The objective of the firm's production function is to maximize profit by using a combination of premium and non-premium outputs expressed as

$$max\ \Pi itjt\ (Pijt, Qijt) - C(Ijt) - C(Mjt, Ljt, Kjt) \quad (2.11)$$

$$subject\ to\ Uc = Ts = f1(Mjt), f2(Ljt), f3(Kjt)$$

where $Uc=Tc$ is the firm's total production capacity utilization to cover total variable and fixed costs and reach the sales target (Tc) to stay competitive. The production function in economy pricing must reach the production capacity utilization Uc based on the firm's input allocation of the raw materials, Mjt, labor Ljt, and capital Kjt. Thus, the production capacity utilization, Uc, is made of three functions, $f1(Mjt)$, $f2(Ljt)$, and $f3(Kjt)$, that represents material, labor, and capital used in manufacturing multi-product units. $(Pijt, Qijt)$ is the value of the output (sales price x quantity of units manufactured) indicated by S, $C(Ijt)$ is the cost of investment, and $C(Mjt, Ljt, Kjt)$ is the landed cost of raw materials, labor, and capital involved in the production function. Expression (2.11) can be written in a Lagrangian form as,

$$\text{Max L}(\Pi\text{jt}) = (Sijtt) - C(Ijt) - C(Mjt, Ljt, Kjt) + \lambda\ [Uc\ (f1(Mjt), f2(Ljt), f3(Kjt)] \quad (2.12)$$

The first-order conditions require that,

$$\delta L/\delta Sijt = 1 - \lambda \text{Uc} = 0 \quad (2.13)$$

$$\delta L/\delta Mjt = C(Mjt) - \lambda\ [f1(Mjt)] = 0 \quad (2.14)$$

$$\delta L/\delta Ljt = C(Ljt) - \lambda\ [f1(Ljt)] = 0 \quad (2.15)$$

$$\delta L/\delta Kjt = C(Kjt) - \lambda\ [f1(Kjt)] = 0 \quad (2.16)$$

The above equations can be rewritten as

$$\lambda = 1/Uc \quad (2.17)$$

$$C(Mjt) = -\lambda\,[f1(Mjt)] \quad (2.18)$$

$$C(Ljt) = -\lambda\,[f1(Ljt)] \quad (2.19)$$

$$C(Kjt) = -\lambda\,[f1(Kjt)] \quad (2.20)$$

The optimal solution involves equating all three equations (2.18-2.20) and takes the form as,

$$\lambda = \frac{1}{Uc} = \frac{C(Mjt)}{[f1(Mjt)} + \frac{C(Ljt)}{[f1(Ljt)]} + \frac{C(Kjt)}{[f1(Kjt)]} \quad (2.21)$$

This equation indicates that the optimal solution involves equating the cost of different inputs of the production function with a series of ratios for materials, labor, and capital. The denominator of each expression transforms marginal costs of production activities into production capacity utilization targets to be achieved. The firm needs to use a specific amount of material, labor, and capital expenses to reach a production capacity utilization target of 70-80% to meet the target revenue for premium and non-premium products as determined by management to have a positive net monetary position (current ratio >1).

Despite the fact that the production functions are product-specific, the production of goods is interdependent because the firm-level human resources and capital stock are fixed at the time of production, and thus the firm must allocate these inputs across the product lines. The allocation is done as a function of the various demand conditions, production technologies, and price of materials (De Loecker, Goldberg, Khandelwal, and Pavcnik, 2012). Interdependency in production may be created because of physical economies of scope, which take place when the firm has a multi-product output (including premium and non-premium) and, therefore, higher productivity levels than when manufacturing only one output.

The input allocations are normally computed by using the parameter estimates and observable variables. The shares of a firm's materials, labor, and capital allocated to a given product line for non-premium or premium goods is constant and independent of input type. This indicates that a firm can manufacture all its outputs by using the same material-labor-capital ratio. Consequently, a firm aiming to profit maximization or cost minimization would not allocate inputs to product lines of multiple goods with such constant ratios. Instead, output demand for multiple goods is estimated to identify input allocation to the product-line level and production functions at the firm level.

As mentioned earlier, the objective of the firm's production function is to maximize profit by using a combination of premium and non-premium multi-product output to meet the production capacity utilization target of 70-80%. This can be achieved, among others, by effectively using the supply chain management that provides value to the firm by improving the manager's ability to accomplish strategic objectives through improved control along the entire supply chain. This enables the organization to forecast demand as accurately as possible and match supply with demand, thus helping in meeting the customer's expectations and optimizing the resources stored and used in production. Supply chain management improves the ability to adapt quickly to market changes and capitalizes quickly on new opportunities. It can also lead to cash-to-cash cycle times for improved cash flows and enables production managers to lower operational costs through better planning and communication.

The New Cost Function Model in Competitive Product-Mix Output

A cost function is a function of input prices and output whose value is the cost of making that output given the input prices. The cost function is often applied using the cost curve by companies to minimize cost and maximize production efficiency. The cost function is a derived function since it is obtained from the production function. Total cost is the cost incurred to produce a given level of output in the short run by utilizing both fixed and variable factors. Marginal cost is the change in the total cost or the total variable cost due to a unit change in the level of output. The long-run cost curves are formed by the short-run cost curves. The long-run average cost curve is U shaped because of the law of returns to scale.

The economic cost of an input is the minimum payment required to keep the input in its present employment. This is considered a payment the input would receive in its best alternative employment. This cost function concept is closely related to the opportunity cost concept. It is usually assumed that inputs are employed in perfectly competitive markets. The firm can get all the input it wants without affecting prices.

If a firm is a perfect competitor in all input markets, and hence the per-unit prices of all its inputs are unaffected by how much of the inputs the firm purchases, then we can say that at a particular level of output, the firm has economies of scale if the firm has increasing returns to scale. Similarly, we can state that a firm has diseconomies of scale if it has to decrease returns to scale. Lastly, it has neither economies nor diseconomies of scale if it has constant returns to scale. With perfect competition in the output market, the long-run market equilibrium will involve all firms operating at the minimum point of their long-run average cost curves.

But if, for different reasons, the firm is not a perfect competitor in the input markets, then there are increasing returns to scale in some segments of output levels. If the firm is so big in one or more input markets that increasing its purchases of an (expensive) input used to manufacture the segment of premium products drives up the input's per-unit cost, then the firm could have diseconomies of scale in that range of output levels. On the other hand, if the firm can get substantial discounts on one or more inputs that are used in non-premium products, then it could have economies of scale in some range of output levels despite it might have decreasing returns in production in that output range.

It is assumed that firms are perfectly competitive in their input markets, and therefore the input prices are fixed in the short run; however, in the long run, they are subject to changes. Let *p=(p1,p2,...pn)>0* be a vector of prevailing market prices at which the firm can buy input *x=(x1.x2,...xn)*. The cost function defined for all input prices, p>0, and all output levels y= f(Rn) used for manufacturing products is the minimum-value function

$$C\,(p, x) = min_{x\epsilon R}\ \ p * x \quad \text{for } f(x) \geq y \qquad (2.22)$$

If the function *x(p,y)* solves the cost-minimization problem, then we have,

$$C\,(p,y) = p,\, x(p,y) \qquad (2.23)$$

Because function, *f*, is strictly increasing, the constraint will always be binding to a solution. Subsequently, we assume the firm operates in a very competitive economy and sells two main outputs: non-premium and premium. Non-premium is sold to the low-end-medium market, which makes around 75% of the total output, and premium is sold to the higher-end market making around 25% of the total output of the firm. Therefore, as per our assumptions, in a competitive economy pricing where a firm can produce both non-premium and premium outputs, the cost-minimization problem used to produce non-premium and premium products is equivalent to,

$$min_{x\epsilon R}\ (np * xi) + (p * xj) \quad \text{for f(Yi)=np*xi and f(Yj)=p*xj} \qquad (2.24)$$

$$subject\ to\ Uc = Ts = f(Yi)+f(Yj)\ where\ Yi = np*xi\ and\ Yj = p*xj$$

where *np* and *p*, are the prices of non-premium and premium inputs *xi* and *xj* used in manufacturing the non-premium output Y*i* and premium output *Yj*. It is assumed that non-premium output Y*i* and premium output *Yj* represent respectively 75% and 25% of the total output of the firm. In addition, *Uc* and *Ts* are, respectively, the capacity utilization and sales target. Using the Lagrangian function, we have that the cost-minimization problem to produce both premium and non-premium outputs is given as,

$$L\,min(C\,(p,np,y)) = (np * xi)+(p*xj) + \lambda[(Yi*Snp+Yj*Sp) - Ts] \qquad (2.25)$$

where *Yi*Snp* is the non-premium output times the final selling price of the non-premium output, and *Yj*Sp* is the premium output times the final selling price of the premium product.

The first-order conditions require that,

$$\delta L/\delta np = 1 - \lambda Yi * Snp = 0 \tag{2.26}$$

$$\delta L/\delta p = 1 - \lambda Yj * Sp = 0 \tag{2.27}$$

$$Yi * Snp + Yj * Sp = Ts \tag{2.28}$$

where $(Yi*Snp)*0.75+(Yj*Sp)*0.25 = Ts$. Equations (2.26) and (2.27) imply that

$$\lambda = 1/(Yi * Snp) \text{ and } \lambda = 1/(Yj * Sp) \tag{2.29}$$

Using the λ values above it implies that,

$$Y_j = Y_i \frac{S_{np}}{S_p} \tag{2.30}$$

Inserting the above expression into (2.28) and rearranging yields,

$$Y_i S_p + Y_i \left(\frac{S_{np}}{S_p}\right) S_p = T_s \tag{2.31}$$

The above equation can be arranged as,

$$Y_i = \left(\frac{T_s}{S_p + S_{np}}\right) \tag{2.32}$$

where the non-premium output is given as $Yi = np*xi$, and *np* is the price of the non-premium input *xi*, therefore we have,

$$np = (x_i)\left[\frac{T_s}{S_p + S_{np}}\right] \tag{2.33}$$

In the same way, by substituting $Yi = Yj*(Sp/Snp)$ into equation (2.28) and rearranging using premium output $Yj=p*xj$ where *p* is the price of the premium input *xj*, we have that,

$$p = \frac{T_s}{x_j * 2S_p} \tag{2.34}$$

The solution for the equations above, (2.33) and (2.34), implies that the price of so-called non-premium inputs, *np*, used in the production of low-end non-premium output *Yi* needs to be minimized, which can be achieved by an aggressive supply chain policy consisting among others on pushing suppliers for discounts on the price of inputs used in manufacturing the non-premium products, in order for the company to sell the final outputs at the promotion price target *Snp*. The other extra reason to minimize the input price, *np*, used in manufacturing the non-premium output is that non-premium product represents almost 75% of the total firm's total output, and the sales price of this non-premium output must be continuously low or discounted to have the desired market share *Ms.*

Meanwhile, the price of other inputs used in making the premium product can be minimized to a certain extent, given that the premium output covers only 25% of the total firm's output. By using this strategy, the company can reach the desired plant capacity utilization target (*Uc*) of about 75-80% to cover total variable and fixed costs that will be translated into reaching the sales target, *Ts,* and the desired market share, *Ms,* to keep the company competitive. In a few words, the demand for inputs used to manufacture premium and non-premium products is considered jointly with the interaction of supply and demand for the total output.

Isocost lines and Product-Mix Output

In a more classical microeconomic way, the cost-minimizing input choices can also be expressed in terms of more classical inputs such as labor and capital. The economic cost of an input is the minimum payment required to keep the input in its present employment. It is the payment the input would receive in its best alternative employment. This cost concept is closely related to the opportunity cost concept in modern microeconomics, which is different from accounting cost, where the total cost to produce a final output is composed of raw materials, inbound freight, labor, variable costs, and fixed overheads, administrative and selling expenses, research and development costs and marketing expenses, etc.

We usually assume that inputs are hired in perfectly competitive markets by getting the best competitive available input price without affecting overall prices in the market. Thus, economic profit is simply a function of K and L, given that all prices (p, w, and v) and technology are assumed fixed in the short run, despite being subject to changes depending on different factors such as competition, promotions, loyalty programs, etc. Assuming output has been determined to be Y, the firm will minimize its cost by choosing a specific point on the Y isoquant. The cost will be minimized by choosing the point where the slope of isoquant equals the ratio of input prices for given capital and labor (w/v). This happens when the rate of substitution in production equals the rate of substitution in the market. The minimized cost in terms of labor and capital is expressed as,

$$Min{:}\ C = wL + vK \tag{2.35}$$

where wL and vK can be further expressed in terms of input labor and input capital, indicated respectively by $wpLp$, $wnpLnp$, and $vpKp$, $vnpKnp$, committed to manufacture both premium and non-premium outputs *Yi* and *Yj* to reach total sales given as *Qij*. Therefore, the new relationship is given as,

$$Min: C = (wpLp+wnpLnp) + (vpKp+vnpKnp) \qquad (2.36)$$

where premium and non-premium outputs in terms of total sales, *Qij*, can be expressed as,

$$Qij=F(Yi, Yj)= f(Kp,Knp; Lp,Lnp) \text{ or } Qij–f(Kp,Knp,Lp,Lnp) = 0 \qquad (2.37)$$

By using the Lagrangian function, the cost-minimization problem to produce both premium and non-premium outputs in terms of labor and capital split between premium and non-premium takes the form of

$$l= [(wpLp +wnpLnp)+ (vpKp+vnpKnp)] + \lambda(Qij–f(Kp, Knp, Lp, Lnp) \qquad (2.38)$$

Here as well, the first-order conditions require that

$$\delta l/\delta Lp = wp - \lambda\ \delta f/\delta Lp=0 \qquad (2.39)$$

$$\delta l/\delta Lnp = wnp - \lambda\ \delta f/\delta Lnp=0 \qquad (2.40)$$

$$\delta l/Kp = vp - \lambda\ \delta f/\delta Kp=0 \qquad (2.41)$$

$$\delta l/Knp = vnp - \lambda\ \delta f/\delta Knp=0 \qquad (2.42)$$

$$\delta l/\lambda = Qij - f(Kp,Knp,Lp,Lnp) =0 \qquad (2.43)$$

The above expressions (2.39-2.43) require diminishing *Qij–f(Kp, Knp, Lp, Lnp) = 0* strictly quasi-concave or Kp = f(Lp, Qij) and Knp =f(Lnp, Qij) strictly convex. Therefore, by using the *Marginal Rate of Technical Substitution* (MRTS), we can express the slope of the isocost of inputs used in the premium product as,

$$\frac{w_p}{v_p} = \frac{\frac{\delta f}{\delta f}}{\frac{\delta K}{\delta L}} = \frac{MP_l}{MP_K} = MRTS_{kl} = -\frac{dKp}{dLp} \qquad (2.44)$$

Along an isoquant, the MRTS indicates the rate at which one input is substituted with another input while maintaining the same level of output. Hence, *MRTS,k,l* should equal *wp/vp* for the minimum cost combination of inputs used for the premium product, and the slope of the isoquant *dKp/dLp* should equal the slope of the isocost line *(wp/vp)*. In the same way, the slope of the isocost of inputs used in the production of a non-premium product is given as

$$\frac{w_{np}}{v_{np}} = \frac{\frac{\delta f}{\delta f}}{\frac{\delta K}{\delta L}} = \frac{MP_l}{MP_K} = MRTS_{kl} = -\frac{dKnp}{dLnp} \qquad (2.45)$$

where the slope of the isoquant *(dKnp/dLnp)* equals the slope of the isocost line *(wnp/vnp)*. The marginal product per dollar spent is equal for all inputs as the cost minimization implies that the marginal rate of substitution between any two inputs of *K* and *L* is equal to the ratio of their prices for both premium and non-premium products. This can be expressed in a simple form for both premium and non-premium outputs as,

dKp/dLp=wp/vp and *dKnp/dLnp=wnp/vnp* (2.46)

The solution to the cost-minimization problem with two inputs consists of raw material inputs indicated as *xi* and *xj*, respectively, used to manufacture non-premium and premium outputs. In addition, labor (L) and capital (K) inputs, indicated as *Lp* and *Kp* are used in the production of the final premium output, and labor *(Lnp)* and capital *(Knp)* are used in the production of a non-premium final output.

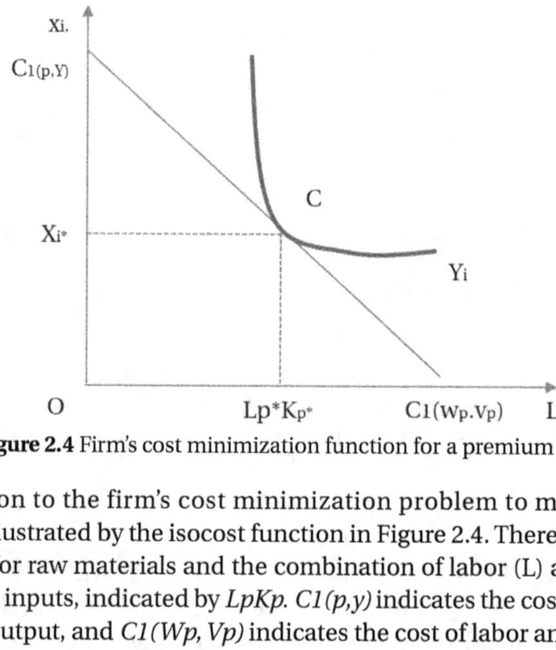

Figure 2.4 Firm's cost minimization function for a premium product

The solution to the firm's cost minimization problem to make a premium output is illustrated by the isocost function in Figure 2.4. There are two types of inputs; *Xi* for raw materials and the combination of labor (L) and (K) for labor and capital inputs, indicated by *LpKp. C1(p,y)* indicates the cost of input for the premium output, and *C1(Wp, Vp)* indicates the cost of labor and capital for the premium output. An interior solution corresponds to the point of tangency, *C*, between the y-level isoquant and an isocost line of the form *xi *p = Yi* for some Yi> 0, which shows combinations of capital inputs *(K)* and labor inputs *(L)* that can be purchased with fixed total cost.

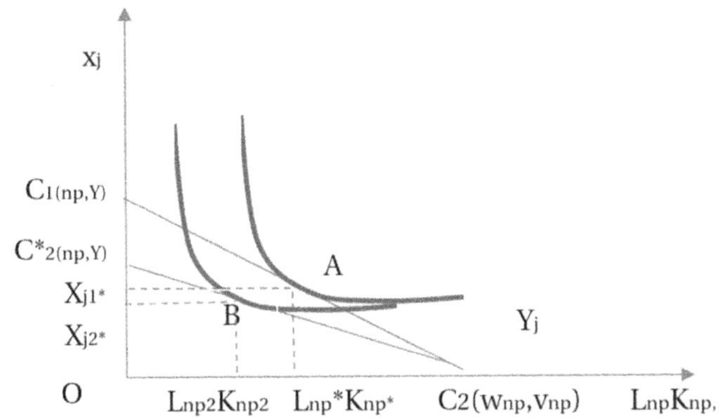

Figure 2.5 Firm's cost minimization function for a non-premium output

Figure 2.5 illustrates the solution to the firm's cost minimization problem to manufacture a non-premium output. This figure shows two types of inputs, *Xj*, for raw materials in addition to labor (L) and capital (K) inputs, indicated by *LnpKnp*. An interior solution corresponds to the point of tangency, *A*, between the y-level isoquant and an isocost line of the form $xj *p = Yj$ for some $\alpha > 0$, which shows combinations of *K* and *L* that can be purchased with fixed total cost.

At the point of tangency, A, the non-premium output is sold at a regular price during non-sales events, which has a regular standard cost higher than the 'promotion' cost during sales events. Therefore, the isocost line of a non-premium product during non-sales events (C1) is higher than the isocost line of a non-premium product during sales events (C2), C1 wp,vp) > C2 (wnp,vnp) and Xi > Xj. The cost of a non-premium product, C2(np, Y), will be lower if the product is sold at a discount during sales events, the firm arranges to buy raw materials from suppliers (inputs Xj) at a lower price, from *Xj1** to *Xj2**. During the promotion of non-premium products, the isoquant will move from point A to point B in Fig. 2.5 as a result of lower input price, C*2(np, Y), but capital and labor inputs will remain pretty much unchanged in the short-run. The isoquant for a non-premium product will move back and forth between tangencies in points A and B based on the frequency of the sales events and the purchasing power of the manufacturing firm to buy inputs from the suppliers.

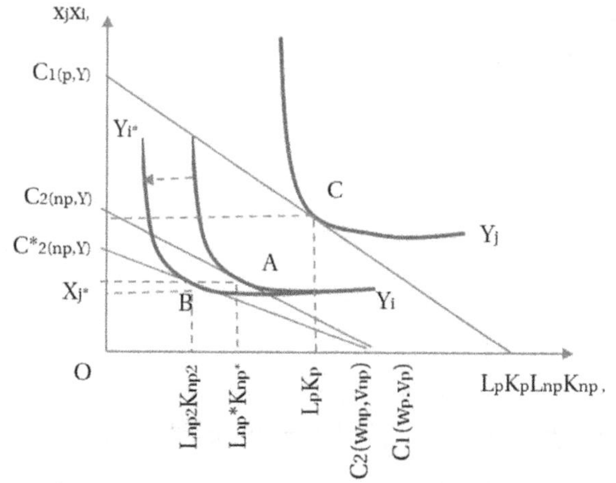

Figure 2.6 Combined firm's cost minimization functions for premium and non-premium outputs

In Figure 2.6, we have the illustration of the combined firm's cost minimization for premium and non-premium outputs in the short run. The input combination of *xixj* for raw materials and for the combined labor and capital, *LpKpLnpKnp,* are indicated by isoquants A and C to manufacture premium and non-premium output levels of *Yi* and *Yj*. During different sales events, the firm, using the same level of inputs but at discount rates for non-premium outputs, will manufacture a higher level of non-premium outputs given by isoquant Y*i** and the same level of premium outputs indicated by isoquant Yj.

In the long run, all inputs, such as raw materials, labor, and capital, will change as the firm tries to reduce long-run costs by implementing a better organizational structure, new technology, a better and more efficient supply chain management, and better planning to reduce variable and fixed overheads. Another way for a firm to reduce long-run costs and be competitive is merging with other companies by offering a larger variety of outputs, both premium and non-premium and a wide range of choices to customers rather than operating separately. It will also eliminate duplicated tasks and positions and reduce administrative, advertising, and promotion costs creating more efficiencies at the consolidation level.

In addition, merging helps reduce a portion of the fixed cost by transferring production capacity (or closing inefficient entities) to other facilities and plants that can use excess capacity. In some cases, in the long run, the production cost can temporarily increase if the firm needs to invest in new technologies and equipment to produce new outputs that are more appealing to customers. However, this cost increase can be controlled and returned to average long-term production cost if the firm introduces other non-premium lower-end outputs that help reduce overall production costs.

In the long-term, short-run and long-run costs will coincide with some short-run cost functions related to some level of fixed inputs. The slope of the short-run cost function will equal the slope of the long-run cost function in the cost-output plane based on the '*envelope*' theorem (Milgrom and Ilya, 2002). The long-run total cost is the 'envelope' of the short-run total cost. If the short-run and long-run cost functions take the same value at the same point in the plane and if their slopes are equal, then they are tangent.

In economy pricing, competitive firms manufacture a combination of product-mix such as premium and non-premium, and the long-run cost of each of these products are separated from each other despite being manufactured by the same company. The long-run total cost of premium output is the envelope of the premium short-run total cost and runs at a higher level than the long-run total cost of non-premium output, which is the envelope of the short-run total cost of non-premium output in the cost-output plane as illustrated in figure 2.7.

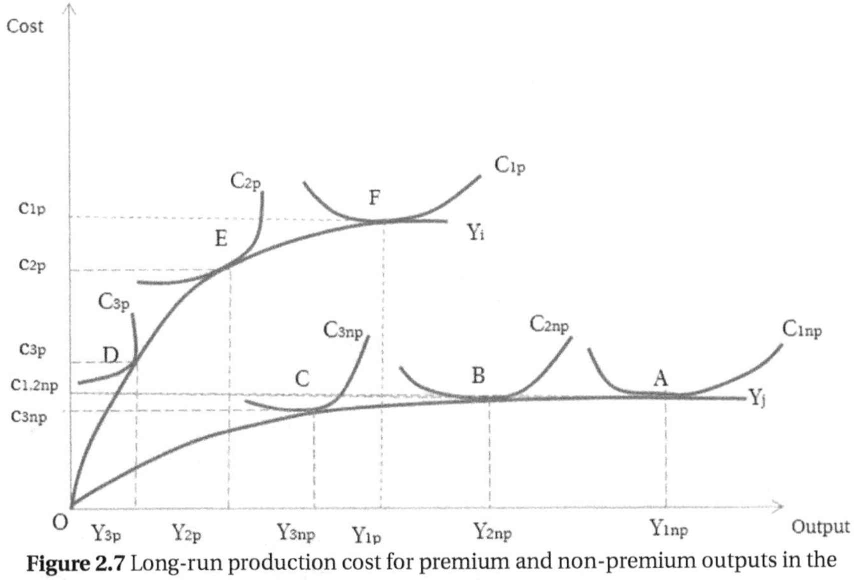

Figure 2.7 Long-run production cost for premium and non-premium outputs in the cost-output plane

Figure 2.7 illustrates the long-run production cost for a firm operating in a competitive market that manufactures two main commodities: a low-medium non-premium output for the mass of consumers and a high-end premium one for a customized high-end segment of the market. The long-run total cost of non-premium output, indicated by *Yj*, is the envelope of the non-premium short-run total costs indicated by *C3np, C2np,* and *C1np* and runs at a lower level than the long-run total cost of the premium output, indicated by curve *Yi,* which is the envelope of the short-run total cost of the premium output indicated by *C3p, C2p,* and *C1p* in the cost-output plane. Both long-run total costs *Yj* and *Yi,* run separately at different levels and don't intersect each other. Short-run total lower costs for non-premium outputs *C3np, C2np,* and *C1np* are used in the production of large volumes of outputs *Y3np, Y2np,* and *Y1np* for mass consumption. Meanwhile, the short-run total cost for the premium products C3p, C2p, and C1p are used to produce small quantities of outputs *Y3p, Y2p,* and *Y1p* for a determined market segment at a much higher cost.

If, for any reason, the long-run total cost of non-premium output, *Yj* intersects the long-run total cost of premium output *Yi,* it means that the cost of non-premium output has been rising significantly, reaching the cost of premium output. In this case, the company needs a new strategy to design a new non-premium product at a lower cost with a lower long-run total cost function than the existing non-premium one to become again competitive in the market. The long-run production cost for premium and non-premium outputs in the cost-output plane indicates how one single firm can differentiate the cost of each product if it operates in a product-mix competitive environment.

Conclusions about the Theory of the Firm in Economy Pricing

The theory of the firm is one of the main concepts in modern microeconomics. This chapter deals with different concepts of the firm theory related to the economy pricing when a firm operates in a very competitive market and produces multi-outputs. This chapter has taken into consideration how effectively a firm can use its production capacity utilization in a dynamic and competitive market. A firm can reach a production capacity utilization of about 70-80% if it tactically uses the sales event pricing strategy for non-premium outputs in combination with the pricing strategy of premium outputs. In fact, by reaching the threshold of 70-80 % production capacity utilization, the firm can easily cover all total variable and fixed costs. By using this strategy, the firm will be able to reach the sales target, generating a stable cash flow and staying competitive in the market.

Another development in this chapter is the volume-based analysis and profitability as strategy companies choose to sell their products in many ways, depending on whether the output is intended for the low-end, high-end market or in between. The strategy of manufacturing and selling non-premium products is to increase the volume and production capacity utilization to generate enough cash and accounts receivables that would be used to manufacture high-quality premium products at a higher cost and which are more profitable.

In the theory of the firm, by using the production possibility frontier is possible to move from short-run to long-run in a successful way if there is an investment in new technology and if the management expertise and supply chain management improves significantly, increasing the economy's capacity to produce both categories of goods at reduced costs. This leads to more potential realization, more production capacity, and economic growth.

We have also seen how under production function and behavioral relationships, the production behavior must adjust to uncertainty and risk. One of the challenges that happen in production is to interpret the factors behind the production decisions and to understand what leads producers to make different choices. The production choices under stringent profit maximization may differ from risk aversion and limited analytic capacities. The same type of technological relationships may result in different outcomes under different behavioral assumptions.

And lastly, in the cost function and isocost lines, we have seen how the cost function is often applied using the cost curve by companies to minimize cost and maximize production efficiency in both the categories of products, premium and non-premium, in a competitive and dynamic market. The long-run production cost in a cost-output plane is also a clear demonstration of how a firm can differentiate the cost of each product by operating in a product-mix competitive environment.

Chapter 3
Pricing Strategy and Market Factors

Introduction

In microeconomics, pricing strategy is a very important topic as it deals with market characteristics and dynamics. For every commodity and service offered in the market, customers are always willing to pay a certain amount to obtain that commodity or service. This chapter will talk about how pricing works in a competitive market and how the pricing strategy is influenced by several factors that might be beyond the firm's control. Here, it will be discussed how a firm adopting price discrimination strategies can reach different objectives. From an organization's perspective, price discrimination can offer many advantages based on the size of the company.

This chapter will discuss another important topic which is the market-based pricing strategy that starts with a target price which is an estimated price for a product or service that customers are potentially willing to pay. This estimate is based on an understanding of customers' perceived value for a product or service and how competitors will price competing products or services. An understanding of customers' behavior and competitors' strategy is increasingly important to design the correct competitive strategies.

The product life cycle and the structure of the industry are other topics that will be taken into consideration in this chapter. Organizations are constantly monitoring and reassessing product life-cycle costs and revenues as the time available to sell a product and recover the investment is getting shorter with changing market preferences and customers' behavior.

An interesting argument in this chapter will be the discussion of product hierarchy and competitive pricing. The hierarchy of the products goes from fundamental needs for every customer to specific and high-end items that satisfy the needs of customers and even exceed customer expectations. An interesting argument will be to explore the evolutionary path from marginalism to competitive pricing and sustained profitability in modern economies. This path uses a more realistic approach than the marginal cost approach, which is more associated with management accounting. The general equilibrium in economy pricing is another area of interest that will be discussed using a different economic logic and perspective.

Price Discrimination and the Dynamics of the Market

A pricing strategy is a firm's method of pricing its product based on market characteristics and dynamics. For almost every commodity or service, there are always customers willing to pay more than others. A firm that sets a single price faces a trade-off between charging all customers a price that some customers are willing to pay and charging a lower price for other customers that are not willing to pay as much as the regular price. A firm adopting price discrimination can reach two objectives. First, by using a price-discrimination strategy, a firm can charge higher prices to certain customers willing to pay more, capturing the consumer surplus (the difference between the common good's price and what the consumer is offering to pay). Second, by adopting a price-discrimination strategy, a firm can charge a lower price to consumers who are not willing to pay the regular price.

From an organization's perspective, price discrimination can offer many advantages, making it one of the common pricing strategies used by local, national, and global companies. However, not all companies can price discriminate. There are at least three conditions for a firm to price discriminate successfully:

First, the firm must have enough market power to charge customers more than the competitive price. In fact, a competitive firm cannot price-discriminate as it cannot charge some consumers more than others for the same commodity because other competitors will easily beat the higher price to increase their share of the market.

Second, the consumers must differ in the price-sensitivity (demand elasticities), and a firm must be able to explore how consumers differ in their sensitivity to charging a different price. To price-discriminate over the volume of units purchased by a customer, the firm must know how the elasticity of demand varies with the number of units purchased.

Third, the firm must be able to prevent or limit the resale of the products when the consumer who buys at a lower price is able to resell the good at a higher price for a personal profit.

There are several benefits for firms using a price discrimination strategy as they can charge the same commodity at a different price to a variety of consumers. Some of the benefits are listed below:

- Profit maximization, by matching prices to the specific characteristics of the market, and its various segments, where the firm can extract some of the consumer surplus available in the market and turn it into producer surplus by increasing the net monetary position.
- Efficient use of infrastructure and better use of space: The price discrimination strategy of charging customers different prices can

benefit firms with high fixed costs associated with infrastructure building, maintenance, and operations. This includes natural monopolies such as gas, electricity supply, and transport services with high fixed costs and can increase profitability by using price discrimination for different categories of consumers. In the same way, price discrimination may also facilitate manufacturing and retail firms to clear their existing stocks quickly when required, therefore making better use of their shop, warehouse, or factory space.

- Price discrimination strategy may also help manage the flow of customers into retail stores more effectively by introducing something like "early bird" prices encouraging shoppers to adjust their shopping times so that queues are shortened at more peak times.
- Sell to international markets by using price discrimination. Firms may be engaged in multi-market price discrimination by charging different prices in various countries because they believe that the elasticity of demand differs. Multinational companies base their prices on different markets and regions on what consumers are prepared to pay in each territory which can vary significantly from country to country. From a modern macroeconomic perspective, international trade of goods and services is likely to be created by price discrimination.

Conversely, from the consumer's perspective, there are several benefits if firms use price discrimination. For a certain category of consumers, lower prices are possible. In fact, from the consumer's point of view, some consumers, especially those in the highly elastic sub-market, may gain consumer surplus because of lower prices. The lower prices could also come because of the application of scale economies in certain industries. Charging lower prices to consumers with an elastic demand can also generate positive externalities to other sectors as a society will benefit if more goods are consumed, and more positive externalities in other industries are generated.

There are also disadvantages for the consumers that are in an inelastic sub-market as they are being disproportionately exploited due to their inelasticity. The most classical case is airfare when high-ticket prices are charged for peak travel seasons compared with off-peak. The same scenario could happen for energy prices or cable/telephone prices where existing and loyal customers, to some extent, often pay higher prices which subsidizes the discounts available to attract new customers.

There are at least three types of classic price discrimination. Perfect price discrimination, also called first-degree price discrimination –is where the firm sells each unit for the maximum amount the consumer is willing to offer, differencing in this way the price each customer pays off. Quantity discrimination, or second-degree price discrimination- is where the firms charge a different price for larger quantities than small ones. And lastly, multimarket price discrimination is also called third-degree price discrimination- where the firms charge different customers different prices in different markets or countries.

It is assumed that marginal cost (MC) is constant across all markets and will equal average total cost (ATC). Profit maximization will normally occur at the price and output where MC (marginal cost) = MR (marginal revenue).

Perfect price discrimination, or first-degree price discrimination, happens when a firm (monopoly) has enough market power to sell its unit at its reserve price. As a result, the firm's marginal revenue curve, *MRd* is the same as its demand curve AD, as illustrated in Figure 3.1

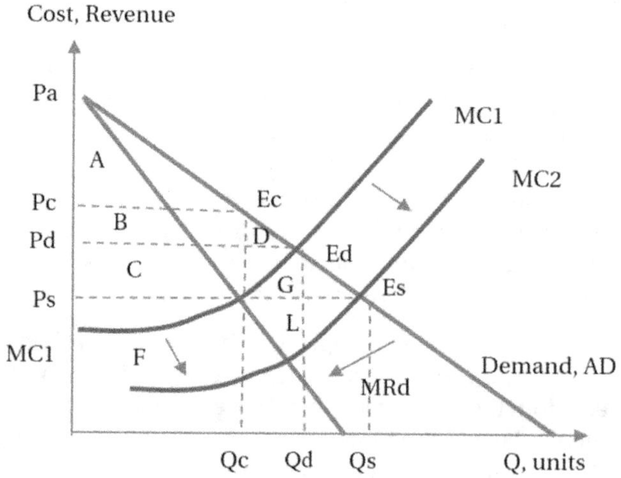

Figure 3.1 Perfect price discrimination

In Figure 3.1, the firm will sell the first unit at a price of *Pa* to the consumer who is willing to pay more for that good. The firm's marginal cost for that unit is *MC1*, and its profit on that unit is *Pa – MC1*. The sufficient condition for the firm to be competitive is to sell the unit at a lower price than *Pa* and have a higher marginal cost for each successive unit it sells. The firm will sell *Qd* units, where its marginal revenue given by curve *MRd* intersects the curve *AD*, and sell those units at a price, *Pd*. The firm will be willing to sell the last unit for *Pc* so that the monopoly can cover the marginal costs on the last unit. In a single-price monopoly equilibrium, the firm is unwilling to sell additional units because its marginal revenue will be less than the marginal cost of producing the units.

However, in a single competitive price for a single standard product, the firm will sell the unit at a lower price, *Pd*, reaching higher volumes given by quantity *Qd*, and achieving the equilibrium at point *Ed*, at the intersection of marginal cost MC1 with demand curve AD. At the competitive market equilibrium, *Ed*, the producer surplus is the total area of C+G, and the consumer surplus is the total area of A+B+D, as illustrated in Figure 3.1

Suppose the firm operates in economy pricing and manufactures a product-mix output such as premium and non-premium products. In that case, it can sell the premium product at *Pa* price, making a substantial profit, and the non-premium product at a lower regular price *Pd,* and during sales events, even at a lower discounted price, *Ps,* moving the marginal cost curve further down to intersect the AD curve with MC2 curve at point *Es,* selling a much higher volume, *Qs,* than at previous equilibrium point *Ed.* In an economy pricing system, the non-premium product is in equilibrium at point *Es,* the producer surplus is the total area F+L, and the consumer surplus is the total area A+B+C+D+G, as illustrated in Figure 3.1.

At second-degree price discrimination, we have quantity discrimination, where the price varies only with the quantity, which means all customers pay the same price for a given quantity. It's also true the fact that not all quantity discounts are a form of price discrimination, as the cost to produce a commodity in large quantities is lower than the cost of producing the same commodity in small quantities. If the quantity discount is not due to cost differences, then the firm engages in quantity discrimination. Figure 3.2 demonstrates the quantity discrimination engaged by a monopoly which, for simplicity, has a linear demand curve for each customer. The demand curve given by AD intersects the vertical axis at $80 and the horizontal axis at 80 units produced daily. The firm operating as a monopoly has a marginal and average cost of $30 per unit given by price point Ps =$30. The figure below shows how the monopoly can maximize its profit by using quantity discrimination and setting two different prices.

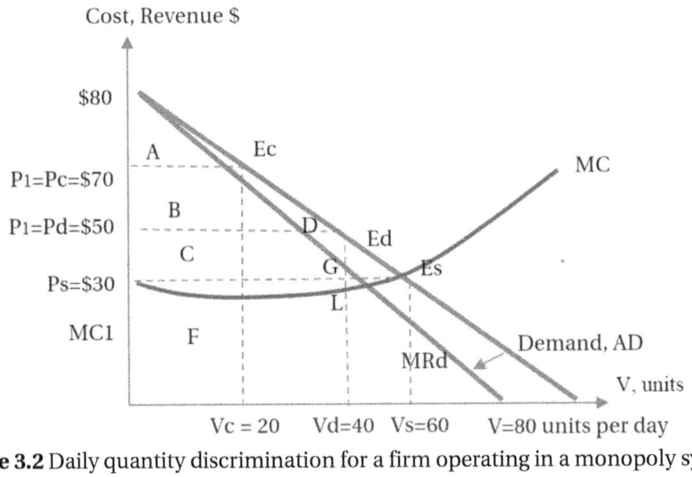

Figure 3.2 Daily quantity discrimination for a firm operating in a monopoly system

Normally the utility monopoly function faces an inverse demand curve given as p = 80 –*V*, where *V* is the number of units. Its marginal and average cost is given as Ps = m = $30. The utility chooses V1 and V2 to maximize its profit. By setting the derivative of profit with respect to *V1*, equal to zero, we have *dπ/dV1 = V2-2V1 = 0*, and the derivative of profit with respect to *V2* equal to zero. By solving these two equations simultaneously, we have the profit-maximizing quantities, V1= 20 and V2 = 40, which correspond to block prices P1 =Pc= $90-20=$70 and P2 =Pd= $50. This means that the firm acting as monopoly charges customers a higher price of $70 for a lower volume in the range between 1 and 20 units for the first price block and $50 for a larger volume of any units beyond the first 20 units in the second block price.

As Figure 3.2 illustrates, based on each consumer's demand curve, the consumer who decides to buy Vc=20 units pay $70 x 20 = $1400 for the first block and $50 x 20 = $1000 for the second block. Suppose a firm acting as a monopoly chooses to set a single price. In that case, it will produce at the point where its marginal revenue equals its marginal cost, selling, let's say, 30 units at $60 per unit. Still, by quantity discriminating, it sells more units and makes a higher profit by setting two different prices, Pc=$70 and Pd=$50.

Third-degree price discrimination is when, in multimarket price discrimination, the firm divides the potential customers into two or more groups and sets a different price for each group. The firm engaged in multimarket price discrimination needs to have the market power to be able to identify groups with different demands and prevent resales. We assume that a monopoly can divide its customers into two main groups based in two different countries. The firm sells a certain volume V1 of its product to the group in the first market (country) and earns revenue of *R1(V1)*, and at the same time, sells volume V2 to the group in the second market (country) and earns revenue of *R2(V2)*. The cost to produce the total volumes sold in both markets, *V=V1+V2*, is given as C(V) (Geoffrey A. J., and Philip J. R., 2011). The standard profit-maximizing function for the monopoly takes the form as,

$$max\ \pi_{V1,V2} = R_1(V_1) + R_2(V_2) - C(V_1 + V_2) \tag{3.1}$$

The first-order conditions corresponding to the above equation are obtained by differentiating with respect to V1 and V2 and setting partial derivatives equal to zero,

$$\frac{\delta\pi}{\delta V_1} = \frac{dR_1(V)_1}{dV_1} - \frac{dC(V)}{dV}\frac{\delta V}{\delta V_1} \tag{3.2}$$

$$\frac{\delta\pi}{\delta V_2} = \frac{dR_2(V)_2}{dV_2} - \frac{dC(V)}{dV}\frac{\delta V}{\delta V_2} \tag{3.3}$$

These equations state that the marginal revenues from sales sold to both groups in separate markets should equal their common marginal cost so the monopoly can have its profit maximized, which is written as,

$$MR_1 = \frac{dR_1(V)_1}{dV_1} = MC = \frac{dC(V)}{dV} = MR_2 \tag{3.4}$$

Therefore, by using multimarket price discrimination, the monopoly maximizes its profit by operating in those markets where its marginal revenue for each market or country equals its common marginal cost. In addition, it can be determined how the prices in both markets vary with the price elasticities of demand at the profit-maximizing outputs. We know that each marginal revenue is a function of the corresponding price and price elasticity of demand. Thus, the marginal revenue in market 1, *MR1,* can be written as $MR_1 = p_1\left(1 - \frac{1}{\varepsilon_1}\right)$ where *p1* is the corresponding price in market 1 and *ε1* is the price elasticity of demand for market 1. In the same way for the marginal revenue in market 2, *MR2,* we have that $MR_2 = p_2\left(1 - \frac{1}{\varepsilon_2}\right)$ where *p2* is the corresponding price in market 2, and *ε2* is the price elasticity of demand in market 2. By rewriting the equation using the expressions for marginal revenue, we have that,

$$MR_1 = p_1(1 - \frac{1}{\varepsilon_1}) = MC = p_2(1 - \frac{1}{\varepsilon_2}) = MR_2 \tag{3.5}$$

By simply rearranging equation (3.5), we have that the ratio of prices in the two countries depends only on demand for elasticities in those countries. Therefore, we can write,

$$\frac{p_2}{p_1} = \frac{1+1/\varepsilon_1}{1+1/\varepsilon_2} \tag{3.6}$$

Assuming that in the second country (foreign country or market 2), the price charged to customers for a single product is, let's say, \$20, and the price charged to customers for the same product in the domestic market 1 is only \$17, we have that,

$$\frac{p_2}{p_1} = \frac{\$20}{\$17} = 1.18 \tag{3.7}$$

This means that the firm believes that the foreign market (2) demand curve is less elastic at its profit-maximizing prices than the demand curve in the domestic market (1); therefore, it charges customers in the foreign market 18% more than domestic customers in market 1. There are also other reasons, except for elasticity of demand, why the multinational monopoly and non-monopoly producers charge customers more in foreign markets than in domestic ones. Other reasons could be that with international transfer pricing, additional factors become relevant such as taxes, repatriation funds, customs and duties, foreign exchange rate, the need to maintain or obtain a competitive advantage in the foreign market, and the ability to work with foreign governments.

However, with the fast-growing process of globalization, world markets tend to settle in one way or another on one price at any given time, given the process of arbitrage. In the last three-four decades, the global market in most countries has seen unprecedented growth related to new trading and selling technologies, new selling applications on mobile devices, online auction bidding, and price comparison websites which means that consumers have increased information about any product, which may reduce the possibility of price discrimination. At the same time, the widespread use of dynamic pricing models by different categories of online sellers and retailers means that time-based pricing has become somehow increasingly common.

Price adjustment and Pricing Relevant

The performance of an organization is largely dependent on its ability to generate revenues, and in order to achieve this objective, setting the right price is critical. Three major influences on pricing decisions are costs, customers, and competitors.

A company cannot sell a product for less than its cost (despite there being multiple cases when a company can sell a certain product for less than its cost), so knowledge of costs and a thorough understanding of cost behavior can enable a company to price its product to receive the maximum benefit. The customers will assist in setting the market price by determining how much they value and will pay for the attributes of the product. Lastly, competitors have a significant influence on price, as their actions and prices will influence the industry dynamics. Companies are increasingly adopting a profit-maximizing approach that considers marginal revenue and marginal cost. In general, prices are affected by both the marketplace and the producer's costs. There are a few categories of costs that affect the producer's costs. Some of them will be discussed below.

Relevant costs for a producer's pricing decisions are a function of the time horizon for pricing. For short-term decisions such as one-time special orders and product emphasis, relevant costs are those that differ between decision alternatives, normally the variable costs. For long-term decisions, fixed costs become relevant because you can adjust and solve problems, such as selling machinery and freeing up cash flows. For long-term decisions, the analysis shifts, and quantitative tools such as capital budgeting can be utilized.

Variable product cost-based pricing or simply **Cost-Based Pricing** is when the selling price is created by adding a markup to the variable costs. This pricing method is suitable for non-competitive markets, as it is focused on recovering relevant costs and ensures an entity is achieving a positive contribution margin. However, this method is not a good fit when fixed costs are a large component of total costs; the company may set a price too low to recover its fixed costs and other general overhead costs not directly attributable to the product, leaving it in an overall loss position. As such, the organization needs to be aware of its fixed costs to ensure the markup percentage is high enough to cover these costs.

Some market-based pricing strategies start with a target price, which is an estimated price for a product or service that customers are potentially willing to pay. This estimate is based on an understanding of customers' perceived value for a product or service and how competitors will price competing products or services. The understanding of customers and competitors is increasingly important because competition from lower-cost producers is continually restraining prices. Products are on the market for shorter periods of time. Customers are more knowledgeable and demanding. Companies must understand their customers' perceived value through close relationships or market research. Companies must also understand competitors' technologies, products, costs, and financial conditions.

With *Cost-Based Pricing* use of poor-quality cost, information can lead to poor pricing and product decisions. Information can quickly become outdated, and costs not properly captured in the accounting system will lead to suboptimal decisions. Another problem with *Cost-Based Pricing* is often referred to as the "death spiral." Assume the volume of sales for a company is falling. This could be a result of a high selling price, which might be related to competitors selling at a lower price due to lower costs. As sales volumes fall, the amount of fixed cost allocated to each unit increases, leading to an even higher cost per unit. If prices are based on costs, then a higher cost per unit leads to a higher selling price, which in turn causes sales to fall even more. Selling volumes can dramatically impact costs. Therefore it is essential to consider not only costs but also market conditions.

Demand-Based Pricing. In contrast to cost-based pricing, demand-based pricing focuses on two things: the value to customers and the demand (competition). If the demand curve is elastic, then slight decreases in prices can greatly increase sales — and vice versa; a slight increase in prices can greatly reduce sales. An elastic demand curve is more prevalent in a competitive environment. If the demand curve is inelastic, prices could rise substantially, and volume would not be affected as much. For example, the price of natural gas could rise, and if it remains cheaper than electricity, volumes would not be impacted significantly. With a monopoly/oligopoly, the organization decides what return it wishes to achieve, given a certain cost structure, and then sets its prices to achieve that return. This approach usually applies to companies with an inelastic demand curve, such as utility companies. Demand-based pricing uses consumer demand to determine a perceived value; this is the core focus of this pricing strategy. It will test consumers' price sensitivity to products to arrive at the final selling price.

There are a few different approaches within demand-based pricing that are listed as follows:

Predatory pricing occurs when a company deliberately prices below its costs to drive out competitors and restrict supply. As competitors may not be able to match the low price, they will subsequently go out of business. At this time, the company with a predatory pricing strategy will raise prices rather than enlarge demand or meet competition. The predatory organization will incur short-term losses for eventually long-term profits. The purpose of this pricing strategy is that deliberate price cutting will force smaller/weaker rivals out of business or prevents new entrants. It is supposed to work in the short term but not in the long term. It is also considered anti-competitive and illegal if it can be proven, but very difficult to prove.

Penetration Pricing involves setting the price low to attract customers and gain market share. The price will be raised later once this market share is gained. Penetration pricing differs from predatory pricing in that penetration is only short-term to gain market share and does not focus on eliminating competition. The key focus is the intent of the pricing strategy that differs between penetration and predatory. The price is set low and, in such a way, can penetrate the market. The low price is set to secure high volumes in sales. The intent of this strategy is to lower costs over the long term by gaining production and distribution economies of scale before competitors. This is normally appropriate for products with long product life, and it may be useful in launching products into a new market.

Price Skimming is when goods are sold at higher prices initially so that fewer sales are needed to break even. Over time, the price is lowered so more customers can buy the product. Selling a product at a high price, sacrificing high sales volumes to gain a high profit from fewer sales, is therefore "skimming" the market. Price skimming is usually employed to reimburse the investment cost of the original research into the product. This type of pricing strategy is commonly used in the electronics markets and is suitable for products that have short life cycles, or that will face competition at some point in the future. This strategy is often used to target "early adopters" of a product or service. Early adopters generally have low price sensitivity; this can be attributed to their need for the product, compensating for their need to economize, a greater understanding of its value, or simply having a higher disposable income. Therefore, early adopters don't mind paying more for the new product. Price skimming is employed only for a limited duration to recover most of the investment to build the product. To gain further market share, a seller will commonly switch and then use other pricing tactics.

Price Bundling consists of offering several products or services for sale as one combined product. If the customer intends to use all the bundled services, it is less expensive than if each product was purchased separately. However, customers often do not use each bundled product or service. This is a common feature in many imperfectly competitive product markets.

Peak-Load Pricing involves the practice of charging a higher price for the same product or service when demand approaches physical capacity limits. This pricing strategy tries to reduce demand to compensate for the limited supply. It is also known as dynamic pricing.

Loss Leader Pricing is a strategy where a product is sold at a price below its market cost to stimulate the sales of other, more profitable goods or services. A loss leader is usually a product that customers purchase frequently, so they are aware that its unusually low price is a bargain. The seller must use this technique regularly if it expects its customers to come back. The retailer will often limit how much a customer can purchase. Some loss leader items are perishable and cannot be stockpiled. They have short life cycles and need to be sold.

Tender/Contract Pricing is the process of making an offer, bid, or proposal or expressing interest in response to an invitation or request for tender. Organizations will seek other businesses to respond to a need, such as the supply of goods or services, and select an offer or tender that meets their needs and provides the best value for money. There is a proposal submitted for a contract/job that is aimed to cover materials and labor costs and generate a profit often undisclosed and in competitive markets. For example, many governments look to tenders for large capital projects. The purchasing department will work with the engineering department to draft the tender offer and ensure that the right technical specifications are listed. They will either offer the opportunity to bid to all companies (open bid) or pick ones they have worked with in the past (closed bid). The bidding companies need to review the requirements of the government project and ensure their proposal fits within those specifications. Then the government will collect all the bids, review them, and assess them based on price and ability to complete the project to a set standard.

Value-Based Pricing is the practice of setting prices based on a trade-off between the perceived value to the consumer and the producer's incentive to produce the product (which is a function of price and cost). Value-based pricing uses value curves, which rank the attributes of the focal firm's cost-volume-profit versus its main rivals to see which firm offers the most value for the price charged. With value-based pricing, the price set could be high in relation to the costs of the product due to the perceived value by the customer, especially when products are sold on emotion, such as in the fashion apparel industry or with products in a niche market. In these instances, sellers begin with high prices with the option of reducing the prices as competition builds in.

Short-Term Pricing Decisions typically have a time horizon of less than a year and include decisions such as: pricing a one-time-only special order with no long-run implications and adjusting product mix and output volumes in a competitive market. By contrast, long-term pricing decisions have a year or longer time horizon and include pricing a product in a market with some flexibility in setting a price.

Target-based costs. Product and service costs can play an important role in establishing a selling price. It is important to know the product or service cost to understand margins and set a selling price that will generate profit for the organization, and then work backward to the target cost for that product. There are several steps of target-based costs: 1) develop a product that satisfies the needs of potential customers, 2) Choose a target price, 3) Derive a target cost per unit by subtracting target operating income per unit from the target price, 4) Perform cost analysis to target cost reduction. 5) Perform value engineering to achieve the target price, by reducing costs and achieving desired quality levels.

Product Life Cycle and the Structure of a Competitive Industry

The product Life Cycle is the sequence of stages a product goes through during its lifespan. Entirely new industries, such as computers and smartphones, have sprung from technologies that are evolving with shorter product lifespans. This has happened so rapidly that these products become obsolete within a few months of their market introduction. Organizations are constantly monitoring and reassessing product life-cycle costs and revenues as the time available to sell a product and recover the investment in it shrinks with changing market preferences and customer behavior.

The life cycle of a product goes through five stages: development, introduction, growth, maturity, and decline. A pricing decision based on life cycle costing factors must take into consideration the fact that between 80% to 90% of a product's lifecycle cost will be incurred during the pre-production stages when the product has not been released to the market and is earning no revenue. The price set for the product will try to recover those initial costs by mapping out the intended prices over each stage. Product life-cycle management aims to maximize profits over a product's entire life cycle rather than to maximize revenues and minimize costs for each life cycle stage.

Product life-cycle management involves managing a product or service through its development, introduction, growth, maturity, and decline stages. The product life-cycle stages correspond to inflection points in the sales curve. It is difficult to identify the stages of a product's life cycle while it is in progress;

these points are easier to identify after the fact. Sales curves differ in shape; some peak and decline quickly without ever manifesting a mature stage (such as clothes fads), while others stay in maturity for decades (such as Levi Strauss blue jeans). Many factors influence the product life cycle, including the nature and timing of product enhancements, the introduction of new technology, pricing, degree of segmentation, and choice of distribution channels.

At least two external factors can shape the nature of the sales curve for a new product: the rate at which consumers adopt it and the degree to which existing and future products can better meet consumer needs. A company can introduce such substitute products to meet consumer needs rather than its competitors; however, the company can be influenced by many factors of financial and non-financial nature that can delay the substitute product. To some extent, the length of life-cycle phases can be managed or influenced individually by companies. Take the case of the maturity phase, which is the most important phase to prolong and lengthen from a financial perspective. During the maturity phase, a product is at its height in demand and is highly profitable for the company. Most companies would take advantage of extending the maturity phase using different strategies such as:

- Increasing product demand within the existing customer base with special exclusive offers
- Encouraging trial versions of the current product so that new customers may be introduced to the product
- Enhancing current product features to make the product more attractive
- Offering special incentives and promotions to attract customers who use alternative brands

There are different scenarios where companies must estimate how much it will cost to supply a one-time special order. This must include all direct and indirect costs throughout the value chain that will change in total by accepting the one-time special order. If the bid for the one-time special order is successful, operating income will increase by relevant revenues minus relevant costs. Two key factors affect short-term pricing: many costs are irrelevant in short-run pricing decisions; short-term pricing is opportunistic.

Qualitative considerations must be factored in when making short-term pricing decisions, such as whether existing customers will be upset with the discounted offers. During the pricing consideration phase, important business decisions require setting the correct price; otherwise, this may result in unfavorable sales outcomes and loss of customers. This goes beyond cost or market-based pricing strategies and also needs to consider the industry's structure and product life cycles.

The Structure of the Industry significantly impacts how an organization sets and pursues its strategy. Competitors' numbers and relative strength will influence a firm's ability to set prices and obtain market share. When one company has strong control over a market, it is called a monopoly: the company can charge what it wants and serve who it pleases to maximize economic profit. True monopolies rarely exist without government regulation.

When a small group of companies can control the market, this is an oligopoly (also called a cartel). These participants can earn profits using implicit collusion to set prices and control the market. However, while explicit collusion achieves the same purpose, it is illegal in most countries. One example of a legal oligopoly that uses collusion to control market prices is the *Organization of the Petroleum Exporting Countries* (OPEC). By coordinating policies and oil exported onto the world markets, OPEC can influence the price of oil, though this power has been diminishing with the development of oil resources in non-OPEC countries.

Private enterprises with this kind of monopolistic power over the market tend to involve government regulation to prevent consumers from being taken advantage of. The concern is that these companies can use their power to charge higher prices, burdening customers unfairly or only serving the most profitable segments of the population. Governments can intervene in these situations using antitrust laws and competition acts and introduce different market regulations to ensure companies cannot abuse monopolistic powers.

Where an industry is not dominated by a single or small group of participants, competition often exists. Perfect competition exists when consumers have a wide range of options available. Individual industry participants have difficulty distinguishing their value proposition from their competition, as their goods and services are largely commoditized. In a perfectly competitive market, market participants tend only to earn moderate profits that are considered average for the industry in which they operate. This is because pricing becomes the predominant competitive basis to maximize profitability. Prices will continue falling until marginal revenue equals marginal cost.

Many industries are somewhere in between the two extremes of a monopoly and perfect competition. This is where competitive markets adopt innovation and creativity, allowing certain market participants to create a competitive advantage, enabling them to achieve sustainable economic growth.

Product Hierarchy and Competitive Pricing

Product hierarchy, as a definition, is the classification of a product into its essential components. The wide variety of products offered in the market is related or connected in different ways to each-other. The hierarchy of the products goes from fundamental needs to specific and high-end items that satisfy the needs of customers. Basic items are normally items that meet the need of every customer. Specific or high-end items are items designed to have an augmented product that exceeds customer expectations.

Today's competition takes place at the basic items level and at the product-augmentation level. The high-end or product augmentation leads the firms to look at the user's total consumption life-cycle, such as the way the user performs the tasks of getting, using, fixing, and disposing of the product. In fact, based on marketing theories, the real competition is not how companies design and manufacture the products but rather what they add to the manufactured output in the form of packaging, services, advertising, customer advice, financing, delivery arrangements, warehousing, and other gears that customer value. These are some of the things that could be considered in the case of product-augmentation strategy.

As firms have higher prices for their high-end or augmented products, they can also offer a 'stripped-down' or an inexpensive product version at a much lower price to stay competitive in a crowded market with so many augmented products. There are also the so-called 'potential products,' where there are possible future augmentations and transformations that different products might undergo. This will prompt firms to search for new ways to satisfy customers and distinguish their offers. Some companies are able not only to satisfy customers but also to exceed their expectations to a higher level. Based on different marketing studies, there are at least seven levels of the product hierarchy:

1-) Need family: The basic need of the family that underlines the existence of a product family.

2-) Product family: those products that satisfy a core need with reasonable effectiveness. In this category, we have a variety of products such as computers and calculators that can-do computation.

3-) Product class: a bundle of products within the product family with certain functional coherence or consistency. Some examples of Product class could be personal computers, i-pads, iPhones, etc.

4-) Product line: this term includes a group of products within a product class that is meticulously related by performing a similar function. They are sold to the same category of customers, are marketed and advertised through the same channels, and fall within a given price range. Samples of product lines are portable wire-less PC, DVD readers, CD-reader, etc.

5-) Product type: the definition of group type is based on a group of items within a product line that shares one of the different forms of the product. For example, palm top computers, 3D television, etc.

6-) Brand: this common term is associated with one or more items in the product line that is used to identify the source or character of the items. For instance, Acer is one PC brand, and Samsung is one brand of smart phone.

7-) Product variant: It is a distinct unit within a brand or product line that is distinguishable by size, price, appearance, or other unique and specific attributes. For instance, same-brand car models such as Jeep Compass, Jeep Patriot, Jeep Wrangler, etc.

Product Mix is defined as the total number of product lines that a company offers to its customers. The product lines may range from one to many, and the company may also have many products under the same product line. All these product lines, when convened together, form the product mix of the company. The product mix is a subsection of the marketing mix and is an important part of a business model, especially for companies operating in a competitive market.

As we already know, the perfect price discrimination equilibrium differs from the standard competitive equilibrium. In fact, in competitive equilibrium, every customer is charged a price equal to the equilibrium marginal cost, *Pc= MCc*. Meanwhile, in the perfect price discrimination equilibrium, only the last commodity is sold at that price. The other commodities are sold at the customer's reservation prices which are greater than *Pc*. Even though some firms choose perfect price discrimination, many more firms set a single price or use other pricing methods to attract customers. One of the main reasons why these firms do not perfectly discriminate is that they incur considerable transition costs, which make them difficult or costly to gather information about each customer's price elasticity.

Generally, a firm operating as a perfect competitor in a given input and output market can buy inputs and sell on output markets, and the amount it produces will not affect prevailing market prices. The competitive firm sees the market price for its product, assumes it will remain the same regardless of how much or how little it sells, and makes its decisions accordingly. If the conditions of input and output markets change, the firm's plans and decisions will change as well. Such a firm is a price taker on both output and input markets.

A competitive firm uses different tools to maximize its profit. Given that both revenue and cost will vary with output, a firm's profit varies with its output level. A firm operating in a non-competitive market with one main product has its profit function written as,

$$\Pi (q) = R (q) - C (q) \qquad (3.8)$$

where *R(q)* is the revenue, and *C(q)* is the fixed and variable cost involved in the production of the main item sold at volume q (Perloff, 2013). If the same firm must operate in a very competitive market and decides to have two diversified products such as premium and non-premium, then its profit function can be written as,

$$\Pi^* (q1+q2) = [Rp\ (q1) - Cp\ (q1)] + [Rnp\ (q2) - Cnp\ (q2)] \qquad (3.9)$$

where *Rp(q1)* is the portion of the revenue of the premium product *q1*, and *Rnp(q2)* is the other portion of the revenue of the non-premium product *q2*. The costs of premium and non-premium products are given respectively by *Cp(q1)* and *Cnp(q2)*. In both competitive and non-competitive markets, the firm will try to maximize its profit by using either one or multi-products.

In a non-competitive market, the firm producing one main product will set its output to maximize its profit. Instead, in a competitive market, the firm will diversify the range of products by producing premium and non-premium items to take advantage of different low- and high-end market segments. It will set the output of non-premium products and the price of a premium product in such a combination as to maximize its overall profit. This firm's profit will be maximized if the firms sell large volumes of non-premium products at a low and competitive price (the price will lower further during sales events) and relatively small volumes of premium products at a much higher price. The combination of these two outputs will create the desired profit. Profit maximization can also be obtained using the first-order condition for a maximum profit for both premium and non-premium products. The premium product will have the first-order condition with respect to selling price *p* given as,

$$d\Pi(p1^*)/dp1 = 0 \qquad (3.10)$$

and the non-premium product will have the first-order condition with respect to quantity sold *q* as,

$$d\Pi(q2^*)/dq2 = 0 \qquad (3.11)$$

Equations (3.10) and (3.11) state that a necessary condition for combined profit to be maximized is that quantity be set at *q2** for non-premium products and price be set at *p1** for premium products. Because profit is a function of revenue and cost, we can state that there is another way to obtain profit. There is another condition to have profit maximization by expressing the profit in terms of revenue, costs, fixed cost, and contribution margin. Given that profit is a function of revenue and cost, we can obtain the necessary condition for profit maximization by setting the derivate of expression *Π(q1+q2) = [Rp (q1) – Cp (q1)] + [Rnp (q2)- Cnp (q2)]* with respect to output equal to zero written as,

$$\frac{d\pi(q_1+q_2)}{dq} = \frac{R_p(q_1)}{dq} - \frac{C_p(q_1)}{dq} + \frac{R_{np}(q_2)}{dq} - \frac{C_{np}(q_2)}{dq} = MR(q_1+q_2) - MC(q_1+q_2) = 0 \qquad (3.12)$$

for $q=q1+q2$, where the firm's marginal revenue for both premium and non-premium products equal its marginal cost for both products $q1$ and $q2$, and the difference between MR and MC is zero. Under cost-volume-profit analysis, the same concept is given by the break-even point that occurs when revenues equal costs.

Determining the break-even point allows a company to determine the level of sales needed to cover all fixed costs and start earning profit. From management accounting, we know that a break-even point can be determined in terms of units of sales or dollars of sales. For a unit of sales, *Break-even (units)=Fixed costs/CM per unit,* and for dollars of sales, *Break-even (dollars) = fixed cost/CM ratio* (Cost Management: Strategies for Business Decisions, Hilton 2004, chapter 4-7). Contribution margin (CM) in management accounting terms is equal to *CM=sales – variable costs.* The break-even point of both premium and non-premium units (*q1* and *q2)* from equation 3.12 takes the form as,

$$Break-even\ U(q_1+q_2)=\frac{Fixed\ Cost_{\ p+np}\ (q_1+q_2)}{CM\ (units)(q_1+q_2)}=\frac{Fixed\ Cost_{\ p+np}\ (q_1+q_2)}{WACM\ (units)q_1+q_2}=$$
$$MR(q_1+q_2)-MC(q_1+q_2)=0 \qquad (3.13)$$

where, WACM is the *weighted average of contribution margin* (*WACM = Total CM/Total units)* that serves to calculate the break-even-point for multiple products in the sales mix. A similar equation can be obtained for break-even dollars using the CM ratio. The *cost-volume-profit* (CVP) analysis is normally used when a company is trying to determine what level of sales is required to reach a specific level of income, also called targeted income. To calculate the required sales level, the targeted income is added to fixed costs, and the total is divided by the contribution margin ratio to determine required sales dollars, or the total is divided by the contribution margin per unit to determine the required sales level in units.

Given that contribution margin (CM) per unit is the amount by which profit will increase for every unit sold past the break-even point, the break-even formula can be adapted to include the target profit as fixed cost such as *Break-even (units)=(Fixed costs + Target Profit)/CM per unit.* The target profit equation for multi products such as premium (q1) and non-premium (q2) derived from equation (3.13) can be written as,

$$Target\ Profit\ Sales\ S_{1+2}(q_1+q_2)=\frac{Fixed\ Cost_{\ (p+np)}+\pi_{1+2}(q_1+q_2)}{WACM\ (units\ or\ ratio)q_1+q_2}>0 \qquad (3.14)$$

where *S1* and *S2* are the targeted sales for the company to reach the target profit *π1* and *π2* for both products for a given fiscal period[1] to be profitable. In fiscal period 1 (year one), the company will reach the forecasted profit π1+2 by selling a combination of quantities, $q_1 + q_2$, of both premium and non-premium products, given the production capacity utilization, until the products are faced out, and in fiscal period two are substituted with other similar, more improved products. The multiperiod sales target to generate profit based on original and subsequent products is given as the sum of all products created over the years, and the profit function takes the form as,

$$Target\ Profit\ Sales\ S_{1+2}(q_1 + q_2 \dots q_{t-n})_{1-t} = \left(\frac{Fixed\ Cost_{\ (p+np)} + \pi_{1+2}(q_1+q_2)}{WACM\ (units\ or\ ratio) q_1+q_2}\right)_{t1} + \left(\frac{Fixed\ Cost_{\ (p+np)} + \pi_{3+4}(q_3+q_4)}{WACM\ (units\ or\ ratio) q_3+q_4}\right)_{t2} + \left(\frac{Fixed\ Cost_{\ (p+np)} + \pi_{5+6}(q_5+q_6)}{WACM\ (units\ or\ ratio) q_5+q_6}\right)_{t-n} + \ldots = \sum_1^n \left(\frac{Fixed\ Cost_{\ (p+np)} + \pi_{k+k*}(q_{n-k}+q_{n-k*})}{WACM\ (units\ or\ ratio) q_{n-k}+q_{n-k*}}\right) \tag{3.15}$$

where *q1* and *q2* are the respective premium and non-premium products sold in fiscal period *t1* and substituted in period *t2* with new, improved premium and non-premium products indicated by q3 and q4, these products are later substituted in period t-n with the newly updated premium and no-premium products indicated by q5 and q6, and so on. The profit will start flowing in the company once the fixed costs in each period are covered by the sales volume of premium and non-premium products to break-even.

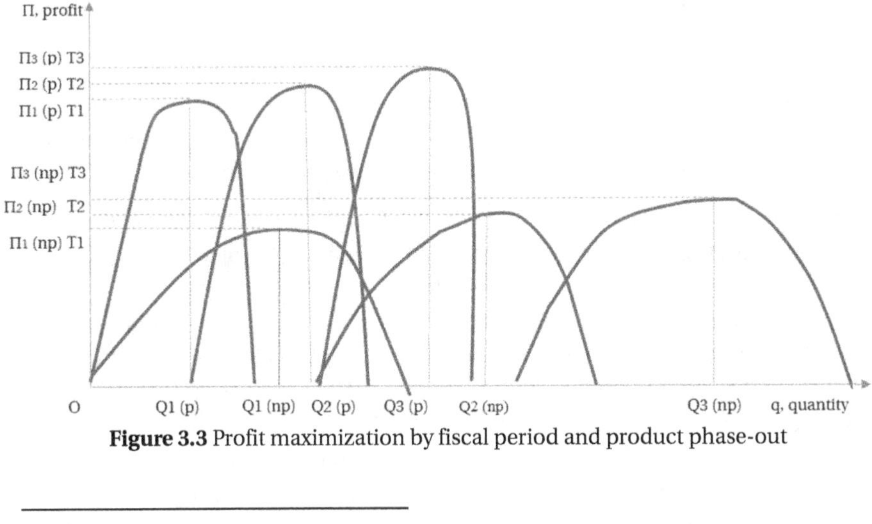

Figure 3.3 Profit maximization by fiscal period and product phase-out

[1] A fiscal period is normally considered a 12-month period with 12 inter-periods of one calendar month each.

Figure 3.3 illustrates the profit maximization curves for each fiscal period (12 months) and the product replacement at the end of each period. The profit curve first rises for each premium and non-premium product, reaching a maximum profit at the peak of each curve when the traditional marginal profit is zero (based on the positive slope of the profit curve). For each of the premium and non-premium products, the profit for all three periods (from fiscal period 1 to 3) in figure (3.3) is indicated as $\pi 1p$, $\pi 2p$, $\pi 3p$, $\pi 1np$, $\pi 2np$, $\pi 3np$, and output is respectively given as *Q1p, Q2p, Q3p and Q1np, Q2np, Q3np*. All the profit curves reach their peak at the point where profit for each of the premium and non-premium products are given respectively by π1np, π2np, π3np, π1p, π2p, π3p, and then they fall, reducing the profit until each of them is phased-out and substituted by another product in the next period of better quality and features. For example, in the figure above, the first non-premium product reaches its peak profit in $\pi 1np$ and with quantity sold *Q1np* in period 1 (during the maturity stage of the product life cycle), then is phased out (during the decline stage of the product life cycle) in period two and substituted by another non-premium product represented by quantity *Q2np* reaching its peak profit at point π2np. This non-premium product is later phased out and substituted with another non-premium product *Q3np* in period three, and so on. A similar process occurs with premium products.

This strategy used by competitive firms guarantees a flow of profit for each period. Non-premium products have lower profits as they are sold out in large volumes at regular and at discounted prices to be competitive. Meanwhile, premium products have much higher selling prices and therefore are sold in limited quantities as they are strategically designed only for certain high-end market segments. The combined profit flows of premium and non-premium products generate enough cash for the firm to cover current expenses and liabilities and create reserve funds for future investments.

Fixed cost is an operating expense that cannot be avoided regardless of the level of production or sales. Fixed costs that make up most of a company's total cost structure are required to achieve higher levels of revenues to break even. Fixed costs are incurred regularly and tend to show little fluctuation from period to period. Companies that have a high level of fixed costs in their entire cost structure are required to achieve higher levels of revenues to break even. Companies with high fixed costs and unchanged variable costs in their production process tend to have the greatest amount of operating leverage. This means that after a company achieves the break-even point, all else equal, any further increases in sales will produce higher profits. Conversely, decreases in sales volume can produce disproportionately bigger declines in profits unless fixed costs are reduced to reach a level of lower break-even point.

Marginalism and Competitive Pricing

Marginalism has for a long time been considered the study of marginal theories and relationships in microeconomics. Marginalism consists of measuring how much additional use and benefit is obtained from incremental increases in the number of goods produced and sold and how much of these measures are associated with the consumer's choice and demand. Marginalism in the study of social and economic science primarily applies differential computations to major problems of rational economic choice and represents a simplification of economic reality. Since the beginning, the theory of Marginalism has had its main objective to explain the incongruity in the value of goods and services by reference to their secondary or marginal utility.

Marginalist ideas have emerged since the early decades of the nineteenth century. However, the proper marginalism wave occurred later in the nineteenth century, during the 1871–77 period, and it focused mainly on marginal utility as a measure of scarcity. During this time, it was formalized a theory of exchange characterized by proportionality between prices and marginal utilities (Maas, 2005).

In the second half of the nineteenth century, three well-known economists in three different countries working independently from each-other contributed to marginalism by setting the basis of a formal theory. The names of these three economists are as follows: Jevons in England, Menger in Austria, and Walras in Switzerland. Jevons first proposed the theory of marginalism in a series of articles published between 1863 and 1871. Similarly, Carl Menger presented the theory of marginalism in his work published in 1871. Menger, among others, tried to explain why individuals use marginal utility to decide amongst trade-offs. Another renowned economist, Léon Walras, was able to present the marginalism theory in his main work, *Éléments d'économie politique pure* (Walras, Léon,1969), published in French and then translated into English, the first part of which was published in 1874 (Jaffe, 1975).

Marginalism outlines both an economical method of analysis and a theory of value. Based on this theory, rational individuals can make economic decisions "on the margin." This economic behavior, as explained by marginalists, is based on the value of the commodity and is determined by how much additional utility an extra unit of a good or service provides (Hutchison, 1978). The development of marginal theory in the nineteenth century, which is commonly used in modern economics, is primarily denoted as the *Marginalist*

Revolution and is seen as the separating line between classical and modern economics (Hutchison, 1953).

Marginalism tries to explain the inconsistency in the value of goods and services by referring to another concept whose secondary value is marginal utility. The interpretation of marginal utility has been commonly described by economists as utility being quantifiable, which means that different levels of utility could be compared along a numerical scale. This interpretation has affected the development of theories of marginal utility and how these theories were received at large by economists. The quantitative concept of utility has allowed for more mathematic standard operations, and further assumptions of continuity and differentiability have significantly increased the reception among economists.

Modern mainstream economic theory regularly assumes that preference structures subject to certain rules use "utility" to associate goods, services, or their uses with quantities and describes utility per se as a quantification. In fact, marginal utility quantifies the satisfaction that a consumer has by consuming additional units of goods or services. In modern economics, the concept of marginal utility is used largely to determine how much of an item consumers are willing to purchase to satisfy their needs. In general, we have a positive marginal utility when the consumption of an additional item increases the total utility and a negative marginal utility when the consumption of an additional item reduces the total utility.

Part of the marginalism theory is also the marginal cost, that is, the change in the total cost that arises when the quantity produced is increased by one unit. In simple terms, the marginal cost is the cost of producing one more unit of a finished good. At each level of production, marginal cost includes variable costs such as the cost of inputs or raw materials, labor, and variable overheads to produce the next unit of the finished good (Vickrey, 2008). Given the production technology - at each level of production and during a certain accounting period - marginal costs include all costs that vary with the production level; meanwhile, other costs that do not vary with the production level are fixed costs and hence not part of marginal cost.

In modern economics, the firm's profitability or operating income is measured by its producer surplus, which is the difference between the amount for which a finished good sells in the market and the minimum cost necessary for the producer/seller to manufacture that good. Using standard microeconomics procedure, the firm's producer surplus can be measured using the supply curve, where its marginal cost curve is above the average variable cost.

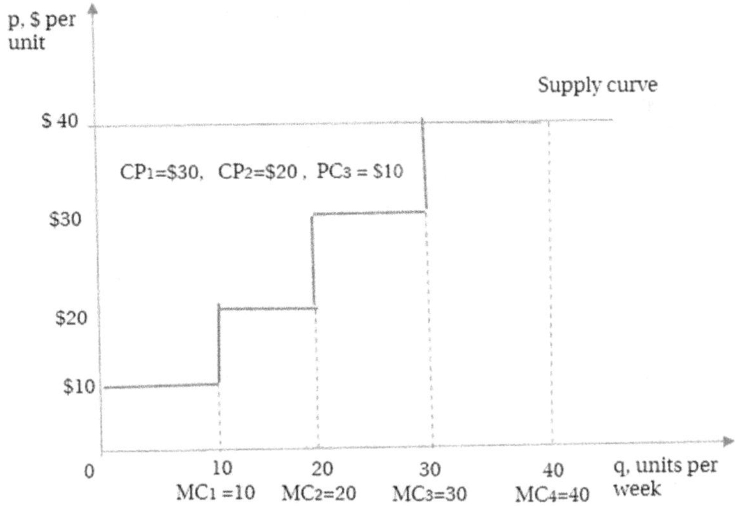

Figure 3.4a Marginal cost and producer surplus

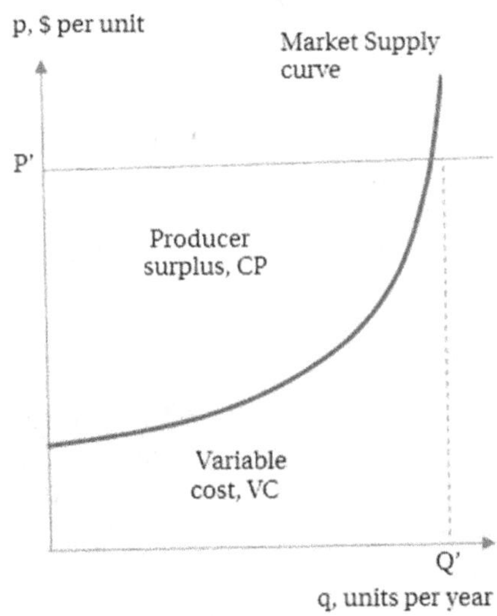

Figure 3.4b Market producer surplus

The firm's supply curve for simplification, as illustrated in figure (3.4a), is designed as a staircase rather than as a standard straight line. The marginal cost of producing the first unit in fig. 3.4a is MC1=$10, which is nothing more than the area under the marginal cost curve between 0 and 10. The marginal cost of producing the second unit is MC2 = $20, and the area under the marginal cost curve is between $20-$30, and so on.

The variable cost to produce four units is computed as the sum of the marginal costs for the first units given as: VC = MC1+MC2+MC3+MC4= \$10+\$20+\$30+\$40 =\$100. If the market price is \$40, then the company's profit from the sale of the first unit with cost MC1 = \$10, is CP1 = p – MC1= \$40-\$10 = \$30, which is company's profit or producer surplus (CP1) on the first unit. The company's producer profit or surplus is \$20 on the second unit and \$10 on the third unit. Meanwhile, on the fourth unit, the market price equals marginal cost, so the firm breaks even. As a result, the company's total profit, CP, from selling four units at \$40 each is the sum of its producer surpluses on these units given as CP = CP1+CP2+CP3+CP4 = \$30+\$20 +\$10 +0 = \$60.

Technically speaking, in Fig. 3.4a, the firm's profit or producer surplus is \$60 and is the area below the market price, p=\$40, and above the marginal cost (supply curve) up to the number of units sold (4). The area under the marginal cost curve, up to the number of units produced, is the variable cost of production. Based on the modern theory of marginalism, the firm is indifferent between producing the fourth unit or not because its marginal producer surplus from the fourth unit is zero.

Figure 3.4b illustrates the market's producer surplus in a more traditional way using the market supply curve. The variable cost of producing the level of output *Q'* is given by the area below the supply curve. The profitability or the market producer surplus is the area above the supply curve and below the market price *p'*, up to the output produced *Q.'* The company's profitability or producer's surplus is calculated by integrating the difference between the firm's demand function (market price line p') and its marginal cost function *MC(q)*, up to the output produced *q'* and is given as,

$$CP = \int_0^{q'} [p - MC(q)]dp = pq' - VC(q') = R(q') - VC(q') \qquad (3.16)$$

where the revenue is given as *R= pq'*. Technically speaking, producer surplus is on general terms related to a firm's profit. The simple equation for profit is the revenue minus total cost. Total cost, *Ct*, can be split into a variable cost, *VC*, and fixed cost, *FC*. Therefore, we have,

$$\pi = R - Ct = R - VC - FC \qquad (3.17)$$

As we can see from the equations above, the difference between producer surplus (3.16) and profit (3.17) is the fixed costs. Thus, in the producer's theory, if the fixed cost is zero, the producer surplus equals profit, which occurs in the long run.

Competitive-Pricing Approach to Explain Marginal Cost Approach

There is also a more realistic approach than the marginal cost approach based on management accounting theories. Determining the cost of a product or service is an important approach in management accounting as it allows management to determine how profitable a product or a job is. Costs are defined as the monetary value of goods and services incurred with the expectation that current or future benefits will accrue from such expenditures. The management of an organization is looking to cost a product or a service in such a way as to accumulate those costs in a more reasonable way that reflects the effort put in place to earn revenue.

The main costing methods used in management accounting are job costing and process costing. Job costing is used in those organizations whose products or services can be uniquely identified. Meanwhile, process costing is used in those organizations whose products are mass-produced. By using the process costing method, the total cost of producing an identical or similar product is divided by the number of units produced to obtain the per-unit cost. Direct materials and direct labor would be traced specifically to the product, then variable and fixed overheads would apply.

In a marginalism world, profit is a function of revenue and cost. Therefore, the necessary condition for profit maximization is by setting the derivate of $\Pi(q) = R(q) - C(q)$ with respect to output, *dq*, equal to zero, and we get the following function,

$$\frac{d\pi(q')}{dq} = \frac{R(q')}{dq} - \frac{C(q')}{dq} = MR(q') - MC(q') = 0 \qquad (3.18)$$

where $\Pi(q)$ is the profit, $R(q)$ is the revenue and $C(q)$ is the cost. The derivate of cost with respect to output is its marginal cost denominated as $dC(q)/dq = MC(q)$. The firm's marginal revenue, *MR*, is the change in revenue it gets by selling one more unit of output: dR/dq. Equation (3.18) indicates that a necessary condition for profit to be maximized is when the firm sets its quantity at q', where the difference between the firm's marginal revenue and its cost is equal to zero, or when marginal revenue equals its marginal cost. The profit will be maximized at q' if the second-order condition holds,

$$\frac{d\pi^2(q')}{dq^2} = \frac{d^2R(q')}{dq^2} - \frac{d^2C(q')}{dq^2} = MR(q') - MC(q') < 0 \qquad (3.19)$$

This means that for-profit to be maximized at q', the slope of the marginal revenue curve, dMR/dq, must be less than that of the marginal cost curve, dMC/dq.

In management accounting, instead, we have that *Operating income* (OI)[2] is given as the difference between a firm's total revenue and the firm's total cost composed of different components and is written as,

$$OI = R - DM - DL - (VOH+VExp) - (FOH+FExp) = NMP\ (cr) > 1 \qquad (3.20)$$

where R is the revenue, DM is the direct material, DL is the direct labor, VOH is the variable overhead, $VExp$ is the variable expense, FOH is the fixed overhead, and $FExp$ is the fixed expense. In addition, NMP is the Net Monetary Position of the balance sheet of the firm, and *cr*, stands for current ratio. The NMP is normally measured by liquidity ratios such as the *current ratio* and is always supposed to be> 1 (current ratio >1) for a firm to cover current liabilities with the current assets and have enough cash flow. This comparison allows us to assess the firm's ability to meet its short-term debts. The operating income of the firm (OI) will also equal the number of units sold to break-even plus an estimated target profit. Equation 3.20 can be written as,

$$\text{OI} = \text{R} - \text{VC-FC} = \text{NMP (cr)} > 1 = \text{(Qbt)Break-even+Target profit} \qquad (3.21)$$

where $VC= DM - DL - (VOH+VExp)$ include the variable costs with direct material (DM), direct labor (DL), variable overhead (VOH), and variable expenses ($VExp$), and $FC=(FOH+FExp)$ include the fixed costs with fixed overhead and fixed expenses, and Qbt is the number of units sold to break-even plus a target profit to achieve an estimated positive budgeted operating income as required by management. In a competitive and multi-product market where the economy pricing is dominated by a competitive number of players that sell premium and non-premium products, we have two case scenarios depending on the frequency of the discount prices offered for non-premium products. We

---

[2] Operating Income and Net Income can be expressed in two different ways, under variable and absorption costing income:

a-) Variable Costing Income

Sales – Variable cost (variable cost of goods manufactured + variable selling) = Contribution Margin (CM) – Fixed cost = Operating income – Interest Expense= Income before Tax – Tax Expenses= Income After Tax – Total Extraordinary Items = Net Income.

b-) Absorption costing Income

Sales – COGS (Variable + Fixed + Fixed OH) =GM – S&A expenses (Variable + Fixed) = Operating Income– Interest Expense= Income before Tax – Tax Expenses = Income After Tax – Total Extraordinary Items = Net Income.

also assume that the period taken into consideration is one fiscal year period consisting of 12 intra-periods:

1-) In the first case scenario, it is assumed that a firm produces multi products, such as one or more non-premium mass production outputs, which are sold at a discount most of the time (higher frequency between 50-90%) and premium goods sold at a much higher price for a determined segment of the market. This firm will maximize the operating income by covering variable costs with the revenue generated mostly from non-premium products and cover the rest of the variable costs and fixed costs with the revenue generated from the high-end premium products during a regular one-year fiscal period. Therefore, the (high frequency) operating income (OIhf) of a multi-product firm manufacturing premium and non-premium goods, with a high frequency of discount price of non-premium products, is given as.

$$\text{OIhf} = (\text{Rnp} - \text{VCnp-FCnp}) + (\text{Rp-VCp-FCp}) = \text{NMP (cr)} > 1 = \text{Qbt} \;\; \text{for} \\ 60\% < \text{Pdisc=NPprob} < 90\% \;\; \text{and} \;\; 10\% < \text{Preg=NPprob} < 30\% \tag{3.22}$$

where *Rnp* is the revenue generated from a non-premium product that covers its variable costs indicated as *VCnp* and a portion of the fixed cost indicated as *FCnp*, and *Rp* is the revenue generated from the premium product that covers its variable costs *VCp* and a portion of fixed indicated as *FCp*. The *NMP* is the net monetary position, and *Qbt* is the chosen output for the firm to break even for both premium and non-premium products and reaches the desired company's profit for the operating income. The firm above operates in a very competitive market and is assumed to have a relatively small volume of the premium product and a large volume of mass-manufactured non-premium products, denominated as *NPprob* in equation (3.22), which is part of revenue *Rnp* with a high frequency (between 60% and 90%) of selling at discount price, *Pdisc*, during the year bringing a much lower operating income and profit. The regular price of non-premium product *NPprob*, denominated as *Preg*, has a lower frequency of selling at regular prices in the range of 10-30%. The high frequency of discount prices of the non-premium product is the price to pay if the company is a new entrant or wants to survive in a very competitive market made of new aggressive entrants seeking to capture market shares.

2-) In the second case scenario, we assume a firm that produces multi product-mix composed of premium and non-premium. The non-premium output is sold at a discount price with much less frequency (between 10-30%), and the premium commodity is sold at a higher price for the high-end segment of the market. The revenue generated by non-premium product/s brings in a high level of operating income which covers the variable costs of non-premium product/s and the portion of the fixed costs, and the revenue generated by high-end premium product/s covers the variable cost of premium product/s and the rest of fixed cost. Hence, the operating income (*OIlf*) of a multi-product firm manufacturing premium and non-premium goods, with low frequency of discount price of non-premium products, takes the form as,

$$\text{OIlf} = (\text{Rnp} - \text{VCnp} - \text{FCnp}) + (\text{Rp} - \text{VCp} - \text{FCp}) = \text{NMP (cr)} > 1 = \text{Qbt} \text{ for } 10\% < \text{Pdisc} = \text{NPprob} < 30\% \text{ and } 70\% < \text{Preg} = \text{NPprob} < 90\% \quad (3.23)$$

where *Rnp* is the revenue generated from non-premium products covering its variable costs given as *VCnp* and fixed costs indicated as *FCnp*. Meanwhile, *Rp* is the revenue generated from the premium product, which can cover its variable costs, *VCp*, and the other portion of the fixed cost indicated as *FCp*. In this case, the non-premium product *NPprob*, which is part of the revenue *Rnp*, will sell less frequently at a discount price *Pdisc* in the range of 10% -30% and will be able to cover both its variable and fixed cost. The regular price of non-premium product *NPprob*, (included in *Rnp)* will have a higher frequency of regular price *Preg* in the range of 70% -90% compared to a discounted price, which will help cover all costs. The firm in the second case scenario will have higher profitability than the firm in the first scenario, operating in a much more competitive and dynamic market. In the second scenario, the market is less competitive, with fewer new entrants due to higher fixed costs and investments.

The marginalism approach says that a necessary condition for a firm to maximize its profit is to set its quantity at *q'*, where the difference between the firm's marginal revenue and its cost is equal to zero, or when marginal revenue equals its marginal cost. Instead, using the competitive-pricing approach, the condition for a firm to stay competitive is not always maximizing its profit for each unit sold but rather having multi product-mix setup categorized by premium and non-premium products to help reach a positive net monetary position (NMP) and choose the quantity of output of both premium and non-premium product mix to break-even and hit the desired target profit.

Financial Troubled Entities and Competition

Based on the modern marginalism theory, every firm maximizes its profit at given output where its marginal profit is zero or where its marginal cost equals its marginal revenue. Based on this theory, a competitive firm can sell as many units of output as it wants at the market price, *p*, given that it faces a horizontal demand curve at this point. The competitive firm's revenue, $R(q) = pq$, increases by *p* it, if sells one more unit of output and its marginal revenue, is equal to p,

$MR = d(pq)/dq = p$. A typically competitive firm maximizes its profit by choosing the right quantity of output such that to satisfy the following first-order condition,

$$\frac{d\pi(q')}{dq} = \frac{dR(q')}{dq} - \frac{C(q')}{dq} = p - MC(q') = 0 \tag{3.24}$$

A competitive firm has its marginal revenue equals to the market price and produces the quantity of output, q', at which its marginal cost equals the market price $MC(q') = p$. The second-order condition requires that the second derivate of the cost function with respect to quantity is positive, given as $\frac{dMC(q')}{dq} > 0$, with the marginal cost curve upward sloping at q'. However, if the firm is maximizing its profit at q', it does not necessarily mean it is making a positive profit. The firm has variable costs; in the long run, fixed and sunk costs are considered. Shutting down the operations can eliminate the variable costs, such as labor and raw materials, but not the fixed or sunk costs. The firm technically will shut down operations if its revenue is less than its short-run variable costs, $R=pq<VC(q)$, which can be written as $p<(VC(q)/q)=AVC$. The general rule is that a firm shuts down operations only if the market price is less than the minimum of its short-run average variable cost.

Differently from marginalism theory, the management accounting approach suggests that if expected sales and marginal revenue begin to decline, a company should take a closer look at the causes of revenue fall. Many reasons could cause the fall in revenue, such as market saturation, price wars with competitors, etc. If this is the case, the company should plan for this by improving the product and allocating more money to research and development to help keep its product line fresh. It could either add additional products or additional features to its existing products to increase the expected decline in sales or marginal revenue. If these measures don't work and sales keep declining, then we will have the symptoms or indications of financial distress.

A company in financial trouble will have a low profit, low cash balances, and high-short debt balances and may have negative operating cash flows. If the company is publicly traded, share prices will decline substantially. In general, different ratio analyses are used to analyze a firm's financial health and provide a sign of trouble, such as:

- Its quick ratio will be very low,
- Its current ratio will be very low,
- Its debt-to-equity and debt-to-asset ratios will be very high,
- Its operating margins and profit margins will be low or negative.

When a company finds itself in a financial distress situation, corrective actions need to be taken based on how serious or pervasive the problem is. In fact, when a firm realizes that it cannot meet its cash obligations, the first step to take is to consider what is causing the cash flow deficiency. Is the problem operational or financial, or both? An operational problem normally implies that daily operations' cash flow is insufficient to cover expenses. Low revenues or high operational and investment costs could cause this. On the other side, a financial problem results when the capital structure of the company is unsuitable because the company might have too much debt, and its principal and interest are absorbing most of the resources from the entity.

Financial distress can be fixed in two ways that can work alone or together: operational and financial fixes (debt restructuring). First, we'll investigate the operational fixes and, later, the financial fixes. An organization will look at its main operations and try to fix the operational problems first by reviewing the current operating strategy. There is a list of factors to consider doing some operational fixes:

- What are the reasons for the revenue's decline? Are competitors offering better, cheaper, or more technologically advanced products? Are price changes and pricing pressures in the industry causing prices to drop and, therefore, revenue to decline?
- Is the company using a combination of premium and non-premium products to mitigate prices and have a more stable revenue?
- Is the mix of products and services correct? Is the company exanimating if a product or service is not profitable, or is it using a disproportionate amount of its resources?
- Have raw materials and other input costs, such as labor and overhead, increased much faster than forecasted, and can the company pass these along to the customer?
- Is the operation inefficient, meaning that are the property, plant, and equipment assets out of date, requiring higher operating costs? Is there excess capacity?
- Are working capital balances too high? Is the collection period for the receivables and the holding period for the inventories too high?

Once this analysis is done, the organization must take corrective action to resolve any identified problems. The objective is to increase the company's free cash flow. The most common definition of free cash flow is the cash the company can generate at the end of an accounting period after it has paid all its expenses and amounts required to maintain its working capital (operating liquidity = current assets – current liabilities) and long-term asset base. The cash is "free" to be paid to shareholders and debtholders without impacting an entity's value. The free cash flow is calculated as operating after-tax cash flow (revenue less cost, less income taxes) less investment in capital assets and working capital.

The entity might take several actions to improve operating cash flow, such as:

- Close unprofitable plant facilities,
- Sell or shut down a product line producing unprofitable outputs,
- Terminate employees and staff,
- Change managers,
- Renegotiate employee or supplier contracts,
- Reduce variable and fixed overhead costs, including wages and salaries, by terminating employees, managers, occupancy costs, and administrative functions,
- Re-engineer the production process to reduce redundancies,
- Use new technology to manufacture the product more efficiently and reduce costs,
- Reduce research and development costs or marketing costs,
- Negotiate with the supplier's payment terms to extend payment due dates or reduce payments,
- Reduce the collection period and accounts receivables so free cash can flow faster into the company,
- Outsource some functional areas of the business,
- Consolidate functions or product lines,
- Sell assets or business divisions that are unprofitable or no longer required in the business.

Below is a simple example of a company that uses operational fixes to generate enough free cash to pay its debtholders and avoid financial distress.

Operational Fixes Sample

Let's assume that a company called *Varing Inc.* has had significant cash flow problems for the past year, 20x8. Due to the market changes, sales have substantially declined in all the company's retail outlets. As a result, management wants to understand how much cash will have available to repay its debtholders for the next year. The forecasted information for 20x9 has been provided below:

Sales	$3,250,000
Operating Expenses	$1,989,000
Depreciation	$550,000
Interest Charges	$140,000
Debt Principal payments	$650,000
Dividends	$300,000
Capital Expenditures	$900,000

The opening and closing balances of selected accounts for 20x9 are below:

Accounts receivable (AR)	$420,000	$310,000
Inventory	$310,000	$250,000
Accounts Payable (AP)	$360,000	$310,000

The corporate taxes are at 20%.

Calculation of the free cash flow:

Sales	$3,250,000
Operating Expenses	($1,989,000)
Depreciation	($550,000)
Net Operating cash flow before income taxes:	$711,000
Income taxes	($142,200)
Add back depreciation	$550,000
Net operating cash flow after tax	$1,118,800
Recovery of investment in AR (420,000-310,000 =110,000)	$110,000
Recovery of investment in inventories (310,000-250,000 = 60,000)	$60,000
Reduction in AP (360,000-310,000= 50,000)	($50,000)
Capital Expenditure	($900,000)
Total free cash flow	$338,800

The company requires an amount of free cash flow equal to $790,000 (Interest charges $140,000 + Debt principal payments $650,0000) to pay the principal and interest obligation for the new year 20x2.

Therefore, we have:

Total payments to debtholders	$790,000
Current estimates of free cash flow	($338,800)
Difference	$451,200

The difference of $451,200 means that the company needs to reduce the operating expenses by $451,200 to have enough free cash flow to pay its debt and interest payments. This could be done through restructuring the company, re-engineering the products, securing another loan with a bank, or trying to do all kinds of operational fixes to generate enough free cash to pay its debtholders and avoid financial distress.

By changing its asset base, reducing liabilities, and lowering costs, a company could hope to emerge as a stronger and better-organized entity that will allow competing more successfully in the industry. However, if the company, through the operational changes, is not able to resolve the cash flow problem, then the entity must consider how to reduce its current obligations. This can be done by carefully considering who are the specific creditors to which it owes funds and how much the entity owns them.

Lastly, management may decide that the company cannot fix its problems by itself but should be acquired by and merged with another firm. By putting the company for sale, the management will hope that an acquirer can be found to pay the right price.

Another major fix for an organization is the financial fix or debt restructuring. Financial fixes are used to reduce an entity's immediate obligations. The most common method used in finance is to restructure the existing debt obligations. In fact, debt restructuring is the process in which a debtor alters the terms and conditions of its existing debt to reduce payments required in the short term. These types of debt structuring are very dependent on how agreeable the creditors are to work with the company to resolve the issues. If these negotiations do not end successfully, then the entity may decide to cease to exist and liquidate itself. It also may force the company to enter formal legal proceedings under *Bankruptcy and Insolvency Act* (BIA) based on the jurisdictions where it operates (R.S.C., 1985, c, B-3). Under this act, the entity needs to prove that it is insolvent. The entity or the debtor is deemed to be insolvent when it is unable to pay the debt based on three criteria:

- The fair market of the debtor's assets is less than the fair market value of liabilities

- The debtor is unable to pay its obligations as they come due (due to cash flow shortage)
- The debtor is expected to run out of liquidity prior to being able to complete a needed restructuring.

Informal negotiations are also part of debt restructuring. In fact, an entity can start informal negotiations with individual creditors to work out a mutually agreeable solution. Successful informal negotiations may result in giving the organization more time to resolve its cash flow problems while getting protected from creditors. In some cases, creditors may agree to settle the obligation for a percentage of the total amount owing, such as 70 cents on the dollar, or even shares might be accepted as an alternative to cash payments to settle the outstanding obligation. Suppose the informal negotiations cannot resolve the debt restructuring. In that case, the entity must go for an in-court formal restructuring proceedings depending on the size of the company and see protection from creditors under *Creditors Arrangement Act* or *Bankruptcy and Insolvency Act*".

If the company has something worth selling, or if there is a potential buyer that would be willing to buy the net operating assets of the company or buy shares while also assuming all the liabilities, then the alternative would be for the entity to be sold. When net operating assets are sold, the cash comes into the company and is used to repay lenders. Any remaining amount is available to distribute to the shareholders as dividends or share repurchases. The selling of net operating assets of an entity is always followed by a wind-up which requires a legal process to dissolve the company in accordance with corporate laws. Alternatively, if the shares of the company are sold, the assets are transferred, and liabilities are assumed as part of the sale, and in return, cash is transferred from the buyer directly to the shareholders.

Dynamic Equilibrium in Economy Pricing

In modern microeconomics, we have seen that supply and demand theory can help understand and eventually predict events that happen in many markets. In competitive markets, the supply-and-demand model is a very useful tool for predicting what will happen to market equilibrium if underlying conditions, such as market trends, consumers' incomes, and the price of inputs, change. The supply-and-demand model is applicable in those markets in which:

- Every market player is a price taker. This means that no consumer or firm is large enough to affect the price of the whole market.
- Firms sell identical products and services. This means that consumers do not prefer one firm's good to another.

- Everybody in the market has full information about the price and quality of goods. This means that consumers are aware of any price changes and inferior-quality goods and will not be willing to trade.
- The costs of trading are low. This means that there are low transaction costs for a buyer to find a seller and trade with him and for a seller to find and trade with a buyer.

These types of markets that have the above proprieties are called *competitive markets.* However, the supply-and-demand model may not be appropriate in markets in which each firm produces and sells a variety of differentiated products, such as premium and non-premium goods, in which consumers know less about the quality and price of products or there are high transaction costs.

Does the supply need to equal demand in a competitive economy? Not always. The quantity supplied is the amount of volume that firms want to sell at a given price during a certain period of the year. The quantity demanded is the quantity that consumers want to buy at a given price during a specified period if the other factors are held constant. The quantity that firms want to sell and the quantity that consumers want to buy at a given price might not be equal to the actual quantity that is bought or sold during a given period of the year.

The intersection of the supply and demand curves determines the equilibrium price and quantity. In economy pricing, the first step is to characterize the equilibrium values as a function of the relevant premium and non-premium variables. We assume that we have a simple demand function for two products, premium, and non-premium, identified as p and np, which takes the form as,

$$Q = D(p, Pnp) \tag{3.25}$$

We also assume that one variable, such as the non-premium price Pnp1, changes causing the supply curve to shift. Then, the supply curve can be written as,

$$S = S\ (p, Pnp1) \tag{3.26}$$

A simple equilibrium can be determined by equating the quantities in supply and demand curves, which can be written as,

$$\text{D(p, Pnp)= S(p, Pnp1)} \tag{3.27}$$

We can characterize how the equilibrium changes by differentiating the equilibrium condition (3.27) with respect to *Pnp1*, using the chain rule at the original equilibrium,

$$\frac{d\,D(P_{np1})}{d\,p}\frac{dp}{d(P_{np1})} = \frac{\delta S(p(P_{np1}), P_{np1})}{\delta p}\frac{dp}{d(P_{np1})} + \frac{\delta S(p(P_{np1}), P_{np1})}{\delta(P_{np1})} \tag{3.28}$$

We can arrange the equation above in a simpler form, as

$$\frac{d\,p}{d\,(P_{np1})} = \frac{\frac{\delta S}{\delta(P_{np1})}}{(\frac{dD}{dp} - \frac{\delta S'}{\delta p})} \tag{3.29}$$

The equation above shows the derivate of *p(Pnp1)* with respect to non-premium product price, *Pnp1*. If the demand curve is *dD/dp <0* and if the supply curve is upward sloping, then δS/δp is positive, so the denominator of equation (3.29) *dD/dp-δS/δp* is negative, and thus the *dp/d(Pnp1)* has the same sign as the numerator in equation 3.29. As *Pnp1* decreases, the equilibrium price falls. Similarly, if *δS/δPnp1* is positive, an increase in *Pnp*1 causes the equilibrium price to fall as well. By using the demand function or the supply function is possible to determine how the effect of *Pnp1* on the equilibrium price can determine the effect on the equilibrium quantity. If the demand function is given as,

$$Q = D\,(p, Pnp1)) \tag{3.30}$$

then, we can differentiate it with respect to *Pnp1* using the chain rule, and we obtain,

$$\frac{d\,Q}{d\,(P_{np1})} = \frac{dD}{dp}\frac{dp}{dP_{np1}} \tag{3.31}$$

If *δD/δp <0*, by the *Law of demand*, then *δQ/δPnp1* will have an opposite sign of that of *δD/δPnp1*. This means that a decrease in the non-premium price, *Pnp1*, during the sale events will move the equilibrium price in the opposite direction of the equilibrium quantity.

We assume that demand and supply curves operate during two short intra-periods in a competitive market where only two products of the same category, such as premium and non-premium, are available. In the first period, indicated as *t*, the premium and non-premium products have regular market prices, but in the second period, indicated as *t+1*, when the sales event is on the price of the premium product remains mostly the same; however, the selling price of the non-premium product gets reduced so the firm can push its demand into customers in order to increase revenue and be competitive. Under this assumption, the demand and supply function of premium and non-premium products in period *t*, denominated as *D(Qp,Qnp)* and *S(Qp, Qnp)*, and their respective prices during the sales events in period *t+1* are given as,

$$\text{D(Qp,Qnp)= D(Pr, Prnp)t + D*(Pr, Psnp)t+1} \tag{3.32}$$

$$\text{S(Qp, Qnp)= S(Pr, Prnp)t+ S*(Pr, Psnp)t+1} \tag{3.33}$$

where *Pr,* is the regular price of the premium product, *Prnp* is the regular price of the non-premium product, and *Psnp* is the sales (promotion) price of the non-premium product during sales events in period *t+1*. The equilibrium price for both premium and non-premium products can be determined by equating the quantities *Qp* and *Qnp* in equations (3.32) and (3.33) and take the form as,

$$D(Pr, Prnp)t + D^*(Pr, Psnp)t+1 = S(Pr, Prnp)t + S^*(Pr, Psnp)t+1 \quad (3.34)$$

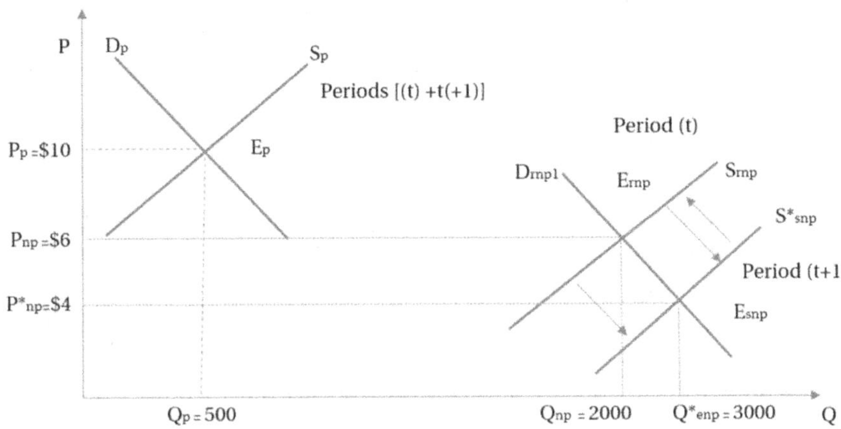

Figure 3.5 Demand and supply curves in equilibrium for premium and non-premium products in a two-period model

The equilibrium equation is an example of an identity of the demand and supply curves. Figure 3.5 illustrates the demand and supply curves in equilibrium for premium and non-premium products for two periods, *t* and *t+1*. The demand (*Dp*) and supply (*Sp*) curves of premium products intersect at the equilibrium point *Ep*, which has a price *Pp = $10,* a selling quantity of 500 units in period *t,* and the same quantity in period t+1 as well, creating a stable equilibrium. The supply curve (*Srnp*) and the demand curve (*Drnp1*) intersect at point *Ernp* reaching the equilibrium at the regular price of $6, which corresponds to a selling quantity of 2000 units in period t, and then intersect at another point *Esnp* reaching the equilibrium at the discounted sales price of $4 which corresponds to the selling quantity of 3000 units in the new period t+1. Once the sales event is completed in period t+1, the equilibrium of supply and demand curves for a non-premium product will move back to point *Ernp* and then return to *Esnp* in the next period if more sales events occur, creating a dynamic equilibrium in a competitive market with premium and non-premium products. Meanwhile, as illustrated in figure 3.5, the equilibrium of supply and demand curves for premium products is more stable and static as it remains at the same point, *Ep*, in both periods, *t* and *t+1*, due to a lack of promotion for this category of product.

Demand Elasticity and Competition in Economy Pricing

Elasticities can be summarized as the responsiveness of one variable because of a change in another variable using a summary statistic. An increase or decrease in the price of an item causes a large or small change in the quantity demanded. The elasticity is the percentage change in one variable, denominated as x, in response to a given percentage change in another variable, y. In fact, the elasticity denominated as *E*, of *x* with respect to *y* is simply given as,

$$E = \frac{Percentage\ change\ in\ x}{Percentage\ chnage\ in\ y} = \frac{\frac{\Delta x}{x}}{\frac{\Delta y}{y}} = \frac{\delta x}{\delta y}\frac{y}{x} \quad (3.35)$$

where Δ is the change in x, so Δx/y is the percentage change in y. Thus, for instance, if *x* changes by 4% when y changes by 2%, then the elasticity of E is 2. If, for example, Δx goes to zero, Δx/y as well goes to the partial derivate, δx/δy. Elasticity is normally calculated at this limit, that is, for an infinitesimal change in x.

The elasticity of demand is the percentage change in the quantity demanded, denominated as *Q*, in response to a given percentage change in the price, *p*. Therefore, the elasticity of demand, denominated by ε, can be characterized as,

$$\varepsilon = \frac{Percentage\ change\ in\ x}{Percentage\ chnage\ in\ y} = \frac{\frac{\Delta Q}{Q}}{\frac{\Delta p}{p}} = \frac{\delta Q}{\delta p}\frac{p}{Q} \quad (3.36)$$

where *δQ/δp* is the partial derivative of the demand function with respect to *p*. For instance, if there is an increase in price by 2% will result in a decrease in the quantity sold by 4%, and the elasticity of demand is ε=-4. We can calculate the elasticity of demand for a linear demand in economy pricing consisting of 2 products, premium, and non-premiums. As mentioned in Chapter 2, in an economy pricing system, an insufficient demand will turn to sufficient demand if promotions and discounts are offered for non-premium products, eliminating excess production capacity. An increase in the frequency of different types of sales events offered by several large firms will increase capacity utilization in the industry and keep inflation low.

A level of utilization to some extent below the maximum production capacity usually prevails, regardless of economic conditions and sales events in any type of industry. In normal conditions, capacity utilization tends to oscillate with the business cycles as firms adjust production volumes in response to changing demand, changing selling prices, and different programs and strategies of sales events to lure customers. As we have seen in Chapter 2, we can have a linear demand function that meets the production capacity utilization condition by using the simplified function Q for quantities Q' and Q'', which represent respectively premium and non-premium products. Therefore, the linear demand takes the form as,

$$Q = Q' + Q'' = Dp'(Pp') + Dnp''(Pnp'') = \text{Sales Target} = Uc \tag{3.37}$$

The demand elasticity in an economy pricing with premium and non-premium products is equal to the linear demand function that reflects the volatile price change of the non-premium product during sales events. Hence, the elasticity in terms of non-premium price changes is given as,

$$\varepsilon = \frac{\frac{\Delta Q}{Q}}{\frac{\Delta p}{p}} = \frac{dQ(p)}{dp(Q)} = \frac{\Delta Pnpd}{\Delta Dnpd} \tag{3.38}$$

where *ΔDnpd* is the change in quantity demanded of non-premium product because of the change in the price of the non-premium product, *ΔPnpd.*

The elasticity demand cannot oscillate forever as it is conditioned by the firm's utilization capacity and limited to the production capacity of the firm. The firm will keep the promotion price of their mass production goods up to the point of the production capacity installed so that it can reach a positive Net-Monetary-Position (NMP). Therefore, the elasticity is given as,

$$\varepsilon = \frac{\frac{\Delta Q}{Q}}{\frac{\Delta p}{p}} = \frac{dQ(p)}{dp(Q)} = \frac{\Delta Pnpd}{\Delta Dnpd} = U_c = NMP > 1 \tag{3.39}$$

Once the full or near-full utilization capacity has been reached, the firm will stop the promotion price and turn to the regular price of a non-premium product until the next sales promotion event or when the production capacity is under-utilized and NMP <1. Furthermore, we can express the demand for premium and non-premium products in terms of costs and NMP as follows,

$$Q = Q' + Q'' = [Dp'(Pp') - (C(Dp')] + [Dnp''(Pnp'') - C(Dnp'')] = Uc = NMP > 1 \tag{3.40}$$

where *Dp', Dnp'', Pp', and Pnp''* are the respective demand and price of the premium and non-premium items, and *C(Dp)* and *C(Dnp)* are the costs incurred to meet the demand for premium and non-premium products. By using equation 3.35, we have the elasticity of demand in terms of premium and non-premium products in periods 1 and 2 given as,

$$\varepsilon = \frac{\frac{\Delta Q}{Q}}{\frac{\Delta p}{p}} = \frac{\delta Q}{\delta p}\frac{p}{Q} = \left(\frac{P'{}_p}{Q'} + \frac{P''{}_{np1}}{Q''}\right) - \left(\frac{P'{}_p}{Q'} + \frac{P''{}_{np2}}{Q''}\right) \tag{3.41}$$

where the price of a non-premium product changes from *P"np1* in period 1 *to P"np2* in period 2, and the price of a premium good, *P'p*, stays the same in periods 1 and 2. The only price change that we normally see in a competitive market is the non-premium price, as the premium price usually stays the same for a much longer period than the price of a non-premium product as the company requires to have a higher profit margin for a premium product to cover part of the cost of non-premium products. Thus, the elasticity of demand in a competitive market will be available mostly for non-premium products that lower the price during the promotion periods to lure customers into buying them, which is given as,

$$\varepsilon = \frac{\frac{\Delta Q}{Q}}{\frac{\Delta p}{p}} = \frac{\delta Q}{\delta p}\frac{p}{Q} = [\left(\frac{P''_{np1}}{Q''_1}\right) - (\frac{P''_{np2}}{Q''_2})] \tag{3.42}$$

where *P"np1*, *P"np2* are the prices of the non-premium product in period 1 and 2, respectively, and *Q"1* and *Q"2* are the respective quantities of non-premium products sold when the price decreases from period 1 to period 2. A price decrease in period 2 of the non-premium-product *P"np2* will proportionally increase the quantity sold from *Q"1* in period 1 to *Q"2* in period 2. In fact, by using the linear demand function, the price of non-premium products from $10 per unit in period 1 will decrease to $8 per unit in period 2, then the quantity sold will increase from 200 to 300 units. Thus, the demand elasticity can be written as,

$$\varepsilon = \frac{\frac{\Delta Q}{Q}}{\frac{\Delta p}{p}} = \frac{\delta Q}{\delta p}\frac{p}{Q} = [\left(\frac{P''_{np1}}{Q''_1}\right) - (\frac{P''_{np2}}{Q''_2})] = \frac{\$10}{200} - \frac{\$8}{300} = \frac{\$2}{ABS(100)} = 0.02 \tag{3.43}$$

where ABS is the absolute value of the quantity change, and ε= 0.02 x 100 = 2 (20%) is the positive demand elasticity. A price decrease of around 20% will cause a less than proportionate jump in the quantity of the non-premium product demanded. The demand elasticity in economy pricing has its limits.

The price for premium products is more inelastic than for non-premium ones. The price of premium products is kept high with very few changes compared to non-premium products, where prices oscillate continuously based on promotions. However, the price cannot go too low for non-premium products. The firm always needs to have current assets available to cover the current liabilities. This means that it needs the cash to cover the short-term liabilities, and this can happen only by lowering the sales price of non-premium products to the point where it can cover current liabilities, which means by having a current ratio greater than 1, as discussed in chapter one, *Current Ratio= Current Assets/Current Liabilities*>1. The demand elasticity for non-premium products produced in large quantities is conditioned (or "elastic") to the point where the short-term availability of cash earned is enough to cover the short-term expenses or simply by having at least a current ratio >1 (quick ratio >1). Hence, we have that demand elasticity for non-premium products meets the following condition:

$$\varepsilon=(\Delta Q/Q)/(\Delta p/p)=(\delta Q/\delta p)(p/Q)=\textit{current ratio}>1 \qquad (3.44)$$

Suppose the price of non-premium products gets further lower, despite selling a larger amount of these units. In that case, the profit margin does not go up, and it reaches a point where the *Current Ratio = 1*, which is not good for the financial health of the company as it can barely cover current liabilities with current assets. Therefore, the price of non-premium products needs to return to the regular price (end-to-sales promotions) where it can reach a *Current Ratio* greater than 1. If the demand, because of price increase, is elastic, which consequently reduces the number of units sold, and the firm may not have a current ratio > 1, then most probably the firm will be looking for new marketing strategies or have product specifications updated by adding new features to the non-premium product to attract more customers.

The elasticity of demand generally varies along most demand curves. The elasticity of demand is different at every point along a standard downward-sloping linear demand curve. On a strictly downward-sloping linear demand curve, the elasticity of demand is a negative number when the selling price of the product is high and a positive number when the selling price is low.

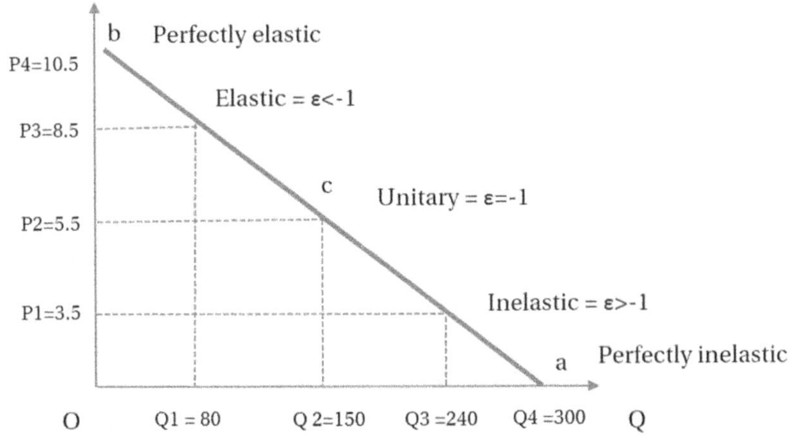

Figure 3.6 Elasticity along the linear demand curve in a traditional economy

Figure 3.6 illustrates the traditional elasticity along the linear demand curve. In a linear demand curve, the higher the price, the more elastic the demand curve is. At the point where the elasticity of demand is zero, the demand curve is said to be perfectly inelastic, indicated as ε=0, where the demand curve hits the horizontal axis at the point Q=a. The demand curve is perfectly elastic where the demand curve hits the vertical axis at point P=b and has unitary elasticity indicated as ε= -1, in the midpoint of the demand curve, at point Q=c. For quantities between the midpoint of the linear demand curve and the lower end where Q=a, the demand is elastic and lies between 0 and -1 where ε>-1. Meanwhile, at a point along the demand curve where the elasticity is between 0 and -1, the demand curve is inelastic. An increase in price from $5.5 to $8.5 will reduce the quantity sold from 150 units to 80 units. As the price rises, the elasticity becomes negative, approaching negative infinity, and when it hits the price axis becomes perfectly elastic.

In an economy pricing system, the elasticity of demand generally varies along the demand curves in a different way than in a traditional economy and is subject to certain conditions. In a competitive environment, the demand curve will most probably never hit the vertical axis, which means it will rarely be perfectly elastic. In the same manner, the demand curve will hardly be perfectly inelastic and hit the horizontal axis as it faces certain restrictions, such as the level of output the firm is able to produce given the utilization capability and how much the firm is keen to reduce the price of the product/s to cover the current liabilities and expenses. Figure 3.7 illustrates the elasticity of demand curves for premium and non-premium products for a typical manufacturing firm producing premium and non-premium products in economy pricing.

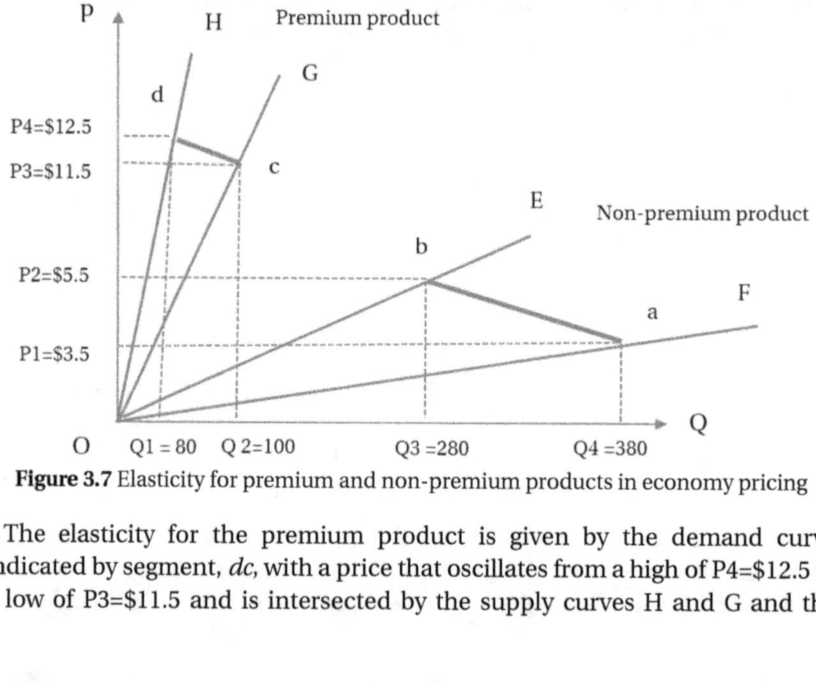

Figure 3.7 Elasticity for premium and non-premium products in economy pricing

The elasticity for the premium product is given by the demand curve indicated by segment, *dc*, with a price that oscillates from a high of P4=$12.5 to a low of P3=$11.5 and is intersected by the supply curves H and G and the quantities sold of Q1=80 units and Q2 = 100 units, respectively. In the same way, the elasticity of a non-premium product is denominated by the demand curve given by the segment, *ba*, with a price that oscillates from a high (regular) of P2=$5.5 to a low (discounted) of P1=$3.5 and is intersected by the supply curves E and F and their respective quantities of Q1=280 units and Q2 = 380 units. The elasticity of demand for the premium product is limited as it cannot oscillate beyond points *d* in the upper end and *c* in the lower end. The same can say for the elasticity demand of the non-premium product, which is limited to point *b* in the upper end and *a* in the lower end.

Suppose the elasticity for premium products oscillates beyond point d, or the price goes higher than planned. In that case, it will sell a lower quantity of premium products than budget, which will not help to keep a steady revenue and cover the current liabilities. In the same way, if the elasticity of non-premium products oscillates beyond point *b* in the upper end, the quantity sold of the non-premium product will be too low to meet the sales budget and cover the current liabilities. If the price of the non-premium product goes too low, beyond point *a*, the volume of non-premium products sold will be higher, but the profit margin per unit will decrease, which might compromise the financial health of the company in the short term. Another reason for the price of a non-premium commodity not to get below point *a*, in Figure 3.7, is the capability of the company to manufacture a large number of products given the installed production capacity and effective utilization capacity.

Hence, in a competitive market, a firm must sell both premium and non-premium products within the elasticity of demand curves denominated by segments *dc* and *ba*, intersected respectively by supply curves *H* and *G* for the premium product and *E* and *F* for the non-premium product. In economy pricing, the price elasticity of demand is limited to the boundaries of price oscillation for premium and non-premium products that guarantee a firm's current ratio is higher than 1.

Conclusions on Pricing and Factor Markets

This chapter has discussed how pricing works in a competitive market and how it is influenced by several factors. A firm adopting price discrimination strategies can reach different objectives, and from an organization's perspective, price discrimination can offer many advantages for small, medium, and large corporations. Suppose a firm operating in economy pricing manufactures both premium and non-premium products. In that case, it can sell the premium output at a higher price, making a substantial profit, and the non-premium product at a lower price to cover current expenses and liabilities. During sales events, for a short period of time, non-premium products can be sold even at a lower price, moving the marginal cost curve further down, which helps increase sales.

In a non-competitive market, the firm producing one main product will set its output to maximize profit. Instead, in a competitive market, the firm will diversify the range of products by producing two or more types of products, let's say premium and non-premium. The firm will set up the price and output of non-premium products and the price and output of premium products in such a combination as to maximize its profit. The profit of this firm will be maximized if the firms sell large volumes of non-premium products at a low and competitive price and relatively small volumes of premium products at a much higher price. The combination of these two outputs and prices will create the desired profit.

The strategy used by competitive firms guarantees a flow of profit for each period. Non-premium products have lower profits as they are sold in large quantities regularly and mostly at discounted prices. Meanwhile, premium products have much higher selling prices and therefore are sold in limited quantities as they are strategically designed only for certain higher-end market segments. And in between, there are several products that fit into different categories to compete in a variety of market segments strategically. The firm's profit, based on the combination of premium and non-premium products (and the products that stand in between) sold during a period, should generate enough cash to cover current expenses and liabilities and accumulate funds for future capital investments.

We have also seen how the economy pricing is dominated by a competitive number of players that sell mostly non-premium products. There are two case scenarios depending on the frequency of the discount price of the non-premium product. In the first case scenario, there is a firm operating in a competitive market which has a non-premium product (or a range of non-premium products) sold between 60% and 90% of the times at discount price generating a much lower operating income and profit. This is the price to pay if the company is new entrant or wants to survive in a very crowed market made of new aggressive entrants that are seeking to capture market share.

Meanwhile, in the second case scenario there is a firm that commercializes non-premium product which sells with less frequency at discount price (between 10% and 30%) and will be able to cover both, its variable and fixed costs. This firm will have a higher operating income and profit than the firm in the first case scenario, operating in a much more competitive and dynamic market. In the second scenario, the market is less competitive, and there are fewer new entrants due to higher fixed costs and investments. In both case scenarios, firms have a premium product selling at a much higher price to cover overhead costs. Firms competing in a cannibalized market will be successful if they are able to have the right combination of premium and non-premium products to generate enough profits and reach a current ratio of > 1.

We have also seen how the demand elasticity in a competitive economy pricing with the premium and non-premium products is equal to the linear demand function that reflects mostly the price change of the non-premium product during the sales events. In addition, in an economy pricing system, the elasticity of demand generally varies along the demand curves in a different way than in a traditional economy, as it is subject to certain conditions. In a competitive environment, the demand curve will most probably never hit the vertical axis, which means it will rarely be perfectly elastic and will hardly be perfectly inelastic and hit the horizontal axis as it faces certain restrictions such as the level of output the firm is able to produce given the capacity utilization rate and how much the firm is keen to reduce the price of products to cover the current liabilities and expenses.

PART II:
The Macroeconomics of Economy Pricing System

Chapter 4

Inflation, Interest Rates, and Unemployment

Introduction

This chapter will take into consideration the macroeconomic effects of economy pricing. It will discuss how inflation, interest rates, and unemployment work at the macro level in an economy pricing system dominated by competition and characterized by different categories of non-premium products in almost all sectors of the economy. This chapter will start by explaining how inflation is determined and what are the causes of inflation. Of course, the rising prices are the source of inflation, although this can be attributed to different factors. The monetary theory normally establishes the relation between inflation and money supply, which means that a rapid increase in money supply will bring price spikes and inflation.

Another section of this chapter will talk about the biggest challenges of recent years, which have been characterized by low inflation until the start of the global pandemic in 2020 and the war in Ukraine in 2022. We will discuss the reasons for low inflation and how a competitive price is created, and its effects on the market.

Later in the chapter, we will consider how low-interest rates have been dominant in the last decade. When interest rates are reduced, more people can borrow more money which causes the economy to grow due to the widening money supply and increasing spending. Another topic covered in this chapter is the low unemployment rate. An unemployment rate below the natural rate means the economy is growing faster than its sustainable natural unemployment rate. However, record-low unemployment rates in recent years have suggested a new kind of relationship between the inflation gap and the unemployment rate.

The phenomenon of slow growth in advanced countries is another topic that will be discussed in this chapter. In many industrialized countries, the rate of growth has recently declined due to different causes such as labor force, capital stock, productivity, etc. The growth rates are also low due to lower fertility rates and shifting spending away from commodities to services or even declining total factor productivity growth. Another discussion in this chapter will be about the inflation-fighting tools in economy pricing by using government programs to keep the price of non-premium products low during high-inflation periods.

The Determination of Inflation in Economy Pricing

Per definition, inflation is a quantitative measure of the rate at which the average price level of a basket of selected goods and services in an economy increases over a certain period of time. It is the rise in the general level of prices where a unit of currency effectively buys less than it did in prior days, weeks, months, or years. Often expressed as a percentage, inflation indicates a decrease in the purchasing power of a nation's currency during a given period.

In normal times, inflation is the rate at which the general level of prices for goods and services is rising and, consequently, the purchasing power of currency is falling. Consumers will have to pay more money to buy the same product in the current period compared to the prior period when the price was lower. In fact, inflation erodes the purchasing power of consumers. Consumers buy fewer products and services with the same amount of money when inflation rises. Inflation can be viewed positively or negatively depending on the individual viewpoint and rate of change.

Those individuals holding tangible assets, like property or stocked commodities, may like to see some inflation as that raises the value of their assets. However, other individuals holding cash may not like inflation, as it erodes the value of their cash holdings and reduces the purchasing power of holding currency. Based on the standard macroeconomics foundations, an optimum level of inflation is required to promote spending to a certain extent instead of saving, thereby encouraging economic growth. The most used inflation indexes are the *Consumer Price Index* (CPI) and the *Wholesale Price Index* (WPI).

It's interesting to take into consideration the causes of inflation. Rising prices are the root of inflation, though this can be attributed to different factors. In the context of causes, inflation is classified into three types: Demand-Pull inflation, Cost-Push inflation, and Built-In inflation.

The Demand-Pull Effect: Demand-pull inflation occurs when the overall demand for goods and services in an economy or industry increases more rapidly than the economy's production capacity. It creates a demand-supply gap with higher demand and lower supply, which results in higher prices. Some of the causes of Demand-Pull inflation are consumption, exchange rate, government spending, and expectations. **Consumption** can cause inflation if consumption and investment rise considerably, increasing the aggregate demand. The prices will increase despite no change in the cost of production. **The exchange rate** also can cause inflation to rise if there is a decrease in a country's exchange rate by causing import prices to increase and export prices to drop. **Government spending** is another factor that can cause inflation to rise if there is a government stimulus where too much money invested into the economy too quickly will make the aggregate demand rise. An increase in the money supply by the government in an economy also leads to inflation. The money supply can be increased by monetary authorities either by printing or giving more money to individuals through stimulus programs. As a result of demand increase, the money loses its purchasing power (Williamson, ch.12). **Expectations** is another factor that can cause inflation to increase if companies raise prices to keep pace with perceived inflation. This will end up causing inflation.

Cost-Push Inflation: Cost-push inflation is a result of the increase in the prices of raw materials and other inputs during the production process. Some factors that cause cost-push inflation are higher wages, supply shock, taxes, and imported inflation. **Higher wages** can cause inflation due to an increase in labor costs. A higher labor cost will make companies adjust their prices to keep up with the profit margins. A rapid wage increase can cause the economy to enter a *wage-price spiral.* Wage increases at an exponential rate can cause price increases, and the value of the currency can drop as more money is needed to purchase goods. A **Supply Shock** is a rapid increase in the cost of raw materials. A classic example of supply shock is the sudden rise in oil prices, which can trigger higher production or transportation costs for companies across all economic sectors. For example, if the oil-producing nations decide to cut down on oil production, the supply diminishes, resulting in price rises and inflation. Another instance is when the crop-producing countries, due to poor weather conditions, are pushed to cut down on crop production, diminishing the supply and leading to higher demand, price increases, and inflation. **Higher taxes** caused by an increase of indirect taxes, such as sales tax and excise duties, can sometimes lead to inflation by forcing prices to go up. In fact, when value-added taxes or duties are applied to products, it leads to higher prices as the consumer ends up paying more for those commodities affected by higher taxes. **Imported inflation** is when trade partners experience inflation which can be transferred over through imports. A typical example is when South Korea goes through a period of inflation and when the United States imports Korean goods such as phones, computers, and TVs in the electronics sector. They are at an inflated overall price level which in turn can inflate other prices in the electronics sector in the United States if enough imported goods are sold. These developments lead to higher costs for commodities and can contribute to overall inflation.

Built-In Inflation. Built-in inflation is another cause of inflation that links to adaptive expectations. As the price of goods and services rises, laborers expect and demand more wages to maintain their cost of living. Their increased wages result in higher costs of goods and services, and this wage-price increase continues as one factor induces the other and vice-versa.

In modern macroeconomics, theoretically, monetarism establishes the relation between inflation and the money supply of an economy. A rapid increase in money supply will bring price spikes and inflation. Because of the money supply increase, prices have jumped quickly, and the value of money has fallen, contributing to economic collapse. There are different types of inflation indexes. Depending upon the selected set of goods and services used, multiple types of inflation values are calculated and tracked as inflation indexes. The most used inflation indexes are the *Consumer Price Index* (CPI) and the *Wholesale Price Index* (WPI).

Wholesale Price Index (WPI) is an indicator of price changes in the wholesale market. WPI calculates the price paid by manufacturers and wholesalers in the market. WPI measures the changes in commodity price at selected stages before goods reach the retail level. It covers around 697 items of Primary, fuel, power, and manufactured products. Most of the items covered under WPI are manufacturing inputs and intermediate goods like minerals, machinery, basic metals, etc.

Consumer Price Index (CPI) is a price index that represents the average price of a basket of goods over time. CPI calculates the average price paid by the consumer to the shopkeepers. It covers around 448 items of rural baskets and 460 items of urban baskets. Most of the items covered under CPI are education, communication, transportation, recreation, apparel, foods and beverages, housing, and medical care (CPI, 2023).

The Producer Price Index (PPI) is another index to measure inflation. The difference from WPI and CPI is that PPI is a family of indexes that measures the average change in selling prices received by domestic producers of goods and services over time. Theoretically, the PPI measures price changes from the perspective of the seller and differs from the CPI, which measures price changes from the perspective of the buyer or final consumer in society.

Inflation has different viewpoints depending on which side you are on and who owns the assets, and what assets you own in a certain period. It could be either a positive or a negative thing, depending upon which side one takes and how rapidly the change occurs. There are wealthy individuals and investors that own tangible assets, such as property or stocks, who like to see some inflation as that raises the value of their assets, and as sellers, they can sell these assets at a higher price. On the other side, some wealthy buyers are interested in buying such assets, although they must pay a higher price because of inflation.

A consistent number of individuals and investors who hold a substantial amount of cash may not like inflation, as it erodes the value of their cash holdings. Inflation in developed economies promotes investments both by businesses in projects and by individuals in stocks of companies, as they expect better returns than inflation (Heijdra, 2017, ch.10). In most industrialized economies, an optimum level of inflation is required to promote spending to a certain extent instead of saving. If the purchasing power of money remains the same over the years, individuals and investors might be indifferent between saving and spending. In some cases, the steadiness of the purchasing power of money over several periods may limit spending, which may negatively impact some sectors of the economy as reduced money in circulation can slow certain economic activities in a country. A balanced line is required to keep the inflation value in an optimum and desirable range.

Having a high, negative, or uncertain value of inflation might, under certain conditions, negatively impact an economy, especially if it is an underdeveloped economy. Certain factors might lead to uncertainties in the market and prevent businesses from making big investment decisions. High and uncertain inflation may lead to unemployment, especially in underdeveloped and developing countries. It might as well promote hoarding as people flock to stock necessary goods at the earliest amid fears of price rise. The practice might lead to more price increases, which in return might result in an imbalance in international trade as prices remain uncertain and impact foreign exchange rates.

The Evolution of Low Inflation in Economy Pricing

One of the biggest challenges of recent years (before the COVID-19 pandemic) has been weak inflation which is simply called low inflation. Theoretically, it is well known in macroeconomics that low inflation limits the scope of monetary policy and may also partially damage the financial system. A few unanswered questions continue to come up when we speak about low inflation. When the global financial crisis erupted in 2008, and growth collapsed around the world, why did inflation not fall further? As growth has picked up in the United States and unemployment has gone down, why has the inflation rate remained still low?

There are many factors to consider to answer these questions; however, one missing factor is the forecasts of the macroeconomic events themselves. The contexts that macroeconomists have relied on to predict inflation primarily use domestic variables dating back to the "Phillips Curve" of the late 1960s, which explained that inflation increases when unemployment falls. But the forces that drive our economy are not only confined within our national or regional borders. The models missed the global events and what is happening across the rest of the world (Roberts, 1995, 975–984). They missed the whole process of globalization, from the global supply chain to technological advances, which have evolved so fast in recent decades.

Over the last two-three decades, the process of globalization has advanced quite rapidly. Trade flows have increased several times, emerging markets have achieved greater economic weight and power, and more and more companies are using global supply chains to shift parts of their production to cheaper locations. Recently, companies that rely heavily on the global supply chain receive their raw materials, work-in-progress, and completed products much faster than decades ago, thanks to the evolution and efficiency of commodity transportation and technological progress. Meanwhile, workers and unions struggle to keep the bargaining power in many countries due to decentralized manufacturing. It is obvious to think that these factors would have an impact on prices. However, none of them are currently captured in the standard frameworks that are used to forecast inflation for major countries such as the United States, Japan, the U.K., Canada, and Eurozone countries.

The inflation rate has been relatively low in the last two decades (except for the pandemic period 2020-2023 due to supply chain disruptions), especially in the U.S. The U.S. inflation rate has been below the Fed's 2 percent inflation target since 2012, and the low inflation is typically related to the probability of falling into deflation, in which, naturally, prices and wages are declining on average. However, prices have been declining in recent years, especially for non-premium products but not wages. Low inflation is not only a phenomenon observed in the United States but also has been a concern around the world, such as in the *Organization for Economic Cooperation and Development countries* (OECD), etc.

Given that inflation cannot be measured by an increase in the price of one product or service, or even several products or services, there are many different indexes to measure inflation, each index signaling different information about inflation. The *Federal Open Market Committee* (FOMC), which is the Fed's main monetary policymaking body in the U.S., prefers to look at *Personal Consumption Expenditures* (PCE) because, among other reasons, the PCE price index covers a wide range of household spending. It is also significant to notice that these indexes are defined as "core" indexes, which exclude food and energy items that fluctuate a lot. Looking at core indexes rather than focusing on a short episode of spikes in inflation helps to understand the inflation trend over a period taken into consideration.

The table below shows the annual U.S. inflation rates for calendar years from 2000 to 2019. Annual rates of inflation are calculated using 12-month selections of the *Consumer Price Index*, which is published every month by the Labor Department's Bureau of Labor Statistics (BLS) in the U.S.

Year	Jan	Feb	Mar	Apr	May	Jun	Jul	Aug	Sep	Oct	Nov	Dec	Avr
2019	1.6	1.5	1.9	2.0	1.8	1.6	1.8	1.7	1.7	1.8	2.1	2.3	1.8
2018	2.1	2.2	2.4	2.5	2.8	2.9	2.9	2.7	2.3	2.5	2.2	1.9	2.4
2017	2.5	2.7	2.4	2.2	1.9	1.6	1.7	1.9	2.2	2.0	2.2	2.1	2.1
2016	1.4	1.0	0.9	1.1	1.0	1.0	0.8	1.1	1.5	1.6	1.7	2.1	1.3
2015	-0.1	0.0	-0.1	-.0.2	0.0	0.1	0.2	0.2	0.0	0.2	0.5	0.7	0.1
2014	1.6	1.1	1.5	2.0	2.1	2.1	2.0	1.7	1.7	1.7	1.3	0.8	1.6
2013	1.6	2.0	1.5	1.1	1.4	1.8	2.0	1.5	1.2	1.0	1.2	1.5	1.5
2012	2.9	2.9	2.7	2.3	1.7	1.7	1.4	1.7	2.0	2.2	1.8	1.7	2.1
2011	1.6	2.1	2.7	3.2	3.6	3.6	3.6	3.8	3.9	3.5	3.4	3.0	3.2
2010	2.6	2.1	2.3	2.2	2.0	1.1	1.2	1.1	1.1	1.2	1.1	1.5	1.6
2009	0	0.2	-0.4	-0.7	-1.3	-1.4	-2.1	-1.5	-1.3	-0.2	1.8	2.7	-0.4
2008	4.3	4.0	4.0	3.9	4.2	5.0	5.6	5.4	4.9	3.7	1.1	0.1	3.8
2007	2.1	2.4	2.8	2.6	2.7	2.7	2.4	2.0	2.8	3.5	4.3	4.1	2.8
2006	4.0	3.6	3.4	3.5	4.2	4.3	4.1	3.8	2.1	1.3	2.0	2.5	3.2
2005	3.0	3.0	3.1	3.5	2.8	2.5	3.2	3.6	4.7	4.3	3.5	3.4	3.4
2004	1.9	1.7	1.7	2.3	3.1	3.3	3.0	27	2.5	3.2	3.5	3.3	2.7
2003	2.6	3.0	3.0	2.2	2.1	2.1	2.1	2.2	2.3	2.0	1.8	1.9	2.3
2002	1.1	1.1	1.5	1.6	1.2	1.1	1.5	1.8	1.5	2.0	2.2	2.4	1.6
2001	3.7	3.5	2.9	3.3	3.6	3.2	2.7	2.7	2.6	2.1	1.9	1.6	2.8
2000	2.7	3.2	3.8	3.1	3.2	3.7	3.7	3.4	3.5	3.4	3.4	3.4	3.4

Table 4.1 U.S. Inflation Rates, historical data (BLS, 2020)

The last column denominated as "Avr," indicates the average inflation rate for each year. As we can see from the table, after the 2008 financial crisis, the yearly inflation on average in the U.S. has been low between 1% and 2.4 %, with the exception of one year in 2011, which has reached 3.2%. Before 2008, the yearly inflation from 2000 to 2008 was, on average, around 3%.

The Central banks, such as the FED, European Central Bank (ECB), Bank of Japan, etc., have been struggling with how to respond to persistently low inflation amid what appears to be the weakening of a foundational economic relationship. Unemployment is at its lowest level since 1969, which should spur higher wages as companies compete for workers. In fact, in the U.S., the average unemployment rate in 2019 was around 3.7 percent. The U.S. unemployment rate held steady at 3.5 percent in December 2019, remaining at the lowest level since 1969 before the COVID-19 pandemic hit the U.S. economy in 2020 and is in line with market expectations. The number of unemployed people for the same period decreased by 58 thousand to 5.75 million, while employment rose by 267 thousand to 158.80 million (*Congressional Research Service report, 2021*). The labor force participation rate was unchanged at 63.2 percent.

Climbing labor costs should eventually get passed along to customers, driving inflation up. Instead, we see that labor cost is contained and moderating. There are other factors and indicators to be added to traditional forecasting models to provide a comprehensive understanding of the inflation process. Some of these factors capture fluctuations in exchange rates, oil, and commodity prices, the world output gap between developed and underdeveloped countries, the difference between potential output and actual output, and the supply chain management role in the global economy. The results show that global factors such as supply chain management and technological process play a very important role in the dynamics of consumer price inflation, but wage inflation still appears to be largely determined by domestic factors.

The unemployment rate in the U.S. in the last few years (2017-19) has been, on average, around 3.6-3.9 percent, the lowest level since 1969. Based on the traditional macroeconomic theory, this should push wages and prices higher as companies must compete to find workers that have the required skills. It is true that labor costs are starting to rise as expected; however, they are not getting passed forward to consumers in the form of higher prices.

There is some background here to understand why this all matters. The Federal Reserve, European Central Bank, Bank of England, and other central banks consider two percent a healthy level for price stability, but they have failed to reach that target due to low inflation for most of the last decade before the pandemic, especially in the industrialized countries. Influenced inflation poses potential challenges on a global scale. This means that Federal Reserve and other central banks would have a more limited ability to control the economy should another recession occur. Larger adjustments in interest rates by central banks might be needed to steady inflation if inflation stays low or goes up quickly (as during the war in Ukraine in 2022) and is less responsive to domestic conditions.

Low Inflation and Supply Chain Management Efficiency

It seems that inflation is increasingly determined abroad, and the global factors that keep inflation domestically low such as global supply chains, could continue for some time, years, or even decades unless regional wars or trade tensions among countries are on the rise and industrialized countries could face a sharp increase in inflation again. In fact, when the global pandemic in 2020-2023 hit all countries, inflation increased rapidly due to continuous lockdowns, shortage of labor force, and supply management issues. The war in Ukraine in 2022-2023 resulted in sanctions against Russia which affected the price of all raw materials causing a general price increase in almost all commodities. The Federal Reserve and other central banks would face a difficult tradeoff between supporting growth or stabilizing prices. Yet this does not mean that the standard frameworks are dead. Conditions at home are still important.

Technological innovation can directly influence the changes in the prices of information and communication technologies, leading to a continued decline in the prices of computers, laptops, i-phones, i-pads, and all sorts of home electronics (Masse and Beaudry, 2016, pp. 1-48). Technological change has a positive impact on competition and market structure as it tends to reduce the barriers to new company creation in many areas, intensify market competition, and thus affect product-price-creation. In fact, the rapid growth of e-commerce worldwide is another way by which digitalization can increase competitiveness and influence inflation (Blix, 2015). New technologies have changed the way consumers think, search for new trends, and compare product prices. Customers benefit from increased price transparency, and comparability, as never before, is being made in a short amount of time thanks to the increase in online shopping trends.

In the same way, technological progress has also increased labor productivity, therefore reducing unit labor costs. With the help of easily accessible information, improved communication, and useful software/applications, it is not hard to imagine that the recent technological innovation and the implementation of powerful EPR systems in many middle-size and large-size corporations have contributed significantly to improved productivity. Nearly any company, whether it is large or small or a start-up, has access to the internet and digital technology and can go global and reach potential customers faster, better, and at a lower cost. In addition, the competition among digital firms is not only increasing but also is invading non-technological sectors, and foreign competition from other countries is reaching domestic markets more easily, which puts pressure to create low, competitive prices in local retail.

In the age of globalization, there is also a new wave of technological progress that has drawn attention among economists, which is called the "sharing economy," by lowering the price of goods and services offered in a crowded market. Despite there being no agreement among economists on the exact definition of the term, the sharing economy usually refers to the idea of a crowd-based market that allows the exchange of privately-owned goods and services. The most representative examples of the "sharing economy" are Airbnb and Uber.

Although we are not able to see this in the official productivity statistics, it is without a doubt that the rise of the sharing economy has improved productivity by allowing the utilization of otherwise idle goods and services, which then has led to a reduction in prices. The study of Georgios Zervas, Davide Proserpio, and John Byers (2017) takes into consideration the impact of the introduction of Airbnb into the Texas market in the U.S. They reported that Airbnb's entry into the hospitality market had had a quantifiable negative impact on local hotel room prices, with lower-end hotels and hotels not catering to business travelers being most vulnerable to the increased competition from Airbnb. This has lowered the price of the non-premium hotel available beds in the hospitality industry. The same can be said about the Uber service, which has lowered the taxi-ride price in large urban areas.

Technological progress in different sectors tends to increase productivity, lowers the rate of wage growth relative to productivity, and delay rising inflation. The continued implementation of technological innovations in the industry serves as a complement to the workforce, and the influence of deflation is straightforward. Higher productivity in the manufacturing sector translates directly into lower production costs.

In chapter one, we have seen that the inflation rate in an economy pricing can be expressed as a function of volumes sold during sales events which offer discounted prices for different categories of non-premium and, eventually, premium products. The inflation rate can be expressed as,

$$\textit{Inflation Rate}=I = \sum_{i=1}^{n} f(Q_{nps}, S(p)_{ev}) \quad (4.0)$$

where *Qnps* is the quantity in volumes of the non-premium products sold at a discount price during sales events on the supply side, and *S(p)ev* is the number of sales events that offer several types of discounts given by *p*, and *i=1,...n* is the number of different categories of non-premium products offered by competitive firms in different industries. The above equation is valid if the competitive firms participating in the sales events offer large volumes of non-premium products at discount prices on the supply side, pushing the demand onto customers. The number of sales events in different industries offered throughout the year with the participation of thousands of competitive firms effectively impact tending to lower inflation rate at the macro level. We have seen in Chapter 1 that the inflation from period *t-1* to period *t* is given as,

$$\pi = \frac{P_t - P_{t-1}}{P_{t-1}} = \frac{\Delta P_t}{P_{t-1}} = \frac{(Ps+Pm+\mathrm{Pr})_t - (Ps+Pm+\mathrm{Pr})_{t-1}}{(Ps+Pm+\mathrm{Pr})_{t-1}} \quad (4.1)$$

where *Ps* is the sales price of the discount stores to customers, *Pm* is the sales price of the product produced by a manufacturer and sold to the discount store, and *Pr* is the sales price of the raw material/s produced by a mining (raw materials) company and sold to the manufacturer. If the discounts store, the manufacturer, and the raw material producer keep the same price or with small changes from period *t-1* to period *t*, then we can say that the inflation is low or inexistent. If we add the technology and supply chain management in the inflation function, we have that equation (4.1) can be written as,

$$\pi = \frac{P_t - P_{t-1}}{P_{t-1}} = \frac{\Delta P_t}{P_{t-1}} =$$
$$\frac{(Ps+Pm+\mathrm{Pr})_t - (Ps+Pm+\mathrm{Pr})_{t-1}}{(Ps+Pm+\mathrm{Pr})_{t-1}} - \theta \frac{tech_t - tech_{t-1}}{tech_{t-1}} - \varsigma \frac{SCM_t - SCM_{t-1}}{SMC_{t-1}} \quad (4.2)$$

where *tech* is the drag of technology onto inflation and *SCM* (Supply Chain Management) is the drag of efficiency of the supply chain management onto inflation from period *t-1* to *t*, and θ and ς are coefficients, respectively, for *tech* and *SCM*. Technological change influences prices via sectoral innovation and reduction in unit labor cost. The *tech* variable in the equation above could be strong enough to lower the overall inflation. The expected inflation rate in the next period, $E_t\pi_{t+1}$, is assumed low as we already accept that in an economy pricing all levels of a production chain-line, from raw materials to intermediate and finished goods, push for stable and low prices thanks to technological innovation and improved supply chain management. The firms operating in a very competitive market believe that new technology and aggressive supply chain management can manage any expected or unexpected inflation rate and any foreign currency fluctuations in the next period unless there are problems such as major causes and events beyond their control (such as wars, pandemics, etc.). The main factors that keep low the inflation rate π, from period t-1 to t, are the changes in technology, value engineering, and efficient supply chain management. The incorporation of these factors into the inflation equation (4.2) will make sense in a fast-paced competitive environment affecting different sectors of the economy.

Supply chain management is the management of the flow of goods and services from raw materials to final consumption and affects the prices of finished goods by lowering the price of raw materials and intermediate goods produced. It involves the movement and storage of raw materials, work-in-process inventory, and finished goods as end-to-end order fulfillment from the point of origin to the point of consumption. In a few words, supply-chain management is a cross-functional approach that includes managing the movement of raw materials into an organization, the internal processing of materials into finished goods, and the movement of finished goods out of the organization to the end consumer.

The job of the supply chain manager is to oversee and manage every stage of the production flow, from purchasing the raw material to the delivery of the final product to customers, including unit labor costs and the fluctuation of exchange rates if raw materials or semi-finished goods are outsourced or purchased internationally. Managing the supply chain allows companies to be able to cut excess costs and deliver products to the consumer faster. This is done by keeping tighter control of internal inventories, production, distribution, and sales, and in many cases, the inventories of company vendors as well (Gali, 2015). Part of the *SCM* process is also the strategic decision to merge with other companies to reduce overhead costs and have better leverage on raw materials and intermediate goods to keep down the price of final goods and be competitive.

Another important task of the supply chain managers operating in a very competitive environment is to keep under control the price of raw materials and work-in-progress inventory to make sure that the final price of finished goods for the same category of products does not fluctuate too much from one period to another. If there is an increase in the raw materials due to a crisis or various shocks, the supply chain managers must source out the raw materials affected by price increase from other sources that offer a lower and more reasonable price to keep the whole chain supply cost under control and be consistent with the estimated budget of output prices from period t-1 to period t.

Central Banks and Interest Rates in Economy Pricing

There is a general knowledge in basic economics that when interest rates are reduced, more people can borrow more money. This causes the economy to grow, widening the money supply and increasing spending on goods and services. Higher demand for goods should make them more expensive, which causes inflation to increase. The opposite holds for rising interest rates, which makes inflation decrease. However, after several years of near-zero interest rates and low and sometimes negative inflation rates in the Eurozone and the U.S., new policies were put in place that followed the 2008 global financial crisis, which incorporated new ideas and proposed new concepts regarding inflation and interest rate in academic circles.

In the aftermath of the 2008 financial crisis, the central banks have had a hard time reaching their inflation targets. It seems that it is not the low policy interest rates promoted by the central bank which cause low inflation but rather the fragile equilibrium of real interest rates. We have seen that the economy's real interest rate under full employment and stable prices, in combination with the zero-lower bound on nominal interest rates, has restricted the effectiveness of monetary policy and has had no effect on inflation, keeping it low or unchanged.

After the 2008 financial crisis, there has been a trend towards deflation rather than inflationary pressures in most of the industrialized countries. In the U.S., the inflation rate after the 2008 crisis peaked in September 2011 at 3.8 percent, while eurozone inflation peaked at 3.0 percent in November 2011, which is about 1-1.8 percent above the inflation target of 2 percent. Both inflation rates have steadily fallen since then, reaching another low point in January 2015 with values of -0.2 percent in the U.S. and -0.6 percent in the eurozone, far below their medium-term target values of approximately two percent (*US Inflation*

Rates, historical data BLS, 2022). Inflation rates have only improved slightly since then, reaching the inflation target of 2 percent in 2018 and 2019, without considering the inflation spike during the COVID-19-pandemic crisis of 2020-2023 and the war in Ukraine that reached high levels between 5-11% in many industrialized countries due to continues lockdowns, factory closures, supply chain disruptions, wars, sanctions against Russia which is a global producer of raw materials.

Another major driver of the global disinflationary process is the remarkable reduction in oil prices and other important raw materials which affects the overall price structure and price level, due to the trickle-down effect via relative prices and wage negotiations. In addition, there has been a decline in core inflation, which excludes energy and food (1.1 percent in October 2015 in the eurozone).

Mainly after the 2008 financial crisis, the central banks have been experiencing difficulties in reaching their inflation targets. Differently from the past, the issue of the central banks is not high inflation but rather inflation rates which seem to be trapped at low values with a tendency towards deflation. From 2008 to 2016, the major central banks in several advanced economies, such as the United States, the United Kingdom, Eurozone, and Japan, get on upon an unprecedented effort to stabilize and inject liquidity into the financial markets. Central banks used conventional monetary tools to cut short-term interest rates to near zero and arranged unconventional tools to provide liquidity and credit market facilities to commercial banks by using quantitative easing (QE) and eventually trying to influence market expectations by signaling future policy through forward guidance. The QE measures used by central banks, along with a lack of demand for the credit given the global recession, have contributed to a decline in real and nominal interest rates to ultra-low levels in the decade that followed the 2008 crisis.

The question that may arise is why central banks' large-scale asset purchases through QE and ultra-low-interest rates have contributed so little to inflation dynamics and have been unable to raise inflation to the inflation target. Here, we can have a few different plausible explanations:

The first classical explanation is that the monetary policy is not expansionary enough, despite the policy rates being near zero, and some central banks' balance sheets were larger than ever after the financial crisis of 2008. A second common explanation is that monetary policy instruments are not enough to push inflation up. A third explanation, based on the New-Fisherian theory, claims that inflation is low because interest rates set by central banks are low and that inflation will rise only when central banks begin to target higher policy rates (Cochrane, 2014, pp. 76-100).

The Neo-Fisherian theory is based on Irving Fisher's theory of interest rates, which explains movements in interest rates by movements in expected inflation (Fisher, 1907). However, it reverses the standard inflation-to-interest rates connection, claiming instead that the interest rates are causing inflation to move up or down. The Neo-Fisherian theory confirms that monetary policy alone is unable to move the equilibrium real interest rate, which is the interest rate that would prevail under normal conditions of full employment and relatively stable prices. If the interest rates cannot help, then inflation is the only economic variable that can help to restore the long-run economic equilibrium if sovereign debt is sustainable.

The logic behind this theoretical idea is that forward-looking economic agents presume a low inflation target from a lengthy period of low central bank interest rates, which leads to nothing more than low inflation expectations and subsequently materializes in low inflation. A lengthy period of low nominal interest rates has not resulted in high inflation (Garcia-Schmidt and Woodford, 2015, pp. 10-86). This theoretical result, however, does not help the efforts of central banks to reach their explicit inflation targets while policy rates are stuck at the zero lower bound and inflation continue to remain low.

Considering a negative equilibrium real interest rate and the zero lower bound on the nominal central bank rate, the Neo-Fisherian theory implies that inflation is low since the equilibrium real interest rate is low and expects inflation to get normalized when the real equilibrium rate eventually increases. In general, a low equilibrium real interest rate limits the behavior of monetary policy by bringing the central bank's policy rate too close to the zero-lower bound. The central banks such as the U.S. Federal Reserve, Bank of England, and the European Central Bank are constrained by the zero lower bounds and have therefore moved to unconventional monetary policy measures like large-scale asset purchases and forward guidance.

Given the persisting of low or even negative equilibrium real interest rates, these unconventional monetary policy measures have somehow become the new standard. As per theoretical results and under normal conditions, higher interest rates are advised for solving the zero lower bound problems and for preventing it from becoming a permanent challenge for monetary policy. This leads us to the question of how the real interest rate could be increased. Given that monetary policy alone cannot move the equilibrium real interest rate, structural and fiscal policies are normally required to address the determinants of the real interest rate, such as productivity, demographic trends, and infrastructure investment.

The inflation has been low precisely because nominal rates had themselves been low. The relation between inflation and nominal rates comes from the Fisher equation, which can be written in a simplified form as:

$$i_t = r_t + E_t \pi_{t+1} \tag{4.3}$$

where $i\,t$ and $r\,t\,t$ respectively denote nominal and real interest rates, while $E\,t\,\pi\,t+1$ denotes expected inflation in period *t+1*. This equation incorporates a long-run positive relation between nominal rates and expected inflation. Given the relation between inflation and nominal rates, some economists have recommended that keeping nominal rates relatively high for an extended period could help to achieve higher inflation. However, according to the "neo-Fisherian" view, central banks after the 2008-9 financial crisis have operated near the effective lower bound, which may not have been an effective strategy for raising inflation (Leeper and Leith, 2016, pp. 25-78). We also have seen that during the same period after the 2008 crisis, most of the economies in industrialized countries have been characterized by low inflation rates, thanks in part to the introduction of new technological processes, continued improvements in production, implementation of modern ERP (Enterprise Resource Planning) system and efficient supply chain management that has helped keep low the price of raw materials and semi-assemblies used to manufacture the final non-premium products.

If the central bank's inflation target is denominated as *π*t+1* and low inflation due to the low price of raw materials is denominated as *πRawt+1*, then the expected inflation in period *t+1* is written as *(π*-πL)t+1*. Thus, we have that $E\,t\,\pi\,t+1$ can be replaced by *Et(π*-πRaw)t+1* and equation 4.3 can be written as,

$$i_t = r_t + \delta_\pi E_t(\pi * -\pi Raw)_{t+1} \qquad (4.4)$$

where *δπ* is the parameter that rules the central bank's responsiveness to off-target inflation. Suppose, for example, that if *δπ* > *1*, the central bank will commit to responding quite aggressively when inflation is off target. But, if *δπ* < *1*, and inflation is deflationary, the central bank may decide not to commit to responding aggressively when inflation is lower than the inflation target, then inflation expectations may become unreliable. The above equation means that the nominal interest rate is determined by the real interest rate and the expected inflation in period *t+1*, which in economy pricing is supposed to be low. Suppose the inflation is expected to be low due to low prices of the mass-produced non-premium products and efficient supply chain management. In that case, the nominal interest rate is equal to the real interest rate.

Given the uncertainty, neo-Fisherians use the fiscal theory of the price level to identify the equilibrium that is likely to be obtained (Woodford, 1995). The neo-Fisherian assumptions could hold in the short run if the government responds to higher rates by either refraining from adjusting surpluses or actively targeting lower surpluses. In addition, the neo-Fisherian mechanism can put the fiscal policy in an awkward and unconventional position since the government must control its influence on nominal prices and actively use inflation to manage the real value of its debt. However, if inflation is low, the equilibria selected would require careful coordination with fiscal authorities since their selection would ultimately depend on how the treasury adjusts surpluses in response to higher nominal rates.

The neo-Fisherian mechanism depends critically on the way government adjusts surpluses in response to the announcement of higher nominal rates. Consequently, control over nominal prices would effectively be assigned to fiscal policy, which could raise questions about central bank independence. Active use of inflation to manage the government's real debt could also lead to the perception that government may try to inflate its debts away merely. But if inflation is kept low for much longer periods, then there is no need for the government to be assigned control over nominal prices. Suppose the monetary policy of a central bank is to cut the short-term nominal interest rate to its effective lower bound and keep it for a long time. In that case, this central bank seeks additional demand stimulus. However, the exact degree of stimulus in the economy is difficult to predict. It may not be possible to choose a length of time for which to commit to the ultra-low-interest rate that does not simultaneously increase the risk of this monetary policy being too short to be effective.

Additionally, a central bank caught in a low-inflation policy trap with a zero nominal interest rate has no monetary tools to use other than unconventional ones if a recession unfolds. However, unconventional policies have not worked to increase the inflation rate for at least a few main reasons. **First**, a negative nominal interest rate will only make the inflation rate lower, as has happened in Switzerland, where nominal interest rates have been negative for some time and have been deflation. **Second**, Quantitative Easing (QE) has not worked to increase inflation, as we have seen at least in Japan, where an extensive QE program in place for a few years has not produced higher inflation (Williamson, 2016). **Third**, forward guidance, which promises more of what they will do in the future and as they continue to keep interest rates low if the low inflation problem persists, will not help to resolve the problem. **Forth,** the increased number of mass-produced non-premium products at low cost and pushed-demand strategies in many industries have kept the price of non-premium products continuously low. As a result, inflation has been low.

There are premises that interest rates will stay low in the future in the hope that this will increase inflation. However, there is no guarantee that inflation will increase due to continues technological progress and the evolving supply chain management that helps keep the price of raw materials low to keep control of the price of final commodities. Therefore, inflation is independent of the interest rates as far as an economy operates as an economy pricing system dominated by low prices of non-premium goods. This does not consider the case of inflation during pandemics, lockdowns, wars, and supply chain constraints, where inflation can quickly go up due to constraints in the market.

The Unemployment Rate in Economy Pricing

According to macroeconomic theories and the Phillips curve theory, when the unemployment rate drops below a certain level, referred to as the natural rate of unemployment (it includes frictional and structural unemployment, and not cyclical), the inflation rate will tend to increase, and continue to rise until the unemployment rate returns to its natural rate. In the same way, when the unemployment rate rises above the natural rate, the inflation rate will tend to decrease. The natural rate of unemployment is the level of unemployment consistent with sustainable economic growth. An unemployment rate below the natural rate means that the economy is growing faster than its sustainable natural rate of unemployment, which places pressure on wages and prices in general upward, leading to increased inflation. (Laurence and Mazumder, 2011). The opposite will happen if the unemployment rate rises above the natural rate, which will put downward pressure on wages and prices in general, leading to decreased inflation. Wages and salaries make up a significant portion of the costs of goods and services; therefore, upward or downward pressure on wages pushes average prices in the same direction based on traditional macroeconomic theories.

However, things seem to occur differently from the traditional macroeconomic theories. The relatively slight decrease in the rate of inflation following the sustained unemployment gap after the 2008 recession recommended a fading relationship between the unemployment gap and inflation. The expansionary monetary and fiscal policies to help reduce the unemployment rate and stabilize prices have been in place equitably for quite some time. The unemployment rate is an approximating estimate of the natural rate of unemployment, and yet the inflation rate based on traditional macro theories has yet to rise to the Federal Reserve's long-term target of 2% per year in the U.S. market. Given this situation, we have that the current state of the economy proposes that either the relationship seen between the unemployment gap and inflation during the recession appears to be continuing even as economic conditions improve, or as suggested, the unemployment gap may no longer be considered an accurate measure of the output gap.

In the U.S.A., the Fed has a dual mandate of full employment and price stability. The unemployment rate in the U.S.A. has been historically low, going up a while to 3.7% in June 2019 from 3.6% in May 2019, which was the lowest since 1969. Inflation, however, has been low in recent years and consistently below the Fed's 2% target. The so-called Phillips curve, which the Fed relies on in guiding its policy direction, argues that as unemployment declines, inflation should rise, a phenomenon that has not occurred during this economic expansion after the 2008 crisis. In recent years, the economy has challenged the Phillips Curve (Rusticelli, 2015). As unemployment has dropped, wages and inflation haven't risen sharply. In some ways, they've weakened. It is supposed to be a connection because low unemployment will drive wages up, and ultimately, higher wages will drive inflation up, yet we have not reached that point. Recent data suggest that, in many cases, the direct connection between unemployment and inflation is quite small or inexistent.

If we consider that the relationship between inflation and the unemployment rate has really weakened, then it would have important implications for economic policy. In fact, it may allow policymakers to employ fiscal and monetary policies more aggressively without putting pressure on hitting the inflation target rate that would have been previously expected. However, a weakened relationship would suggest that if inflation begins to accelerate, a larger and more sustained period of higher unemployment may eventually be necessary to stabilize inflation.

In addition, further research and time are necessary to determine if the weakened relationship between inflation and unemployment seen after the recession is a temporary phenomenon specific to the financial crisis or if it is a more lasting shift in the strength of the relation between unemployment and inflation. In the United States, which is still the largest and most developed economy in the world, the Federal Reserve was not able to meet its own inflation target in the last decade, before the pandemic started in 2020, despite the unemployment rate falling to levels consistent with the natural rate of unemployment, which may suggest that unemployment gap is no longer considered an accurate representation of the output gap. There are some explanations for this:

One first possible explanation of the weak relationship between inflation and unemployment is that the long-run sustainable rate of unemployment after the financial crisis of 2008 is lower than it was in the past. This rate is a representation of the maximum sustainable employment without generating an overheating economy via wage and price pressures. Additionally, there are several non-monetary factors, such as demographic trends, technological progress, and globalization, that can affect the sustainable unemployment rate. This explanation states that the economy of industrialized countries can sustain lower unemployment rates without producing any inflationary pressures.

A second possible explanation is that the sensitivity of inflation is relaxed in the economy, which means that the Phillips Curve in the last decade, especially after the 2008 financial crisis, was lower than it was several decades ago. In fact, estimates of the Phillips Curve propose that in the past, inflation was mostly linked to how much slack or inactivity was in the economy. In the past, as the unemployment rate declined, wages and prices were under pressure to increase. However, more recently, new estimates concord that the Phillips Curve is basically flat, which means that prices are stable and less responsive to slack.

This might be due to the trend in the labor market bargaining or competition from imported commodities and economy pricing that makes firms less willing to increase prices, especially those of non-premium products. (Gordon, 2011). This explanation could suggest that we are less likely to see inflation generated by slack, such as that indicated by low unemployment rates and economy pricing.

A third possible explanation is that lower inflation expectations are considered a new factor behind the muted inflation rates. In fact, prices may not rise as much if firms and households do not expect much higher inflation in the future. Therefore, the public may start revising their inflation expectations downward, given that actual inflation has been consistently below the central banks' two percent target over the last few years.

According to Hornstein and Kudlyak (2020), unemployment is low because the rate at which people exit unemployment is high or because the rate at which people enter unemployment is low, which is different from the previous business cycle peaks when unemployment was low due to high rates at which people were leaving the unemployment status.

Low unemployment rates can also be explained in terms of economy pricing based on the substantial number of products sold at a discount rate. As seen in chapter 2, for a given firm, the combination of the linear demand function for premium and non-premium products is equal to the total production capacity utilization during a fiscal period which is supposed to reach about 70- 80 percent of total production capacity utilization rate deemed to cover total variable and fixed costs and reach the sales target. From chapter 2, we know that the linear demand function for a firm that produces premium and non-premium products meeting the sales target in a competitive market is given as,

$$Dp(Pp) + Dnp(Pnp) = Sales\ Target = 80\%\ Uc \qquad (4.5)$$

where *Dp and Dnp* are the respective demands for premium and non-premium products; *Pp and Pnp* are the respective prices of premium and non-premium products. This equation can be written in terms of total cost made up of variable cost (which varies according to the quantity of the goods produced and include inputs such as labor and raw materials) and fixed costs, which is independent of the quantity produced (fixed costs consist of monthly building rent and monthly leasing fees on machinery, including sunk costs, etc.). Therefore, the firm's expected profit manufacturing both premium and non-premium products can be written as,

$$\Pi = [Dp(Pp) + Dnp(Pnp)] - [(AVC + AFC)] \qquad (4.6)$$

where *AVC* is the total variable cost, and *AFC* is the total fixed cost. The total variable cost can further be broken down into raw materials, the quantity of labor employed by the firm, and real wage to produce premium and non-premium products; therefore, the firm's expected profit is given as

$$\pi = [D_p(P_p) + D_{np}(P_{np})] - [(R_p + L_p W_p) + (R_{np} + L_{np} W_{np})] + (AFC + L_f)] \quad (4.7)$$

where *Rp* and *Rnp*, *Lp* and *Lnp*, *Wp* and *Wnp* are the respective raw materials, labor, and wage used to produce premium and non-premium products, respectively. Meanwhile, *Lf* is the fixed labor or administrative office labor as part of the total fixed cost.

The production capacity utilization of 70-80 percent deemed to cover total variable and fixed costs and reach the sales target is composed of roughly 20-30% premium and 70-80% of non-premium products. This means that the firm must commit larger amounts of labor in the forms of salaried and hourly wage employees to manufacture and run the operations of non-premium product categories. The higher the component of a non-premium product that makes up 70-80 percent of production capacity utilization, the more resources the firm will put in terms of labor, wages, and raw materials to produce the non-premium category. As a result, the firm will increase the labor force in operations by hiring new employees at a minimum or above the minimum wage to keep up with the demand for non-premium products, especially during sales events. Meanwhile, the number of office staff or salaried employees, as part of fixed costs for the company, which enjoy higher salaries, will remain stable.

Simplifying equation (4.7), we have that *Uc* and *Π* of the firm operating in a competitive market depend mostly on the production of the non-premium products that, combined with the premium products, make the firm profitable. However, most of the resources and labor are directed to the production of non-premium products that make up between 60% and 80% of total production. Therefore, the profit portion of non-premium products by using the function of the production capacity utilization is given as,

$$U_c = \pi_{np} = [D_{np}(P_{np}) - (R_{np} + L_{np} W_{np})] \text{ where Uc=70-80\%} \quad (4.8)$$

where *Rnp, Lnp, Wnp* are the respective raw materials, labor, and wage used to produce non-premium products and, *Uc* is the production capacity utilization, and *Πnp* is the profit derived from non-premium products. The number of firms, *Fi*, operating in *n* markets, producing *i* non-premium products that meet the sales target by reaching 70-80% of capacity utilization rate, *Uc*, will have the profit function for each firm *Fi* given as,

$$\pi_i = \sum_{p=1}^{n} p_i \, [A(D_{np})(\text{L})\text{-}(wL_{np})] \text{ where } \sum_{p=1}^{n} F_i = \sum_{p=1}^{n} U_c \quad (4.9)$$

where *Dnp* is the demand for non-premium products, *L* is the quantity of labor the firms employ, *A* is a factor that shifts the profit function and reflects the technology, and *wLnp* is the quantity of labor times wage (per hour) involved in the production and distribution of non-premium products. A higher value of *A* means that the firm can produce more output from a given amount of labor and sell more for a relatively stable or unchanged price for a given amount of output.

The distribution of *A* is discrete, and there are *K* possible values of *A* indexed by i; *pi* denotes the probability that *A=Ai*. Thus, the firm's expected profits are:

$$E(\pi) = \sum_{p=1}^{n} p_i \, [A(D_{np})(\mathrm{L})\text{-}(w_i L_i)] \qquad (4.10)$$

where *L* and *w* denote the quantity of labor and the real wage if the realization of *A* is *Ai*. The firm meets its expected profit; thus, it is risk neutral. Given that the firm sells non-premium products during sales events, it also meets the NMP >1 (Net Monetary Position) condition, as the firm can cover current liabilities with the current assets. Selling large volumes of non-premium products means that firms need to have a large infrastructure and employ many employees to work on the production facilities, distribution centers, customer services, and logistical support. The larger the number of firms that produce, distribute, and sell non-premium products in different sectors, the larger the number of active people employed by these firms that are paid at minimum or above the minimum wage, and the lower the rate of unemployment in the economy.

Let's assume that *N** is the full employment, N is the actual employment, and that the unemployment rate denominated as *u* is that portion of the labor force that has not been employed. Therefore, the unemployment rate can be written as u*-u = (N*-N) / N* ...(ii), where *u*-u* is the unemployment rate. Meanwhile, B=*(Pnp*-Pnp)/Pnp* is the change in non-premium product prices during the year. Thus, the Phillips curve relationship in terms of non-premium discounted prices indicated by *B* can be written as,

$$B = \frac{(P_{np}^{*} - P_{np})}{P_{np}} = \frac{\varepsilon(N^{*} - N)}{N} = \varepsilon(u^{*} - u) \qquad (4.11)$$

where ε is the responsiveness of non-premium product prices to the unemployment rate. If we consider the Phillips curve relationship in terms of production capacity utilization indicated as *Uc*, and unemployment rate, *u*, we have that this relationship indicated by *Puc* is given as,

$$P_{uc} = \frac{\varepsilon\prime(U_C^{*} - U_C)}{U_C} = \varepsilon'(u^{*} - u) \qquad (4.12)$$

where, Uc^* is the full production utilization capacity, Uc is the current capacity utilization, and u^*-u is the unemployment rate. The term u^*-u is the unemployment rate, and ε' is the responsiveness of the production capacity utilization of a firm manufacturing large volumes of non-premium products to the unemployment rate. A higher level of capacity utilization in different industries leads to lower unemployment rates.

The standard Phillips curve relates the rate of inflation with the rate of unemployment. In fact, the Phillips curve argues that unemployment and inflation are inversely related: as levels of unemployment decrease, inflation increases. The relationship, however, is not linear. Graphically, the short-run Phillips curve traces an L-shape when the unemployment rate is on the x-axis, and the inflation rate is on the y-axis.

In an economy pricing system and in a market dominated by a variety of non-premium products, the Phillips curve relationship in terms of capacity utilization, which is used mainly for non-premium products denominated as *Ucnp,* and unemployment rate denominated as *u,* still has an L-shape as revealed in figure 4.1.

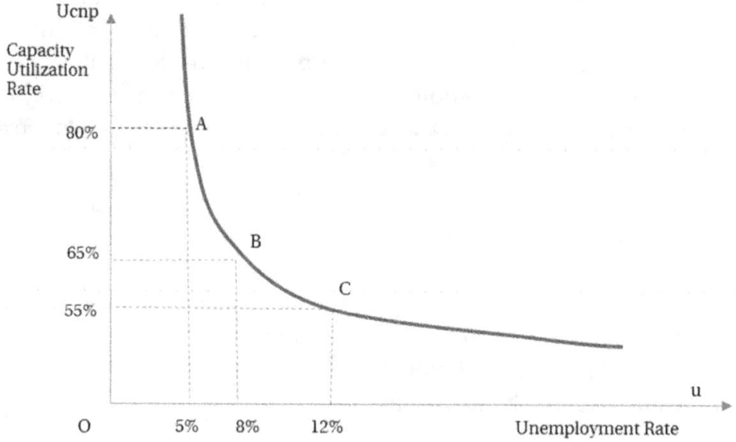

Figure 4.1 The relation between Unemployment Rate and Capacity Utilization Rate in Economy Pricing

Figure 4.1 illustrates several firms in several sectors producing different categories of products at different competitive and non-competitive prices. The firms having non-competitive prices have a low-capacity utilization rate of around 55%, which results in a high unemployment rate in the economy at about 12%, as indicated by point C in figure 4.1. At point B the firms increase the production utilization capacity at 65% when they start to manufacture and sell more non-premium products at more competitive prices than premium products, which causes the unemployment rate in different sectors to decrease to 8%. And finally, at point A, the firms - due to technology improvements, outsourcing, and supply chain efficiency - produce and sell large volumes of non-premium products reaching the capacity utilization rate of 80% and fewer premium products, causing the unemployment rate in the economy to decrease further at 5%.

An economy pricing that is dominated by mass production and large sales of non-premium products during sales events, low inflation, and high-capacity utilization rates has the capability to keep the unemployment rate low. The rate of unemployment stays low as the inflation rate is low due to the stability of prices for a major part of non-premium products that dominate the market. The capacity utilization rate for many competitive firms in an economy pricing system continues to have a growing trend which means that the average employment rate tends to be stabilized at a higher level thanks to technological progress, efficient global supply chain management, acquisition and merger, availability of resources, outsourcing, cheap (borrowing) money, and competitive forces that have reigned the global economy in the last few decades.

Slow Economic Growth in Industrialized Countries and Outsourcing

The phenomenon of slow growth rates in advanced countries is not new. Potential growth is defined as the rate of growth that an economy can sustain in the medium term (normally fiscal period) without causing extra inflation. We could think of several possible explanations for the continued slow growth in advanced economies in the last two-three decades, especially after the 2008 global financial crisis. In many industrialized countries, the rate of growth has recently declined due to different causes such as labor force, capital stock, productivity, etc. In fact, the growth rates are low due to mostly lower fertility rates and shifting spending away from commodities to services or even a decline in total factor productivity growth. For example, the growth rate of a big industrial country such as the U.S. has slowed by more than half from 3.2 percent per year during a three-decade period 1970-2006 to only 1.4 percent during a decade period 2006-16, and only half of this GDP growth slowdown is believed to be accounted for diminished productivity growth (the growth rate has been measured between quarters with identical unemployment rates) (Gordon, 2018).

Advanced economies are more likely to have lower population growth rates due to lower birth rates (from a low infant mortality rate) compared to developing countries with high population growth, which puts more pressure on government resources such as healthcare and education. The decrease in fertility rates after the baby boom years of the post-WWII in the advanced economies explained the expanded access to high education of the baby boomers, which pushed back the age at which young people were willing to create a family. The liberalization of many professions for women, the new educational and professional opportunities for young women, along with growth in overall wages meant that women were more likely to delay marriage.

The consequences of these decisions helped create smaller families with fewer kids (standard family of four), lower fertility rates, higher standard of living, and more rights for women. Slowing population growth and aging have lowered working-age population grow rates in industrialized countries. The participation of women, part-time students, and older workers (over 65 years) in the labor market has increased the rate of the active population in the last three decades. It has also increased the participation of young-women and old workers in part-time employment in addition to part-time students, which has reduced the average number of hours that employed people are working, especially in-service sector. However, as a population continues aging, it will further lower potential employment growth due to older specialized workers leaving the labor force as they retire and increasing the gap to replace them.

Another factor that has contributed to slow growth in advanced countries is the shifting of spending away from commodities to services. In the last two hundred years, industrialized countries have become very efficient at producing all kinds of basic and non-basic goods (non-premium and premium) like clothes, food, furniture, vehicles, TVs, computers, smart-phones thanks to technological progress, company-governance improvements, the international movement of capitals, cost reduction and efficiency on supply chain management. The consequence is a steady reduction in the price of those goods relative to services which have helped people in advance countries take advantage of the savings to purchase more services like education, healthcare, leisure, entertainment, and travel. This has created the perfect condition for the composition of expenditures to move away from goods toward services. Advanced countries still consume more goods and services than third-world countries or developing countries, but the price of these goods has decreased a lot faster, and the share of total expenditure has fallen relative to services.

Another factor that contributed to slow growth in advanced countries is the capital stock. Lower trend growth of capital stock has reduced the rate of growth in advanced economies since the 1980s. Trend growth in the capital stock has declined in Japan, the United States, and the Euro area, which has reduced the capital stock's contribution to the potential growth rates by around 0.5 percentage points. A large share of the decline in investment has come from public and residential investment, not business investment. There are at least two reasons that explain the slow growth of capital stock related to population growth. **First,** lower labor force growth necessitates less capital stock to equip workers adequately. **Second**, the slowing growth in the general population lowers the need to invest in new housing and public infrastructure. The decrease in public investment also reflects more conservative management of public finances following the accumulation of government debt after the 2008-2009 financial crisis.

Excess savings can lead to slower growth. There are several factors that can lead to excess savings over investment demand in industrialized countries. **One factor** is that the aging population in developed western countries will tend to save more for retirement and spend less on consumption which can put pressure on lowering the interest rate and reduce investment as fewer capital goods will be needed to invest in production to produce consumption goods. **A second factor** is an inequality in savings among those that make a minimum wage and those that are wealthier and get paid bigger salaries in advanced countries. The minimum wage earners save less than other employees and professionals that earn higher incomes. That excess income of the wealthier people as soon as it is earned is saved and is normally used for future investment in capital goods, such as houses, cottages, boats, luxury vehicles, shares, bonds, etc., putting downward pressure on the interest rates.

A third factor is that there is a decline in investment goods which means that today's dollars of savings can be purchased more capital than before, triggering excess savings over investments (Summers, 2014). This is true, especially for those firms that invest more in technological progress, advanced products, and services, software applications, etc., and less in physical capital. This will shift the structure of the economy towards a service-oriented economy with less demand for capital goods. In fact, lower growth in demographics and low productivity means a lower trend in desired investment and less production capacity expansion, which could lead to less future capital stock and less production and output.

A fourth factor is that consistently weak demand in developed countries may lead to limited productivity growth and a shift of the labor force from the manufacturing sector to the service sector with lower labor force participation. The weak demand and low inflation in developed countries normally lead to a higher rate of outsourcing production capacity in developing countries to keep the costs of final goods down and the price of commodities stable. Hence, another factor that contributes to slow growth in advanced economies is a slow growth trend of capital stock in developed economies and an increase trend of capital stock exportation in developing countries to help outsource part of the production in those developing countries where there is cheaper labor force and abundance in raw materials.

In chapter 1, at the microeconomic level, we have seen that the equation which indicates the final price of the buy-product, *Un,* sold to the final customer in the superstore based on three levels of demand-push for a non-premium product could be written as,

$$PU_{(s)np} = [P_a + L + VFOH + \boldsymbol{P_m}] + [PM_m + L_m + VFOH_m + \boldsymbol{P_{(r)np}}] + [P_r + L_r + VFOH_r + \boldsymbol{PI}] \quad (4.13)$$

where the final sale price *PU(s)np* of non-premium product sold to the final customer is a combination of three-levels of demand-push to reduce price coming from the discount superstore, the manufacturer of non-premium goods, and raw-material suppliers. The first level of demand-push is at the superstore level by pushing the demand into customers using different pricing strategies and marketing models of discount prices. The first part of the equation above on the right side indicates *Pa* as the profit margin of the superstore, *L* as labor, *VFOHA* as the variable and fixed overhead of the superstore (including the selling administrative costs), and *Pm* as the wholesale price the superstore buys the products from the manufacturer.

The second part of the equation above indicates the second level of the demand-push at the manufacturing level, where the manufacturer is asked to reduce the price of final products in order to support the superstores' sales events. *PMm, Lm,* and *VFOHm* are, respectively, the profit margin, labor, variable and fixed overhead (including administrative cost) of the manufacturer to produce one unit of *Un,* and lastly, *P(r)np* represents the across-the-board price the manufacturer buys raw materials from different suppliers and mining industry to produce its output.

The third part of the equation above indicates the third level of discounted price and demand-push when the manufacturer asks their suppliers of the raw materials and intermediate subassemblies to reduce the price of raw materials used to produce non-premium products so they can support the sales event of the superstore, where *Pr, Lr, VFOHr* are respectively the profit margin, labor, variable and fixed overhead (including administrative cost) of the extraction company and *Pl* is the price to buy land to extract minerals including the mining rights and loyalties.

The superstore could use a different strategy to meet the target cost and keep the desired profit margin. This is the outsourcing strategy. In fact, the outsourcing strategy consists of agreeing with the manufactures to significantly reduce the wholesale price by outsourcing some subassemblies of product specifications of the non-premium product to developing countries where labor, fixed and variable overheads are much cheaper. This strategy can go even further by outsourcing the manufacturing of the entire non-premium product completely to developing countries, so the superstore can better position itself with respect to its competitors during sales events.

As a matter of fact, if the manufacturer decides to buy the subassemblies directly from developing countries in agreement with the superstore to reduce the target cost of a non-premium product, indicated as *PU(s)np,* using the two levels of demand-push, the final price will take the form as,

$$PU_{(s)np} = [P_a + L + VFOH + \boldsymbol{P_m}] + [PM_m + L_m + VFOH_m + \boldsymbol{P_{(r)dev}}] \tag{4.14}$$

where *P(r)dev* is the price of raw materials or subassemblies purchased from developing countries at a much lower price compared to the price of raws and subassemblies purchased and made in industrialized countries. In the equation above, we can see that the superstore has eliminated the profit margin, labor, variable, and fixed overhead of the third level of demand-push by directly outsourcing subassemblies to developing countries. The discounted price of the non-premium product can be reduced further if the superstore decides to buy the non-premium product entirely from a developing country using the same product specifications as if it was manufactured in an industrialized country. The non-premium product manufactured in a less developed country uses cheaper specialized labor and less variable and fixed overheads. Therefore, the discounted price of the non-premium product *PU(s)np* using only one level of demand-push can be written as,

$$PU_{(s)np} = [P_a + L + VFOH + \boldsymbol{P_{manuf}}] \tag{4.15}$$

where *Pmanuf* is the discounted price of non-premium products outsourced and purchased directly from developing countries and sold in the superstore. This equation shows that the superstore has eliminated the profit margin, labor, variable, and fixed overhead of the second and third level of demand-push by outsourcing the non-premium product directly to developing countries.

The outsourcing of two levels of demand-push of the supply chain in developing countries has eliminated the higher cost of production of raw materials, subassemblies, and finished goods in industrialized countries. This, in return, has reduced the production capacity of the industrialized countries and has increased the production capacity of the developing countries hosting the outsourced manufacturing facilities. The reduced production capacity in industrialized countries has slowed growth as the manufacturing sector gets smaller and smaller with a less specialized manufacturing labor force in favor of a cutting-edge service-oriented sector that is currently dominating the advanced countries.

Inflation-fighting Tools in Economy Pricing

Inflation is an important parameter of an economy. Low and stable inflation is good for the economy as it helps money keep its value and makes it easier for consumers to plan how to spend their money. In the economy pricing system, most of the industrialized countries, in addition to low prices, have had record low inflation, low-interest rates (especially after the 2008 financial crisis), low growth rates, and record low unemployment rates. However, inflation can rise quickly due to unpredicted factors and external shocks such as wars, famines, diseases, and political unrest, as happened during the global pandemic years of 2020-2023, where the global supply chain was disrupted and caused a general increase of almost all prices in many countries. The task of national governments is to keep inflation within a reasonable range, despite the external shocks, to help growth and reduce unemployment without comprising the purchasing power parity (PPP) of the currency.

Several traditional methods are used to control inflation, with some being more effective and easier to control than others, such as Price controls to fight inflation, Contractionary monetary policy through higher interest rates, Open Market Operations, and Lower Energy, Trade, and Procurement Costs.

Price controls are normally government regulations on prices for goods and services and wages. Price control is considered by many economists as a tool of direct economic intervention to impose pricing and manage the affordability of certain goods and services, such as gasoline, food, and rent. Price control makes several basic goods and services more affordable for consumers; however, it can lead to disruptions in the market, less profit for producers, and eventually lower quality for certain goods and services under price control. Price controls set by the government can impose price maximums, referred to as price ceilings, and minimum prices, called price floors. Although the reasons for government pricing policy may be affordability and economics stability, price control may have opposite effects (Taussig, 1919). The negative long-term effects of price controls have been known to lead to shortages, rationing, worsening of product quality, and the arising of an illegal market to supply price-controlled goods through informal channels. If the prices imposed by the government are set too low, the producers may experience losses, and this can often lead to a drop in the quality of goods and services available in the market. The price-controls distort the allocation of resources. In fact, price ceilings prevent prices from exceeding a maximum, which could cause shortages, and price floors prevent prices from below a certain minimum, which can cause a surplus. Another problem with the imposed price control is the trade-off between the need to have a certain program generally perceived as fair and the need to have adequate flexibility to maintain efficiency. Efficiency requires making frequent adjustments, which could be subject to bureaucracy administering controls.

The **Contractionary Monetary Policy** is another indirect method to control inflation. The main objective of the contractionary policy is to reduce the money supply in an economy by increasing interest rates. The central bank will increase interest rates to slow economic growth by making the credits and loans more expensive, which reduces consumer spending, and businesses reduce their investments. Rising interest rates help rise the interest rates paid on government securities, which help investors buy government securities that have higher interest rates and are less risky than riskier equity investments with lower rates.

Open Market Operations (OMO) is another monetary tool to control inflation. OMO refers to a central bank buying and selling Treasury securities to increase or decrease the money supply and adjust interest rates. The bank's balance sheet increases when it buys securities and shrinks when it sells them. This monetary tool promotes liquidity in financial markets and puts downward pressure on interest rates when the central bank buys securities while selling securities does the opposite. Central banks, through Open Market Operations (OMOs), can continue to raise interest rates and decrease their balance sheet to better control demand and reduce inflationary pressures.

Lower Energy, Trade, and Procurement Costs are more direct tools to control inflation. Government policies and regulations can influence the price of many goods and services. For example, the government can reduce tariffs for certain goods imported from other countries, which helps companies reduce their prices, and consumers get their best price for every dollar they spend. Government can end certain regulations in the transportation industry that increase shipping costs and encourage the production of renewable energy to push the price of electricity down.

The role of the central bank is to maintain price stability and control inflation. However, it's not easy to bring inflation under control without triggering a recession, especially if the government continues to use fiscal policy and excessive spending, which could worsen inflation pressures. If the central bank quickly increases interest rates to fight inflation, this may cause a higher cost of borrowing and, eventually, an undesired recession.

Promotion of non-premium products at a discounted price:

There is also another method that is used to control inflation by selling more non-premium products in different industries at an affordable or discounted price. Non-premium brands are normally referred to as those products that highlight different elements and characteristics, such as price discounts, affordability, and reliability, which tend to be more important for value-conscious consumers and are offered at different low and medium price-ranges. Price and quality ratings can help consumers create their utility 'function' and influence how consumers perceive the quality of a product. For non-premium products, consumers use price to assess the product's overall quality when objective quality is difficult to assess. Affordable pricing for non-premium and basic products is what is needed during the recession and rising inflation. Each firm can easily identify in revenue the affordable non-premium products sold at regular prices or at discount prices.

Assuming a firm has few non-premium items, *n*, that sells at discount price, *Punp*, during sales events. The sales revenue of this firm indicated as *Rs*, operating in economy pricing that sells non-premium discounted, non-premium, and premium products at regular price is given as,

$$R_s = \sum_{i=1}^{n} P_{unp} q_u + \sum_{i=1}^{n} P_{np} q_{nP} + \sum_{l=1}^{n} P_P\, q_p \text{ where qu> qp and qu=ku} \quad (4.16)$$

where, *Punp* and *qu* are, respectively, the discount price of units *Un* and quantity sold of non-premium products during sales events. Meanwhile, *Pnp* and *qnp* are, respectively, the regular price and quantity sold of non-premium products during non-sales events, and *Pp* and *qp* are the regular price and quantity of premium products. *Ku* is the capacity utilization of the superstore to reach a satisfactory level of revenue to meet the net monetary position condition (NMP>1).

The portion *Punp qu* in the equation (4.16) that point to the sales discounted price and quantity of non-premium products determines the inflation control tool to fight the rising prices in an economy pricing system. We assume that there are many firms, *Fi*, operating in different sectors of economy pricing offering discount price *Punp* for non-premium products with a total sales revenue for all premium and non-premium products given as,

$$R_s = \sum_{i=1}^{n} F_i \left[\sum_{i=1}^{n} P_{unp} q_u + \sum_{i=1}^{n} P_{np} q_{np} + \sum_{l=1}^{n} P_P\, q_p \right] \quad (4.17)$$

To put pressure on firms to keep inflation low, the government can choose to reduce corporate tax for all those firms in different industries that, during the rising inflation period, sell non-premium or basic products at discount prices for the portion *Punp qu* in the equation above.

Suppose the revenue for a firm operating in economy pricing for non-premium discounted, non-premium and premium products are made respectively of 45%, 30%, and 25% of total sales. In that case, the government can choose to reduce corporate taxes based on the sales of non-premium discounted products that have a price increase based on the inflation target of the industry in the range of no more than 2-3% from month to month, or from quarter to quarter, to keep the inflation down. For example, if the corporate tax is 26%, and the firm at the end of the month has total sales of non-premium discounted products reaching 45% of overall sales, then the corporate tax could get reduced from 26% to 14.3% calculated as 26% -(26% x 45%) = 26% - 11.7%=14.3%. This fiscal policy will motivate the firm to sell more non-premium products at a discounted price. This fiscal tool is important, especially in those industries that produce basic needs, such as food, clothes, baby products, personal care products, basic services, etc., that could help keep the inflation low for essential products. In some cases, the government can increase corporate taxes, for a limited time, to those oil-producing corporations that reach extraordinary profits due to unreasonable and unjustified fuel price increases that affect almost all sectors of the economy.

During inflation-rising periods, many firms operating in the non-premium-product environment can choose to participate in the government program on corporate tax reduction for the portion of non-premium products that has a steady price increase of 2-3% from one period to another. The higher the number of firms producing and trading non-premium products participating in this government program, the lower the overall inflation in the economy from one period to another. The total number of firms that operate in an economy affected by rising inflation in different sectors can be divided into those firms that produce non-premium products and participate in the price-control government programs with tax reductions and those firms that produce premium and non-premium products but do not participate in price-controlled programs and do not get a tax reduction. This function can be given in the equation below as,

$$Total\ firms = \uparrow Tax_{red}[\textstyle\sum_{i=1}^{n} F_{inpr}\ G_{npr}] + \downarrow No\ Tax_{red}[\textstyle\sum_{i=1}^{n} F_{inp} G_{np} + \textstyle\sum_{i=1}^{n} F_{ip} G_{p}] \tag{4.18}$$

where *Finpr* is the number of firms that produce and sell non-premium products indicated as *Gnpr*, which are eligible for the corporate tax refund, and *Finp* and Fip are the number of firms that produce and sell non-premium and premium products respectively indicated by *Gnp* and *Gp*, that are not eligible for tax reduction as they do not participate to price-control programs. The higher the number of firms producing and trading non-premium products participating in the Tax corporate reduction programs (*TAXred*), compared to other firms that do not participate in these programs, the lower the overall inflation in the economy.

The inflation rate for economy pricing, which consider the average price of a non-premium product during sales and non-sales events that are part of the government program to keep inflation low, based on the consumers' price index (CPI), can be written as,

$$InflationRate = \frac{Avr\ \sum_{i=1}^{n}(CurrentCPI - BaseYearCPI)}{Avr\ \sum_{i=1}^{n} BaseYearCPI} * 100 = \frac{Avr\ \sum_{i=1}^{n}(P_{unpc} * q_u - P_{npb} * q_p)}{Avr\ \sum_{i=1}^{n} P_{npb} * q_p} * 100 \tag{4.19}$$

where *Punpc* is the price of a non-premium product at the current period, and *Pnpb* is the price of a non-premium product at the beginning of the period, which is referred to as the base-year period. The non-premium quantities sold at the current period and at the beginning period are given respectively by *qu* and *qp*. The difference in price between the current period, *Punpc*, and the beginning of the period, *Pnpb*, should be, on average, between 2-3% (2.5%) to be eligible for government programs of price control, which can be written as,

$$Low - InflationRate = \frac{Avr\sum_{i=1}^{n}(P_{unpc}{*}q_u - P_{npb}{*}q_p)}{Avr\sum_{i=1}^{n}P_{npb}{*}q_p} * 100 = 2.5\% \tag{4.20}$$

The corporate tax reduction could be considered an indirect subsidy for firms participating in government price-control programs that manufacture and sell non-premium products to keep the price stable. In fact, tax reduction funds could help these firms recover part of the rising cost of raw materials during the inflation period, which is an incentive for these firms to keep the price of non-premium products at reasonable levels. This program gives time to firms operating in economy pricing and selling non-premium products to streamline the supply chain during the period of high inflation to better control costs. More other firms can join these government programs, so they can keep the price of non-premium products low, despite the rising cost of raw materials, to defend market share for those non-premium products that they have a competitive advantage. Once the inflation rate returns to the acceptable average of 2-3% on annual bases, then price-control programs can be ended.

Conclusions

In this chapter, we have seen how inflation, interest rates, and unemployment work in an economy pricing dominated by competition and how firms bring to different market categories of premium and non-premium products to stay competitive. Before the COVID-19 pandemic, recent years have been subject to low inflation in most industrialized countries. Due to low inflation, the central banks such as Federal Reserve in the U.S. and European Central Bank (ECB) in Europe have been stressed about how to respond to persistently low inflation amid what appears to be the weakening of a foundational economic relationship.

It is a general opinion that inflation is increasingly determined abroad, and the global factors that keep inflation domestically low such as global supply chains and technological progress could continue for months, years, or even decades. We have seen how the technological progress in different sectors has increased productivity, lowered the rate of wage growth relative to productivity, and as a result, delayed rising inflation. In fact, the introduction of technology innovation in the industry has been a complement to the workforce, lowering the labor cost and therefore creating deflation in different kinds of goods and services. Late in the chapter, we saw how supply chain management (SCM) managed the flow of goods and services from raw materials to final consumption and how it has affected the prices of finished goods by lowering the price of raw materials and intermediate goods. The SCM has allowed companies to be able to cut excess costs and deliver products to the final consumer faster and cheaper, which is achieved by keeping tighter control of inventories, production, and distribution centers.

We also went likewise through the concept of low-interest rates and their relation to inflation. The monetary theory normally establishes the relation between inflation and the money supply of an economy, which means that a rapid increase in money supply will bring price spikes and inflation. Since the 2008 financial crisis until the start of the pandemic and the war in Ukraine in 2022, many central banks have kept interest rates low to stimulate economies around the world. By keeping the interest rate low, a central bank caught in a low-inflation policy trap with a zero nominal interest rate has no monetary tools other than unconventional monetary policies if a financial crisis spreads out and hits the economy. As it was mentioned in this chapter, unconventional policies had not been proven to increase the inflation rate. A negative nominal interest rate will only make the inflation rate lower, as it happened in Switzerland. In addition, Quantitative Easing (QE) has worked to keep the cash flowing to the banks and economy running but has not helped increase inflation.

The inflation was low due to continues technological progress and supply chain management. Especially an enhanced supply chain management keeps the price of raw materials low, which helps control the final goods' price. Based on this, we can say that inflation is independent of interest rates as an economy is competitive and operates at low-price levels.

The low unemployment rate in a competitive economy was another theme that was taken into consideration in this chapter. We have seen that there is a weak relationship between inflation and the unemployment rate. The long-run sustainable rate of unemployment after the financial crisis of 2008 was lower than it was in the past. An economy pricing system dominated by production and sales of non-premium products and operating in a low inflation environment has the trend to keep the rate of unemployment low, thanks to technological progress, global supply chain management, availability of resources, and cheap money.

Another topic in this chapter discusses how the reduced production capacity in industrialized countries has slowed growth as the manufacturing sector gets smaller, using a less specialized labor force in favor of an innovative service-oriented sector that is helping advanced countries to become service-oriented economies. And lastly, the subject of inflation-fighting tools. It is interesting to notice that during inflation-rising periods, many firms operating in a non-premium-product environment can choose to participate in a government program on corporate tax reduction for the portion of non-premium products that has a control price increase from one period to another. The higher the number of firms in different sectors producing and trading non-premium products participating in this program, the lower the overall inflation in the economy from one period to another.

Chapter 5
Monetary Policy in an Economy Pricing System

Introduction

This chapter is about how monetary policy works when inflation, interest rates, and unemployment rates are kept low in an economy pricing system characterized by a high level of competition between firms in different sectors. The chapter will start with the relationship between money growth and inflation. It will consider the Quantity Theory of Money (QTM) and the optimum quantity of money as proposed by Friedman in the 1960s and how this theory has evolved in the last decades. Later in the chapter, we will talk about the Quantity Easing and Quantity of Money in Circulation and how unconventional monetary policy is supposed to influence the quantity of money in circulation through Quantitative Easing (QE).

Further in the chapter, the relationship between monetary policy and low-interest rates will be analyzed. As we know, monetary policy is the macroeconomic policy managed mostly by the central bank, which involves the supervision of money supply and interest rate to achieve macroeconomic objectives like controlling inflation, reducing liquidity, help consumption and growth. An interesting segment in the chapter is the study of central bank independence. The idea of central bank independence for many economists has meant, above all, independence from direction by short-term concerns and interference of politicians. From here, then we go to the analysis of the central bank rules and the introduction of a new central bank rule called the Solvency Curve, which is based on a new concept of how an economy can fight the recession and return to normality.

Another topic that will be discussed in this chapter is the relationship between the Treasury and the Central Bank. Here will be introduced the concept of a *New Monetary Authority* designed to replace the Central Bank and which will be supervised and administered jointly by the treasury and government.

Money Growth and Inflation

From the monetary theory, we know that money supply may affect inflation. Based on this theory, inflation can happen if the money supply grows faster than the economic output under otherwise normal economic circumstances.

Nevertheless, inflation can also be affected by factors beyond the money supply. The theory most discussed when looking at the relationship between inflation and money supply is, without a doubt, the quantity theory of money (QTM), despite the fact that there are other theories that challenge it.

The quantity theory of money suggests that the exchange value of money is determined like any other good, with supply and demand. The basic equation for the quantity theory is called the Fisher equation, which was developed by American economist Irving Fisher (Friedman and Schwartz, 2008). In its simplest form, the quantity theory of money was formulated in terms of the equation of exchange. Let M be the total stock of money, P the price level, T the amount or the number of transactions in volumes of goods and services carried out using money, and V the velocity of circulation of money, then the formula that states the quantity theory of money can be expressed as,

$$MV = PT \quad (5.1)$$

Years later, economists replaced T with the real output Y (or Q), usually quantified by the real Gross Domestic Product (GPD). Based on this formula, the standard Quantity theory of money states that the money supply and price level in an economy are in direct proportion to one another. When there is a change in the supply of money, there is a proportional change in the price level and vice-versa. On the other side, there are other economists that criticize the quantitative theory of money, arguing that money velocity is not stable, and in the short-run, prices are sticky, so the direct relationship between money supply and price level does not hold. Some interesting variants of the quantity theory suggest that price changes, inflation, and deflation occur proportionately to increases or decreases in the supply of money. So far, there are no credible empirical analyses that can prove this variant of quantitative theory, and a good number of economists do not support this view.

Economists of the caliber like Alfred Marshall, A. C. Pigou, and Maynard Keynes had a different approach to the quantity theory focusing on money demand instead of the money supply. They claimed that a certain portion of the money supply would not be used for transactions; instead, it would be held for the convenience and security of having cash on hand. Keynes reformulated the classical *Quantity Theory of Money* (QTM), and according to him, money does not directly affect the price level. Also, a change in the quantity of money can lead to a change in the rate of interest. Further, with a change in the rate of interest, the volume of investment can change. Normally the portion of cash is commonly represented as k, a portion of nominal income as PY. Therefore, the Keynesian equation for money demand is represented as:

$$Md = kPY \rightarrow M(1/k) = PY \quad (5.2)$$

where Y is exogenous, and k is fixed in the short run.

In the *Quantity Theory of Money* (QTM) and the optimum quantity of money as proposed by Friedman in the 1960s, we have that money moves around the economy mainly in the form of cash and cheques (Friedman, 1969). It can be assumed that the speed at which money moves around the economy, *V*, is constant. But technological advances have made it much easier and faster to move money around and exchange it for goods and services. Data from the Fed's statistical service, FRED (*FRED, Economic Data*, St Louis, Fed 2019), shows that *V* has become significantly more volatile since the 1960s, especially at the beginning of the 2000s with the technological advances and the introduction of electronic monetary transactions such as *Electronic Funds Transfer* (EFT). The velocity of money has been mostly related to people's behavior and the structure of the financial system. There are visible patterns to show that the velocity of money is not constant, even in the short run.

On the other hand, by focusing on the QTM, we have that *P* which is the price level in a credit-money economy, can have its volume change either with or without direct central bank intervention. In addition, the monetary authority cannot raise the supply of money without the cooperation of the private sector. As we mentioned above, *V* is the velocity or speed at which money changes hands which until recently has been assumed constant. If *P* is rising faster than 2-3 percent yearly, then it means that there is too much money in the economy for the level of output (GDP), so the central bank is supposed to reduce the quantity of money in circulation, *M*, in order to bring the inflation down.

The quantity of money, *M*, is created largely by banks when they lend and not by the central bank. The central bank (like FED, Bank of Japan, Bank of Canada, European Central Bank, etc.) can influence the rate at which banks create money by controlling the Central Bank's rate, which banks lend reserves to each other. Thus, if commercial banks must pay more to obtain reserves from the Central Bank to fund their lending, they will raise the borrowing interest rates on loans to customers, consequently reducing demand for loans and hereafter reducing the quantity of new money being created. Therefore, less money will be created, fewer loans will be issued to customers, less spending will be done by customers, and inflation is likely to fall.

In open market operations, a central bank can raise the Central Bank's rate by selling securities for dollars, which will help withdraw a large quantity of money, *M*, from circulation. In the same way, to reduce the central bank's rate, the central bank can buy securities for newly created currency (such as U.S. dollars) which will increase the number of dollars in circulation. The central bank's Open Market Operations can also influence the currency/dollar exchange rate. Increasing the central bank rate will tend to raise the dollar exchange rate, and reducing the central bank rate will tend to lower it.

Quantity Easing and the Quantity of Money in Circulation

Another unconventional monetary policy that is supposed to influence the quantity of money in circulation is *Quantitative Easing* (QE). A QE is nothing more than an unconventional monetary policy, used mostly during the financial crisis in 2008-9, whereby a central bank purchases at-scale government bonds or other financial assets to inject money into the economy to expand economic activity or simply keep running the economy to avoid recession.

As per monetary economics, the enormous infusion of money because of QE operation would create inflation, or even worse, would cause hyperinflation and the collapse of the domestic currency such as the U.S. dollar. However, QE did not create hyperinflation or even much in the way of any inflation. Despite large amounts of purchases of MBS (Mortgage-Backed Securities) from 2009 to 2014 through QE operations, the Fed has struggled to raise inflation to its 2 percent target. Between December 2008 and March 2010, the Federal Reserve started the LSAP (large-scale asset purchase) program called also QE1 by purchasing more than $1.7 trillion in assets, representing almost 22% of the $7.7 trillion stock of long-term agency debt, MBS agency securities and other Treasury securities outstanding. By November 2010, the Fed declared the start of another QE program called the "QE2" program consisting of purchasing $600 billion of long-term Treasury securities to sustain economic growth, bank loaning, and increase the employment rate.

It is interesting to note that when QE first started in 2009 through the purchase of MBS and other securities in the secondary market, economists were still using a model of bank lending known as the "money multiplier." This theory suggested that of each new deposit, including QE deposits, a bank would keep 10 percent as reserves and lend out the remaining 90 percent. However, when the Fed bought securities from primary dealers such as banks and investors, it was thought that 90 percent of the new money it created would be lent out as new loans to the mass of consumers. This would spur spending and investment in the economy, bringing it out of recession and raising inflation to target. Therefore, economists expected that if a central bank such as Fed would infuse large quantities of money into the economy, the "money multiplier" would do the rest. Unfortunately, the "money multiplier" theory did not work with QE. This theory failure changed the "money multiplier" effect in the real economy. In fact, it seems that the money multiplier is simply a mathematical relationship between loans and deposits and cannot necessarily stay constant. The QE operations caused banks' reserves to increase dramatically, but it did not make them lend to the public as was hoped to happen.

In addition, even lowering the interest rate to zero or near zero did not help commercial banks lend a large amount of money to the public. After the financial crisis of 2008, damaged banks simply didn't want to lend, and damaged businesses and households were not ready to borrow. In fact, they wanted to reduce their debts rather than increase them. This phenomenon was called the "balance sheet recession" by the economist Richard Koo (2014). Consequently, although M is increased by the infusion of QE to buy the MBS (Mortgage-Backed Securities), V slowed to a crawl. In fact, increasing M when no one wanted to borrow may itself have slowed the velocity of money in circulation. The fast-economic growth and rising inflation that might have been expected from a large increase in bank lending simply did not materialize. However, the huge amounts of purchases of *MBS (Mortgage-Backed Securities)* and other securities through QE during the 2009-2014 period in the U.S., Europe, and other developed countries helped save the main commercial banks from total collapse and kept the economy running. Interest rates stayed low, and so did the dollar exchange rate.

Using the concept of economy pricing, we have that in an economy pricing dominated by premium and non-premium commodities, and the Fisher equation 5.1 can be written in a simplified form as,

$$M\,Vt = \Sigma i(Pnp\ Qnp + Pp\ Qp) \quad (5.3)$$

where M is the total amount of money in circulation on average in an economy during a period, say a year; Vt is the transaction which is the velocity of money that is the average frequency across all transactions with which unit money is spent, reflecting the availability of commercial banks, and the choice made by customers as to how fast they turn over their money. In other words, the velocity of money or the velocity of circulation of money measures the number of times the average unit of currency is used to purchase goods and services within a given period. On the right side of the equation above, we have Pnp, Pp, and Qnp, Qp, which are respectively the price and quantity of non-premium and premium products of the i-th transactions in economy pricing.

In an economy pricing dominated by non-premium goods, which are sold at reasonably low prices throughout the year, the inflation is kept low. The inflation could get even lower if, during the year, there are a substantial number of sales events that reduces further the prices of non-premium goods. Low inflation will keep low V, which is the velocity of money in circulation, despite the increased number of transactions due to low prices of non-premium goods. The best route to increase V is to increase the quantity of money M or infuse M in the economic system so consumers can include it in their consumption basket of semi-premium and premium goods at higher prices.

The central bank purchasing of MBS (*Mortgage-Backed Securities*) through QE to help commercial banks with liquidity should also be in combination with the purchase of "subsidy government bonds." The "subsidy government bonds" are created for subsidy purposes to help government inject money directly into the real economy by running large subsidy programs for unemployed or low-income families during a recession. This will help people buy a variety of non-premium products rather than basic groceries and move up their basket purchase to premium products at a higher price. This will increase the velocity of money in circulation, create jobs and keep inflation low.

As mentioned above, if the central bank would infuse large quantity of money into the economy to buy long-term agency debt such as *MBS* securities and other Treasury securities, then the total stock of money *M* can be further split into QE stock money for MBS and treasury securities, and QE money for subsidy programs. Therefore, the Fisher quantity theory of money formulated in terms of the equation of exchange, including the QE effects in the economy, can be expressed as,

$$\uparrow (Mqem+Mqes) \downarrow Vt = \Sigma i(\uparrow Pnp\ Qnp + \downarrow Pp\ Qp) + \uparrow Cqe \qquad (5.4)$$

where *Mqem* is the stock of money infused in the system to purchase the stock of long-term agency debt, MBS agency securities, and other Treasury securities. *Mqes* is the new QE program to buy "subsidy government bonds" so the government can use the cash to inject money directly into the real economy to run large subsidy programs during recession periods, such as wage subsidies, unemployment subsidies, unemployment insurance, family, and child support subsidies, etc. A portion of the subsidy money in *Mqes* is used for large corporations' bailouts as well, such as big commercial and investment banks, big automaker companies, etc. In addition, in the U.S.A., the U.S. Congress during the 2008-9 financial crisis approved a $787 billion economic stimulus package to boost economic growth by granting $288 billion in tax cuts, $224 billion in unemployment benefits, and $275 billion for "shovel-ready" public works. All these government subsidies, bailouts, and stimulus programs are part of the *Mqes* factor in the equation above, as this is cash money injected directly into the real economy to avoid recession and financial instability.

On the right side of the above equation, we have *Pnp, Pp,* and *Qnp, Qp,* which are the respective price and quantities of non-premium and premium products of the i-th transactions in economy pricing. Meanwhile, *Cqe* is the quantity of money received by commercial banks from the central bank through QE that has not been lent out and is sitting as cash in the banks' balance sheet. The higher the $\uparrow$*Cqe,* the lower the velocity, $\downarrow$*V,* of money in circulation. This means that banks' reserves have increased dramatically due to QE operations (infusion of $\uparrow$*Mqem*) but did not make them lend to the public as the public is afraid to borrow and spend. Once the recession is over and the economy starts to grow slowly, the QE program will start gradually decreasing until it stops completely. Therefore, Fisher's equation can be formulated as,

$$\uparrow (M) \uparrow Vt = \Sigma i(\uparrow Pnp\ Qnp + \uparrow Pp\ Qp) + \downarrow Cqe \qquad (5.5)$$

where *M* this time is the total amount of money in circulation on average in the economy during a given period without any money injection from the central bank, and *Vt* is the velocity of money which represent the average frequency across all transactions. On the right side, *Cqe* is still the quantity of money received by commercial banks from the central bank through QE that is decreasing (↓) as the banks have started to lend out loans to firms and the public. Meanwhile, *Pnp, Pp,* and Qnp (↑), Qp (↑) will be increasing as both premium and non-premium goods are in high demand after the recession, and therefore the velocity of money *Vt* (↑) will increase as well and consequently will increase the total amount of money in circulation given by *M*. Hence, from equations 5.4 and 5.5 we can see that the increase on the amount of money in circulation, *M*, and the increase on the velocity of money *Vt*, depends mostly on the capability of the public to borrow and then spend in premium and non-premium products and the ability of banks to keep enough cash in their balance sheet so they can lend out without compromising their financial health.

Monetary Policy and Low-Interest Rates

Monetary policy is the macroeconomic policy managed mostly by central banks. It involves the supervision of the money supply and interest rates. It is a powerful macroeconomic tool in the hands of a government of a country through the central bank to achieve macroeconomic objectives like controlling inflation, reducing liquidity, increase consumption and growth.

The objective of monetary policy is to preserve the value of money by keeping inflation low, stable, and predictable. This is achieved by actions such as changing the interest rate, buying or selling government bonds, regulating foreign exchange rates, and changing the amount of money banks are required to maintain as reserves. The government's actions through the central bank are focused on realizing the macroeconomic goals of the government. Many economists and researchers believe that if the supply of money is adequately regulated, it leads to favorable economic impact and stability. Therefore, it becomes necessary to regulate the circulation of money (Fullwiler, 2006).

Monetary policy could be formulated in different ways; however, it is based on inputs gathered from a variety of sources. The monetary authority that controls the monetary policy may look at macroeconomic numbers such as gross domestic product (GPD) and inflation, industry/sector growth rates, as well as geopolitical developments in international markets—including regional wars and tensions, oil embargos, and war trade tariffs with specific countries. Monetary authorities are normally given policy mandates from the government and parliaments to achieve stable GDP growth, keep inflation and unemployment rate low, and maintain foreign exchange at a predictable range. For example, the Federal Reserve (Fed) oversees monetary policy in the United States and has what is generally referred to as a "dual mandate," which consists of achieving maximum employment and keeping inflation at a stable range (Hallowell and Williamson,1961).

In addition, it is the Fed's responsibility to achieve stable economic growth and keep inflation in check and keep long-term interest rates relatively neutral.[1] The Fed's role is to be the lender of last resort, providing commercial banks with liquidity and regulatory inspection to prevent them from bankruptcy and panic spreading in the financial services sector and capital markets. It's interesting to highlight some of the factors that are relevant in understanding the role of monetary policy in an environment of low-interest rates and low inflation:

First, in the industrialized countries, there has been a trend decline in the fundamental equilibrium real interest rate since the 1980s. In general, the real equilibrium rate is the rate required to match the desired levels of saving and investment. The combination of different factors, such as low population growth, rising life expectancy, and an aging population, have acted through multiple channels to increase the desired savings and reduce desired investments. A decrease in desired investment impacts slower productivity growth and, possibly, shifts in the structure of the aggregate production function. During the global financial crisis of 2008-9, the risk increase provided a disincentive to invest, reinforced precautionary saving, and boosted a portfolio shift to less risky assets, such as sovereign bonds, etc.

Second, the financial crisis has also affected desired savings and desired investment levels. Many banks, firms, governments, and households have focused on repairing their balance sheets and have been cautiously careful when making investment decisions. The low equilibrium real interest rate has been compounded by weak nominal developments after the financial crisis of 2008. The global financial crisis has resulted in considerable changes in labor markets and relaxed capacity utilization. The post-crisis focus of many governments in industrialized countries has been on keeping a low unemployment rate, low-interest rates, steady inflation, and stable capacity utilization in the manufacturing sector.

In the post-crisis period of 2008, central banks focused on economic stabilization and adopted an accommodative monetary policy which has been mostly characterized since 2014 by a combination of conventional and unconventional monetary policies such as a-) a near zero or a negative policy rate; b-) a massive asset purchase program; c-) targeted longer-term refinancing

---

[1] In theory and in general, the *neutral interest rate* is the rate at which monetary policy is neither stimulating nor restricting economic growth.

operations (TLTRO); d-) forward guidance on the path of policy instruments. In addition, under conditions in which monetary policy rates may or may not be effective, fiscal measures have an especially powerful macroeconomic impact, both by providing stabilization in the event of adverse shocks and supporting the return of target inflation eventually.

It's interesting to mention that many consumers in developed economies are continuously hunting for sales promotions most of the time during the year. They more than welcome steady prices and low inflation. However, the problem is that low inflation means interest rates, on average, could remain low. Keeping interest low won't be of great help for central banks, as it diminishes the central banks' ability to fight recessions using its traditional tool, which is – cutting its target for the interest rate on overnight loans between banks (central bank funds rate). The difference between the central bank's funds rate and its effective lower bound (which is roughly zero or less) has been decreased. In fact, in the U.S.A., the Fed's monetary policy of the estimate of the neutral level of the federal funds rate, which is the interbank interest rate at which the monetary policy is neither contractionary nor expansionary, has decreased from 4.2 percent in January 2012 to less than 2.5 percent in June 2020, in the first year of the global pandemic crisis. However, the interest rate increased rapidly in 2022 to fight inflation due to the war in Ukraine and the increased price of raw materials.

The main monetary tool that, traditionally, the Fed and other central banks have at their disposition is the interest rate or the federal funds rate. Based on this tool, when the federal funds rate was above the effective lower bound, the Fed could reduce it to support the economy during downturns and recessions. However, this tool can be ineffective when the funds' rate neared its effective lower bound, as happened during the 2008-2009 recession. In this case, the Fed began using two new monetary tools—large-scale purchases of longer-maturity Treasury and government-backed mortgage securities (quantitative easing) and statements about its plans for short-term interest rates (forward guidance).

The main reason the Fed decided to use these two tools was to aim at putting downward pressure on long-term interest rates, such as mortgage rates and corporate bond rates. However, other central banks, differently from Fed, have arranged other tools such as pushing their short-term policy rates below zero, turning them into negative rates, and aiming rates on long-term maturity securities by committing to buy them at a predetermined price- yield-curve-control. The *Yield-Curve-Control* (YCC) is a monetary tool in the U.S. market that is intended to control interest rates along some portion of the yield curve. The yield curve is usually defined as the range of yields on Treasury securities from three-month Treasury bills to 30-year Treasury bonds. YCC may as well affect the long-term rates directly by imposing interest rate caps on maturities, such as those related to bonds. Given that bond prices and yields are inversely related, it will imply a price floor for targeted maturities. If bond prices of targeted maturities remain above (below) the floor, the central bank cannot do anything as the price of bonds is driven by strong bond demand. However, if bond prices fall (rise) below (above) the floor, the central bank will intervene by buying targeted-maturity bonds in order to increase the demand, which will increase the price of bonds.

During the first years of the pandemic-COVID-19 recession in 2020 and 2021 (before the start of the war in Ukraine, which led to a quick jump in inflation), some central banks, such as Fed in the U.S.A., resumed both large-scale securities purchases and forward guidance. The Fed's two possibilities consisted of changing its statutory maximum employment and price stability mandate, which means that Fed can raise or lower the two percent inflation target. However, the security purchases and forward guidance would remain key parts of the Fed's monetary strategy. In addition, many economists were doubtful about the usefulness of negative rates in the United States and weren't ready to adopt the yield-curve-control.

It is also a well-known fact that low inflation can threaten central banks' ability to fight recessions. Low inflation is a problem because it contributes to low-interest rates, which (because of the effective lower bound) reduce the scope for interest rate cuts. The two new instruments adopted by the Fed during the financial crisis—quantitative easing and forward guidance—were much faster and more effective in managing the financial crisis. These unconventional monetary policies should become a permanent part of central banks' new monetary strategy. To preserve unconventional monetary policy effectiveness, it is critically important for central banks to keep inflation and inflation expectations close to the target.

In a competitive market, inflation has become unresponsive to job market pressures which means that the Federal Reserve can get it wrong if they are on the side of pushing unemployment lower without risking an undesirable increase in inflation, despite the fact that it is unlikely to happen. On the other hand, lower inflation means interest rates keep staying lower, leaving the Fed and other central banks with fewer monetary tools and unable to cut rates in response to a weak economy. The low inflation in competitive markets because of competitive prices - as mentioned in chapter four - is mostly determined by managing the supply chain, which allows companies to be able to cut excess costs and deliver products to final consumers much faster. This is achieved by keeping tighter control of internal inventories, cost reduction, high efficiency on distribution process and warehousing, and indirect control on suppliers' inventories.

Since the financial crisis of 2008, growing globalization and global supply chain management have played an increased role in determining consumer price inflation in many countries. Better handling of globalization in inflation models will help improve forecasts and explain the growing gap between profits and the labor share of national income. Overall, while consumer price inflation is increasingly "determined abroad" and is mostly related to the global supply chain, wage inflation is still largely a domestic process.

In conclusion, we have that there are four major factors that have characterized a modern developed economy after the 2008 crisis: 1-) economy pricing (an increase of multi-product enterprises offering a variety of non-premium and premium products); 2-) low inflation; 3-) low unemployment; 4-) low-interest rates. Below is a discussion of these factors:

1-) We have seen that the economies of advanced countries have entered a new phase called "economy pricing," where most of the mass-produced non-premium products are sold at a discounted price during certain periods of the year, called sales events. The discounted prices are a result of decreased production costs thanks to technological progress, global supply chain efficiency, and low commercial barriers.

2-) Industrialized countries in recent years have had steady inflation due to the mass production of non-premium products that had kept the price of non-premium goods low and guaranteed affordable prices. In fact, technological progress in different sectors tends to increase productivity, lowers the rate of wage growth relative to productivity and, as a result, delay rising inflation. The continued introduction of technological innovation in the industry serves as a complement to the workforce, and the influence of deflation is straightforward. Higher productivity and efficient management of the global supply chain in the manufacturing sector has translated directly into lower production costs and steady inflation.

3-) The unemployment stays low as the firms in need of reaching production capacity utilization of 70 or 80 percent are deemed to cover total variable and fixed costs and are required to sell more non-premium goods during promotion sales events than premium goods. This means that firms have to commit a larger amount of labor, mostly in the forms of hourly wage employees at minimum wage (or above minimum wage) than salaried employees, to manufacture the category of non-premium products. This widespread non-premium phenomenon decreases the rate of unemployment in addition to increased service-oriented sectors.

4-) In the post-crisis period of 2008, most of the central banks focused on economic stabilization and adopted an accommodative monetary policy that low borrowing costs have typically characterized. There is a combination of conventional and unconventional monetary policies, such as a near zero or a negative policy rate, massive large-asset purchases of long-maturity treasury securities, and purchases of government-backed mortgage securities and other financial security programs.

Should Central Banks be Independent?

The idea of central bank independence at the dawn of the twentieth century meant, above all, independence from direction by the short-term concerns and interference of politicians. Instead, central bankers would be allowed to set an independent monetary policy on bringing down inflation and installing a regime of confidence in monetary stability of what is called 'anchoring price expectations.' The central bank was given independence from the executive and legislative branches. With money's value changing value quickly because of the collapse of the Bretton Woods system and the withdrawal of convertibility of gold into U.S. dollars in the early 1970s, independent central banks became the guardians of inflation and price stability. The ending role of gold as a liquid dollar claim and the end of the unified fixed exchange rate regime from 1968 through 1973 emphasized even further the independence of the central banks.

There are **advantages** and **disadvantages** to having an independent central bank. Having an independent central bank clearly has many advantages. Some of the **advantages** can be listed below:

1-) **Deficit spending**: a considerably large number of Governments (if not all) are affectionate in undertaking big projects even though such projects may not be completely supported by economic fundamentals. The big projects consist of building large-scale roads, highways, bridges, railways, ports, airports, subways, schools, hospitals, airbases, military installations, etc. In this case, the government should not have pampered with deficit spending, but it did, as it could not cover large expenses with tax revenues. These occurrences and future commitments to invest more in large projects would become more common if the government had full control of the monetary policy. Governments have the capability to issue bonds to match their deficit, which can be bought by central banks through open market operations. The bonds issued by the government can increase the level of public debt and debt service (interest payments on the debt issuance). However, deficit spending can be consistent with public debt remaining stable as a proportion of GDP (Gross Domestic Product) as long as the level of GDP steadily grows.

2-) **Inflation**: Controlling inflation is the primary objective of any central bank. One way to control it is the need to control the money spent by the government. If the governments can make decisions regarding public spending in the economy, they will tend to spend more money than they could cover from taxes. For example, governments may increase public spending by providing free health care, childcare benefits, and retirement benefits despite the fact that they don't have the financial resources to implement such decisions. This makes us think that governments will lead to use the popular option of money printing to finance deficit spending, which will ultimately lead to higher inflation than expected and, eventually, economic recession. Hence, in industrialized countries, to prevent this, central banks have been made independent of government authority.

3-) **Business cycle and political cycle**: business cycle operates in a completely different way from the political cycle, which is based on an election every 4-5 years. The business normally operates based on business cycles. The periods of boom and recession in the economy do not coincide with the political cycles and elections. Politicians may be easily influenced during election years and try to have popular decisions. For example, if in one election year, there is much more inflation than in a normal year, they might be tempted to skip the necessary decision to raise the interest rates to fight the inflation as a central bank would do in similar conditions. Therefore, it is possible that politicians will not act properly or delay the decisions regarding monetary policy in improving the economy during election years if the monetary decisions are unpopular. This is another reason why the central bank needs to be independent. Usually, central banks can make tough and unpopular decisions regardless of the election cycle. The monetary policy and elections are not naturally correlated. Therefore, it is better that the decisions regarding the economy be taken independently

Separating the central bank and monetary policy from the government has many advantages that have been listed above. However, there are some **disadvantages** as well that are listed below:

1-) **Secretive**: The biggest criticism against the independence of central banks is that their operations are very reserved and reticent. There is no opening to the public regarding the central banks' meetings. Quite often, their actions and decisions are completely unexpected and hard to predict by financial analysts and business operators. It is believed that some financial crises in some countries have taken place because the central bank took unexpected actions. To prevent this from happening, central banks need to ensure that their decisions are transparent and based on economic logic. Their policies should not be secretive but rather transparent to the government, stakeholders, the public, and professional experts in finance.

2-) **In Favor of big banks and big corporations**: There is reason to believe that all the policies and actions taken by central banks are in favor of large corporations and big banks and not in favor of the small businesses and common people. For example, the main central bank's goal is to reduce inflation. However, after the 2008 financial crash, the central banks used the policy of quantitative easing to save mostly the big banks and big corporations from going bankrupt, with a high risk of creating inflation.

3-) **Concerns over the independence of central banks.** A well-known central bank like the ECB has been continuously criticized for projecting too rigidly the target of low inflation when the biggest problem in Europe was unemployment which has a higher rate than the U.S.A., and low economic growth. There are concerns about the wider impact of monetary policy by central banks, which could impact low-interest rates on the distribution of income between savers and borrowers. The main fear of a central bank, 'inflation,' was no longer a major issue for many years for ECB, at least until the global pandemic of 2020 and the war in Ukraine of 2022 hit the real economy. Instead, a major issue in recent decades has been stagnation and the prolonged liquidity trap.

As we can see, there are pros as well as cons to having independent central banks. There is a widespread general opinion that advantages could outnumbering disadvantages. The independence of the central bank has been widely regarded as better than the alternative, and this is why many central banks across the world have witnessed increased autonomy. However, the typical monetary model assumed that political parties were fiscally irresponsible regarding monetary policies and thus needed independent central banks to bring more responsibility in managing money and debt. It turns out that in recent decades, we have not seen a persistent increase in debt but rather repeated efforts to control debt and be monetary and fiscally responsible in main developed areas such as the Eurozone, Australia, the U.K., Canada, Japan, and the U.S.

The interpretation of models of the independent central bank in the 1970s, 1980s, and 1990s was nothing more than a mere partial interpretation of the financial reality at the beginning of the twenty-first century. Many of the independent central bank theories have become recently obsolete due to the new monetary reality. In fact, in the last two-three decades, the inflation and unemployment rate in industrialized countries have been stable. Central banks of major industrialized countries that once were putting up a fight against inflation were struggling to keep inflation at two percent and avoid deflation until the supply chain disruptions due to COVID19-pandemic and war in Ukraine changed everything during 2021-2023.

Most of the central banks have started bond purchases to flush the credit system with liquidity to stimulate demand and raise inflation. The low inflation and low unemployment rate came as a result of the remarkable efficiency gains achieved through globalization, technological progress, and the vast pool of new workers who were attracted to the world economy through the integration of China, Korea, Taiwan, Vietnam, and other Asian export economies, and the weakening of trade unions, to which the anti-inflation campaigns, deindustrialization, and high unemployment of the 1970s and 1980s powerfully contributed.

So, now the question is: do we still need an independent central bank? Or What a new central bank would look like?

In a new monetary reality dominated by economy pricing with low inflation, low-interest rate, and low unemployment, I would recommend having a more transparent and limited process controlled by administrative orders between treasury departments and central banks. This should reduce or abolish the concept of the central bank as being the 'lender of last resort' and eliminate central banks' ties to large financial corporations. The new process of administrative orders between the treasury department and central banks would empower voters to exercise greater control over the political fortunes of such a process by allowing the central banks to collaborate with governments under the control of a democratic process. In fact, I suggest that the newly transformed central bank should be called the '*National Monetary Authority*' or simply '*Monetary Authority*' with shared administrative orders with the treasury department under government supervision and being transparent to the public regarding monetary policies. The '*Monetary Authority*' should not be independent but rather have shared monetary policies and responsibilities with the treasury department under government supervision and ultimately report to the national parliament for major changes in monetary policy.

New Central Bank Rules: The Solvency Rule Curve

Central banks, for the most part, in the past, have conducted monetary policies by adjusting the short-term nominal interest rates in response to various shocks, using the money stock as the main indicator. Taylor (1993) proposed a simple interest rule based on two variables. The first variable is the nominal interest rate which can rise more than one-for-one with inflation so that the real rate increases when inflation rises, and the second variable is the interest rate, to fall when output is below normal and rise when output is above normal. Taylor's rule was designed to be linear in inflation and in the percentage departure of output from its natural rate. The classic representation of Taylor's rule is written in a simplified form:

$$It - \pi t = r^* + a(\pi t - \pi t^*) + b(\ln Yt - \ln Yt^*) \qquad (5.6)$$

Where It is the target short-term nominal interest rate, πt is the inflation, πt^* is the desired rate of inflation, r^* is the assumed equilibrium rate of interest, and Yt is the real output, Yt^* is the logarithm of the potential output, a is the coefficient on inflation and b is the coefficient related to output. The Taylor rule says that with coefficients a=b=0.5, the central bank should raise the interest rate above its long-run equilibrium level in response to inflation exceeding its target and to output exceeding its natural rate. The Taylor rule was based on the principle that an increase in inflation by one percentage point would push the central bank to raise the nominal interest rate by more than one percentage point.

During the financial crisis of 2008, other alternative rules to the Taylor equation were created. One of them is called the *Solvency rule,* which was based on the insolvency of the system. The new perspective on the solvency rule presented by Brancaccio and Fontana (2011 and 2015) after the financial crises of 2008 states that a central banker follows a new 'rule' which is aimed at controlling the solvency conditions in the economic system rather than altering interest rates due to the changes in the economy. Because of this rule, the inflation target and, eventually, the output gap are neglected. Regarding the interest rate, we assume that the interest rate is kept low and is conditioned by the solvency of workers and firms that represent financial stability in the system. Differently from the Taylor rule, the solvency rule represents more a benchmark than a mechanical formula.

As we know, the interest rate fell close to zero during the financial crisis of 2008-9 and then again during the first year (2020) of the global COVID-19 pandemic of 2020-2021, where central banks made heavy use of unconventional tools such as "quantitative easing" (QE) to boost the economy. Quantity easing

(QE) was mostly based on the logic of buying bonds, mortgage-backed securities, treasury notes, and other assets to inject money into the financial system. The bond purchases helped lower longer-term interest rates as debt soared, especially government debt. The large number of government bonds purchased by central banks as part of the QE program helped set the price for most private debt, maintained a certain level of stimulus in the economy, and tried to exert downward pressure on interest rates.

However, neither the money supply nor private sector credit grew more quickly, and what is most important, it did not ignite money supply growth, despite banks having access to large amounts of liquidity. For the most part, banks did not use cash injections to increase lending but rather repaired their balance sheets. It was hard to determine whether injected money was spent on GDP or existing assets, like securities, stocks, or real estate. But if QE did not cause faster GDP growth, neither did it fuel inflation.

The quantitative easing policies undertaken by the central banks of the major developed countries since the beginning of 2008 have contributed to the reduction of systemic risk following the bankruptcy of Lehman Brothers. The QE, especially in the U.S., have contributed to 1) Lower interest rates for corporate bonds and mortgage rates; 2) stabilized stock market valuation in terms of price-earnings ratio; 3) Increased confidence in investor's expectations for a steady return on their investments; 4) stabilize the job market; and 5) a slow but steady GDP growth.

The QE is composed of different programs used by central banks as they need them. For example, the Central Bank of Canada (BoC), during the first year of the pandemic crisis of 2020-2021, before the war in Ukraine started in 2022, and inflation spiked up, used the following QE programs: i) The Commercial Paper Purchase Program (CPPP), ii) Contingent Term Repo Facility (CTRF), iii) Provincial Bond Purchase Program (PBPP), iv) Term repo operations and v) Corporate Bond Purchasing Program (CBPP). All these QE programs added assets to the BoC and, at the same time, injected a large amount of liquidity into the market. Selling these BoC's assets would mean removing liquidity from the market

If the short-term nominal interest rates are kept continuously close to zero, and the inflation rate is below the inflation target due to the economy pricing and the efficiency of the global supply chain, the new role of the central bank is to decide how and when to support the market liquidity. The central bank can support the market liquidity by using the QE tool and by following the new solvency 'rule,' which is aimed at controlling the solvency conditions in the economic system till the commercial banks increase their lending to public and firms are able to borrow again after repairing their balance sheets and aim to have positive expectations on their investment returns. Therefore, the solvency rule or the new representation of the central bank's rule is presented as follows:

$$Bqe' = r' + a(\pi t - \pi t^*) + b(\ln Yt - \ln Yt^*) + c(Lt - Lt^*) \qquad (5.7)$$

where *Bqe* is the quantitative easing" (QE) to boost the economy by buying bonds, mortgages-backed securities, and other assets to inject money into the financial system, *Yt* is the real level of output, *Yt** is the desired level of output, *Lt* is the real bank lending to the public, *Lt** is the desired bank lending to the public, *r'* is the interest rate, *πt* is the real inflation below the inflation target, and *πt** is the desired inflation target. The central bank's new solvency rule during and after the financial crisis has its intention to control the solvency condition of commercial banks and big corporations rather than interest rates. Interest rates will automatically be set low as soon as a downturn or a financial crisis hits the economy to protect the solvency of workers, families, and firms and stabilize the system. With the new central bank's solvency rule, interest rate, inflation, and the output gap are all ignored to give room to money injection into the system through QE to stabilize it.

The QE will continue until financial stability has been reached, commercial banks and large and medium corporations have repaired their balance sheets, and private firms and the public have reached confidence to start borrowing again. The QE will be gradually reduced or stopped when the desired bank lending to the public, *Lt**, is reached despite the fact that the inflation might not have yet hit the inflation target. The relationship between the central bank's rule of QE and the commercial bank-lending-to-public, *Lt,* is illustrated in Figure 5.1 in the form of L shape curve.

At the beginning of the economic downturn, such as the financial crisis of 2008 and the global pandemic of 2020-22, the central bank's monetary strategy was to set interbank interest rates close to zero and start the Quantity Easing (QE) by buying bonds, mortgages-backed securities, Treasury notes, and other assets to inject money into the financial system. This monetary policy was supposed to help the central bank increase the size of the balance sheet through an increase in its monetary liabilities (base money), holding constant the composition of its assets. There is a shift in the composition of the assets of the central bank towards less liquid and riskier assets, holding constant the size of the balance sheet. The less liquid and more risky assets can be private securities and bonds, as well as sovereign or sovereign-guaranteed instruments such as treasury notes, government bonds, and other assets.

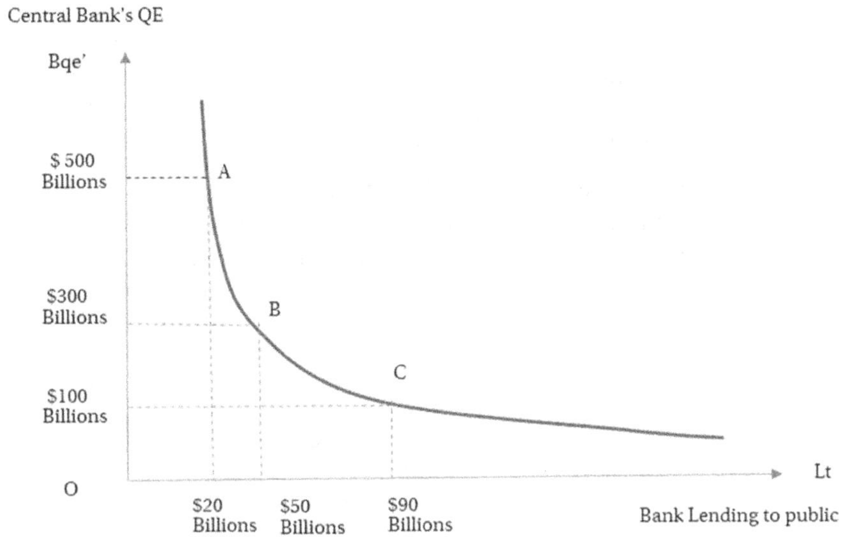

Figure 5.1 Central Bank's new solvency rule curve

As illustrated in Figure 5.1, the new solvency rule curve shows that at the peak of the financial crisis at point A, the central bank purchased about $500 billion dollars per quarter of private security assets and bonds. The bank-lending-to-public is, at minimum, at around $20 billion dollars, as the public and private firms are not ready to borrow money from banks, despite interest rates being kept close to zero (benchmark interest rate is at 0.25 percent) and inflation is very low. As the financial crisis gradually winds down, the QE moves from point A to point B, with purchases at about $300 billion per quarter (from $500 billion), and again the QE moves from point B to C, with purchases at about $100 billion per quarter and the confidence in public start increasing as firm's balance sheets are repaired. Thus, bank lending to the public increases from $20 billion in appoint A to $50 billion in point B and reaches $90 billion in point C.

The central bank's solvency rule, demonstrated in Figure 5.1, does not take into consideration inflation and interest rates as they are at a minimum during an economic downturn and do have little impact on stimulating the economy. The central bank could slow the pace of QE to a pace that keeps the desired level of a stimulus rather than trying to use extra downward pressure on interest rates. This could easily be done by reinvesting the proceeds of maturing assets rather than creating yet more money to buy security assets.

In addition to QE, the central bank also controls the commercial banks' reserve requirement, which consists of how much of their funds they're required to keep as monetary reserve compared to what they lend out to the public. Lowering the reserve helps the commercial banks lend out more of their money, which increases the supply of money, and in return, allows interest rates to fall. Lower interest rates are an incentive for people to borrow and spend to stimulate the economy in addition to market confidence, build-up savings, and increase balance sheet repairs.

The Central banks in many industrialized nations, such as the U.S., the U.K., Canada, Japan, and the Eurozone, are barred from buying government debt directly from their own governments and allow the governments to run large budget deficits. Instead can buy government bonds from other companies and investment funds that hold government debt in the secondary market. There is a two-phase process; first, the government sells bonds to private entities, and second, the private entities, in return, sell them to the central bank. By doing so, the central bank does what is called "monetizing the debt" and indirectly helps government hold large public debt.

There is a difference between the QE and money creation that is normally understood as "money printing." The term *printing money* typically indicates the newly created money by a central bank to directly buy government bonds to finance government deficits or pay off government debt. Instead, the original idea of QE, especially during the 2008-9 financial crisis, was to use the newly created money to buy financial assets such as long-term securities and mortgage-backed securities other than government bonds. In addition, the central bank could also "sterilize" government bond purchases by paying interest to banks for reserve deposits. This monetary policy tool (QE) will remove the domestic currency from circulation previously injected by the purchase of government bonds. The net effect of this tool is to raise bond prices, lowering borrowing rates for mortgages and other loans, blocking eventually inflationary increase in the money supply. An indirect effect of QE is also to lower rates on sovereign bonds.

The distinctive characteristic between the two monetary policy tools - the QE and debt monetization - is that with the former, the central bank creates money to stimulate the economy and not to finance government spending. Also, a central bank has the final objective of reversing the QE once the economy has recovered from the financial crisis by selling government bonds and other financial assets back into the secondary market.

Interrelation between the Treasury and Central Bank

There are significant differences between the role of the central bank and the treasury. The main role of a central bank is to provide banking services for commercial banks and lend money to banks, taking assets as collateral. Many industrialized countries have implemented specific reforms designed to grant their monetary authorities greater independence from their government and direct political influence. The Central bank independence is normally guaranteed by legislation and the institutional framework that govern the bank's affiliation with elected officials, in most cases with the minister of finance. Central bank legislation consists of specific procedures for selecting and appointing the head of the central bank. Usually, the minister of finance will appoint the new governor in consultation with the central bank's board and the existing governor. The central bank legislation specifies the banks' governor's term of appointment. A substantial number of independent central banks have in their legislation a 3-5 years fixed non-renewable term for the governor of the central bank. In return for their independence, the central bank, as per its legislation, is regularly accountable at some level to government officials, either to the Ministry of Finance or to Parliament. For example, in the U.S.A., the Board of Governors of the U.S. Federal Reserve is nominated by the U.S. President and confirmed by the U.S. Senate. In the same way, in the European Monetary Union, the European Central Bank (ECB) is primarily accountable to the European Parliament as the representation of EU citizens but also must regularly report to the Council of the EU, which represents Member State governments, as reflected in the Statute of the ECB.

Differently from a central bank, Treasury is an institution that is considered a government body that manages the government's money where the government has its bank account into which the government deposits its receipts (tax revenues primarily) and the account from which it pays its obligations such as disbursing money for different government project (like building schools, hospitals, roads, bridges, etc.), paying employee salaries, buying goods and services from the private sector, etc. The Department of Treasury in many countries is part of the Ministry of Finance under total control of the central government.

The Department of the Treasury usually manages government spending. It collects the government's tax revenues, distributes its budget, issues its bonds, bills, and notes, and basically, in some countries, it authorizes printing the money. In general, the Treasury Department is led by a Cabinet-level appointee who advises the president or the head of the state on monetary and economic policy. In many developed countries, the Treasury does not have the authority to create money, as that's the responsibility of the central bank. However, the treasury takes revenues such as taxes, borrows additional money as necessary, and pays out the government's obligations.

The treasury department also has a specific department that could enforce tax law, such as the *Canadian Revenue Agency* (CRA) in Canada, the *Internal Revenue Service* (IRS) in the U.S., the *HM Revenue and Taxes* (HMRC) in the

U.K., etc. There's no direct relationship between Central Bank and Treasury. As part of a government body, the Treasury regularly supervises either directly or indirectly the central bank's actions. Often the central bank will serve as a "deposit banker" for the Treasury; that is, the government's bank account will be kept at the central bank. This means that the central bank is responsible for accepting and making payments on behalf of the Treasury (Lavoie, 2013).

In the U.S., as in many industrialized countries, the Department of the Treasury and Central Bank work together to preserve a stable and solvent economy. The central bank usually serves as the government's banker, processing transactions for the treasury. These transactions include accepting electronic payments for taxes, issuing payroll checks to government employees, and clearing checks for tax payments and other government receivables. Another important function is that the central bank and the treasury work together to borrow money when the government needs to raise cash (Wray, 2012).

The central bank often operates treasury securities auctions on behalf of the Treasury for securities such as Treasury Notes, Treasury Bills, Treasury Bonds, and Treasury Inflation-protected securities (TIPS), Treasury Floating Rates Notes (FRN). The central bank operates as an independent non-profit entity. However, it creates a profit. After its expenses are paid, the remaining profits are paid to the Treasury, which uses that money to fund government spending.

The central bank in developed countries, by legislation, is not allowed to buy treasury securities directly but rather indirectly in the secondary market. This makes the central bank typically one of the largest, if not the largest, buyers of the Treasury's debt (treasury securities). Given that the central bank is the largest buyer of government bonds, it has a central role in setting interest rates for the government and interest rates for the economy at large. The central bank uses as a benchmark the interest rate on Treasury debt, which is then filtered down to the rest of the banking system. In addition, the central bank has an enormous role in determining how much the government can borrow and if the government debt is sustainable in the long term. If the central bank does not agree to buy large amounts of government debt, then the treasury must collect more taxes to offset the government spending not covered by government bonds.

The central bank is also responsible for managing the nation's currency and, in many cases (but not always), is the issuer of the currency that the Treasury accepts for tax receivable and pays its own obligations to other entities. Therefore, the central bank can affect the value of that currency – by devaluating or evaluating it - and therefore affect the value of Treasury debt relative to other assets. A stylized central bank balance sheet is illustrated in Figure 5.2

Liabilities	Assets
Banknotes (monetary base)-L1	Government balances and government Treasuries-A1
Commercial Bank Reserves- L2	Foreign Assets (net)-A2
Liabilities held by Treasury -L3	Central Bank Operations (net)-A3
Capital and Reserve – L4	Other assets -A4

Figure 5.2 Stylised Central Bank Balance Sheet

Each component of the central bank's balance sheet, made of liabilities and assets, has an important role in the operation of the central bank, treasury, and the wider economy. The banknotes-L1 (also named liability L1) are the liabilities issued by the central bank that is in circulation and held by the public and by commercial banks. Normally, banknotes enter circulation through commercial banks, which draw down banknotes in exchange for reserve balances held at the central bank. The private sector and the wider population obtain banknotes through direct withdrawals from commercial banks or agents.

Commercial bank reserves (L2) are overnight balances that banks hold in an account at the central bank, which are considered a claim on the central bank. Banknotes and commercial bank reserves are considered the most liquid, risk-free assets in the economy (Gray, 2011). The safest way that commercial banks can independently reduce the total quantity of reserves in the system is by exchanging reserves with banknotes. Central banks, on the other side, must impose reserve requirements on commercial banks that hold reserve accounts with them. Nowadays, there are at least five roles for reserve requirements at the central bank: monetary policy purposes, liquidity management purposes, structural liquidity purposes, central bank revenue purposes, and sectorial behavior purposes (Bindseil, 2004).

Liabilities held by the treasury (L3) are the outstanding amount of the central bank notes (Federal notes in the U.S.) and the central bank accounts held by the Treasury. Like private corporations in the private sector, central banks are required to have capital and reserves as well. Like in the private sector, central banks carry capital on the balance sheets and capital buffer (net worth calculated as the difference between the value of total assets and total liabilities), which is used in the channel in which the central bank absorbs losses.

Government assets such as U.S. Treasuries (A1) are assets held at the central bank by the government and denominated in domestic currency. Regarding foreign assets (A2) held by central banks, we have that this category of assets is denominated in a non-domestic currency. Central banks usually hold foreign reserves for a variety of purposes, such as intervention in the FX market, the necessity to meet external obligations on foreign currency debt, and, eventually, to cover trade balances. Regarding the Central Bank Operations, there is frequently a unique category of reserves consistent with the central bank's achievement of its desired operational target and ensures that payment can be made between commercial banks. In fact, it is through central bank operations that the central bank can control the availability of reserves to the system.

Putting in an accounting perspective, operations that provide reserves to commercial banks will show as *assets* of the central bank; meanwhile, operations that reduce the total of reserves held by the commercial banks will show as *liabilities*. Other assets (A4) of the central bank are those items that cover other elements of the central bank's balance sheet, such as investments in portfolios and property. The balance sheet of the central bank must balance all the time, and based on the assets and liabilities illustrated in Figure 5.2, we have that:

$$L1 = A1 + A2 + A3 + A4 - L2 - L3 - L4 \quad (5.7)$$

In the central bank's balance sheet, the monetary base L1 is equal to the total assets A1, A2, and A3 minus the total liabilities L2, L3, and L4. The central bank also acts as a banker for the central government in addition to maintaining balances for the commercial banks. The government deposit funds at the central bank are housed under liabilities and are like the reserve accounts, despite being treated in a different way as they are not subject to reserve requirements and are not remunerated. The government deposits at the central bank fluctuate continuously. In fact, when the government, due to the fiscal policy, increases its balance at the central bank through collecting taxes or issuing debt, it does at the expense of the commercial banks. If the government reduces its balance through expenditure, investments in infrastructure, or paying salaries, it does so by increasing the reserves available to commercial banks.

There are also situations when government spending is not financed by taxation, debt sales, or borrowing but rather by the central bank, which lends to the government to offset the deficit in the fiscal account. By operating in this manner, the central bank credits the reserve accounts of commercial banks with reserves in lieu of funds from the government. The offsetting asset in the central bank is an accounting entry that is due to the central bank from the government. The central bank, in this way, has directly financed the government. However, many industrialized countries have legislations in place that prohibit the direct financing of government debt by central banks. Central banks are permitted to purchase government debt in secondary markets for other policy purposes.

Regarding the treasury's balance sheet, we have that it shows the government's assets, liabilities, and net position, which is a representation of a more comprehensive understanding of the government's financial position. Government assets included on the Balance Sheets are resources of the government available to meet future needs. Some of these assets reported in the Balance Sheets are cash, loans receivable, PP&E net (plant-property and equipment), inventories, and other monetary assets.

There are also other resources available to the government that goes beyond the standard assets presented in these Balance Sheets, which include government lands and Heritage Assets, in addition to the government's sovereign powers to tax and set monetary policy. Regarding government liabilities, they consist of government obligations resulting from past actions that demand financial resources. Some of the common government liabilities reported on the balance sheet are government debt securities held by the public and accrued interest, government employee benefits payable, environmental and disposal liabilities, loan guarantee liabilities, benefits due and other payables, contingencies, and other commitments. Figure 5.3. below illustrates a stylized condensed government balance sheet with all the assets and liabilities by each item and category.

Government Balance Sheet	
Assets (by category)	**Liabilities (by category)**
Cash and Monetary assets	Accounts payable
Accounts and taxes receivable, net	Government debt securities held by the public and accrued interest
Loans receivable, net	Government employee benefits payable
Inventories and related property, net	Environmental and disposal liabilities
Property, plant, and equipment, net	Insurance and guarantee program liabilities
Debt and equity securities	Loan guarantee liabilities
Investments in government-sponsored enterprises	Other liabilities
Other assets	
Total assets	**Total liabilities**
Stewardship of land and heritage assets	Contingencies and Commitments
	Net position
	Funds from Dedicated Collections
	Funds other than those from Dedicated Collections
	Total net position
	Total liabilities and net position

Figure 5.3 Stylised Government-Treasury Condensed Balance Sheet

As reported in the government balance sheet, the government's responsibilities, policy commitments, and contingencies are part of the total government liabilities, and they include different classes of social insurance programs, long-term fiscal projections, and a wide range of other programs under which the government is supposed to provide benefits and services to the public, especially to the category of underprivileged people. As seen in the chart above, at the end of the treasury balance sheet is the *Net-Position* line, which is the residual difference between assets and liabilities, and represents the cumulative results of operations since the beginning. The second-last line is called the *Total-Net-Position* and is the sum of the *Net-Position* line and funds from dedicated and non-dedicated collections.

Whenever the treasury collects taxes and other revenue, it credits them to the corresponding funds from dedicated collections that will be used to meet a government purpose. If the collections of taxes and other sources of receivables exceed the payments to the treasury beneficiaries, the excess revenue is invested in Treasury securities or deposited in the *General Fund*, which is eventually held at the central bank. The government has exclusive access to financial resources due to its sovereign power to tax and borrow through generating tax revenues and issuing treasury debt securities in the secondary market, which are purchased by private entities and by the central bank as well. The central bank, through the holding of Government balances and government Treasuries in its assets (A1 category), is one of the biggest sources of financing indirectly treasury and national government programs.

From Central Bank to National Monetary Authority

The central bank has not always been an independent entity. Looking back to historical facts in the U.S. during the eighteenth-nineteenth century, looking at the early years of the U.S. monetary system, we could see the government's fiscal and monetary operations were much simpler. At that time, the U.S. did not have a central bank, no primary market, and no debt limit. When the government decided to spend, it issued its own securities (legal tender notes) to the public, promising to take the notes back when tax payments from public and private firms were due. A *Legal Tender Note* was nothing more than good money used for payment of a debt that was recognized by the government or the law of the land.

The U.S. Congress, at the beginning of the twentieth century, developed the *Federal Reserve Act* or the Federal Reserve System, the central banking system of the United States to increase the economic stability in the United States by introducing a central bank that was able to oversee monetary policy and given power over the money supply in the country's wide economic base. In fact, by December 23, 1913, American President Woodrow Wilson signed the *Federal Reserve Act* into law, which created a decentralized central bank meant to balance the interests of private banks, private corporations, and the general public with no interference from the central government and politics (Meulendyke, 1998).

The U.S. Treasury was able to inject into the system unconvertible bills for government expenditure and then withdraw the bill (legal tender notes) when taxes came due. Hence, it is forthright to believe that the funding capacity of the government was not limited to taxes that the public owns, and taxes were not intended to be a funding mechanism. Tax liabilities were a fiscal tool created by a government to generate a demand for a desired currency (such as coins or bills) until taxes were paid to the government and bills drained out of the economy and confirming the expectations of the population about taxes (Tymoigne, 2014). Taxes will make the population willing to accept the government's legal tender notes in payment for goods and services.

Prior to the existence of the Federal Reserve System in the United States, the Treasury carried out many monetary functions. After the creation of the Central Bank, the Treasury has often been deeply involved in monetary functions, especially during the earlier years. Later, in March 1951, there was an agreement between the Treasury and the U.S. Federal Reserve System, known as *Treasury-Federal Reserve Accord*, where the central bank was no longer required to support the securities market at any level. In effect, the 1951 accord established that the Central Bank would act independently and exercise its own judgment as to the most appropriate monetary policy.

The accord re-established the Federal Reserve's independence and paved the way for the Fed's control of monetary policy as the nation's central bank. The Fed will manage the money supply and influences interest rates. However, the central bank was required to work closely with the Treasury and would be fully informed of the Treasury's needs in managing and financing the public debt. The Fed in the United States is in constant contact with the Treasury Department, which, among other things, is responsible for the management of the public debt and its various cash accounts.

The 2008-2009 global financial crisis and the evolution of the economy pricing system have changed how monetary policy is done and how the central bank manages the money supply. The low inflation rate, low-interest rates, and low unemployment rate have left central banks with very few monetary policy tools and significantly reduced their independence. The standard central bank monetary policies of buying and selling government bonds on the open market to reach a desired target for the interbank interest rate have not given the expected results.

Technically, suppose the recession continues even when a central bank has lowered interest rates to nearly zero. In that case, the central bank can no longer lower interest rates but can use an unconventional monetary tool which is quantitative easing (QE), to buy financial assets without reference to interest rates. In fact, by using quantitative easing, the central bank can buy financial assets and securities from commercial banks and other financial institutions, which helps raise the price of those financial assets and lower their yield while simultaneously increasing the money supply. This unconventional monetary tool (QE) contrasts with conventional open-market operations, as it involves the purchase of more risky assets than government bonds at a large scale over a pre-determined period.

Hence, the amalgamation of the central bank and the Treasury into one government sector or the creation of a national monetary authority inside the government sector can be done without a loss of overview for sovereign monetary policy, especially if the Treasury is required to tax the public and issue government bonds to fund itself.

What is the role of the proposed **National Monetary Authority**?

The role of the new "National Monetary Authority" is to have shared administrative orders with the treasury department under government supervision and be transparent to the public regarding monetary policies. For simplicity, the "National Monetary Authority" (NMA) will be called "Monetary Authority" (MA). The new 'Monetary Authority' should not be independent but moderately a separate government entity under government supervision and have shared monetary policies and responsibilities with the treasury department. The Monetary Authority (MA) will be focused on increasing its holding of government treasuries mostly on the secondary market rather than on the primary market. It will still be indirectly involved in Treasury funding through three classic channels:

First, the Monetary Authority (MA) will still be able to finance the primary dealers that participate in the treasury's auctions. Through this channel, the MA will accept treasuries as collateral for repurchase agreements (repos)[2] or by buying treasuries outright. The commercial banks will directly buy government treasuries in the open-market operations, and the MA will guarantee that there are enough reserves and supply the commercial banks with temporary repos, which is a matched purchase of treasury security debt with the requirement to repurchase later. Commercial banks will normally use these agreements to finance the purchase of government debt securities or other investments in the open market. The MA will then repurchase the debt securities from commercial

---

[2] The standard definition of a *Repurchase Agreement*, which is usually called, '*repo*,' is a form of short-term borrowing for dealers in government securities. A repo is created when a dealer sells government securities to investors, usually on an overnight basis, and buys them back the following day at a slightly higher price. The difference in price is nothing more than the implicit overnight interest rate. Repos are basically used to raise short-term capital. The repos are also a standard tool used by central bank in open market operations.

banks at a discount rate, called the *repo rate.* These *repo rates,* like *prime rates,* will be set by the national Monetary Authority and supervised by the government. The repurchase agreements are strictly short-term investments with a maturity period based on the *repo rate.*

Second, the National Monetary Authority will still be actively involved in setting the yield curve of treasuries by focusing on the short end of the curve and influencing expectations about future short-term rates. The yield curve can also be set by buying and selling long-term treasuries in the secondary market.

Third, the Monetary Authority will still be a major player in the primary and secondary market because it buys new Treasury securities (treasuries) to replace their maturing Treasury securities, which helps to ensure that the refinancing of the Treasury goes well as planned. Treasury securities are debt obligations issued by the U.S. Department of the Treasury to finance government spending as an alternative to taxation. Treasury securities include Treasury bills, notes, and bonds.

The repo rate system will still be a major tool Monetary Authority uses in open market operations to control the money supply within an economy by increasing or decreasing available funds. On the one hand, a decrease in repo rates will encourage commercial banks to sell securities back to the Monetary Authority in return for cash which will increase the money supply available to the general economy. On the other hand, by increasing repo rates, the Monetary Authority will be able to decrease the money supply by discouraging banks from reselling these securities.

Other functions of the National Monetary Authority would still include the issue of money, lender of last resort to commercial banks, lender of last resort to government, the set of reserves requirement for commercial banks, quantity easing, etc. Let's analyze some of them in more detail.

- **Issue of money**: the new Monetary Authority will still have responsibility for issuing notes and coins based on the money demand that will be used by commercial banks and the entire private sector in the economy.
- **Lender of last resort to commercial banks**: The Monetary Authority will have the capability to lend sufficient funds to commercial banks to avoid liquidity shortages and financial crises. This will help maintain confidence in the whole banking system and the private sector as well.
- **Set reserve requirements**: This is the amount of cash that the regulated commercial banks must have on hand each night. The Monetary

Authority will continue to use this monetary tool to control how much banks can lend.

- **Custody and Management of Foreign Exchange Reserves:** Another function of the Monetary Authority (MA) should be the management of the foreign exchange reserves of the country. It should be the official custodian of gold and foreign currencies. The MA should be able to sell gold at fixed prices to the monetary authorities of other countries and buy and sell foreign currencies at international prices. In countries where a fixed-exchange-rate regime exists, the role of the MA in accordance with the central government would be to fix the exchange rates of the domestic currency in terms of foreign currencies.
- **Lender of last resort to government and fiscal agent and adviser to the government**: the new Monetary Authority will have the ability to intervene on the open market and buy government bonds if the government fails to sell enough bonds in the open market and cause the shortfall. This MA function will give bond investors more confidence in buying government bonds that will help the government to borrow at lower interest rates. The role of an MA is also to act as a banker, fiscal agent, and adviser of the central government from whom it depends. As a banker to the government, the MA will keep the deposits of the central government and makes payments on behalf of governments without paying interest on government deposits. It should as well buy and sell foreign currencies on behalf of the government. As a fiscal agent of the government, the MA should make short-term loans to the government for a period not exceeding 90 days. However, this limit may be bypassed if the government needs medium-term loans of 6-12 months. It floats loans, pays interest on them, and finally repays them on behalf of the government. By doing this, it can manage the entire public debt.
- **Use open market operations**: the new MA can still use the open market operations to buy and sell securities from member banks. This monetary tool helps commercial banks to change the amount of cash on hand without changing the reserve requirement. Commercial Banks and Monetary Authorities will be able to buy and sell government bonds and mortgage-backed securities in the open market to stabilize the banking system. The expansionary monetary policy of lowering interest rates (sometimes they are lowered so much that they become negative) stimulates growth, preventing or shortening a recession. In fact, the U.S. Federal Reserve added $4 trillion to its balance sheet using QE after the 2008-9 financial crisis and began reducing its stockpile of mortgage-backed securities only after October 2017.

- **Clearing House for Transfer and Settlement:** another important role of the MA should be to act as a clearing house for the transfer and settlement of mutual claims of commercial banks. Given that the MA will hold the reserves of commercial banks, it should also be able to transfer funds from one commercial bank to another to facilitate the clearing of cheques. To transfer and settle claims of one bank upon others, the MA operates a separate department called the "clearing house," mostly in big trade centers.

Jointly Operations: National Monetary Authority and Treasury Department

There are other functions or targets of the new *Monetary Authority* that will be overseen jointly with the *Treasury* under government supervision, such as inflation control, growth, unemployment rate, and the management of interest rates during a recession. As we have mentioned before, an economy pricing system dominated by fierce competition normally has low inflation due to improved global supply chain management, low unemployment rate, and low-interest rate. Therefore, the role of the new Monetary Authority will be to check jointly with the Treasury the three main parameters of economic stability: inflation, unemployment, and interest rates. Treasury and Monetary Authority will be jointly responsible for these objectives and targets:

- **Target low inflation**: in an economy pricing system dominated by effective global supply chain management, technological progress, and continuous improvement is unlikely that the inflation will be higher than 2% (+1/-1) unless there are external shocks such as wars, pandemics, supply chain disruptions, etc. Low inflation creates greater economic stability and preserves the value of money and savings.
- **Target growth and low unemployment rate**: technological progress, effective supply chain management, and fast movement of capital and financial resources are the ideal conditions for mass production of non-premium products sold at discount prices. In fact, technological progress tends to increase productivity, lowers the rate of wage growth relative to productivity, and as a result, delay rising inflation. Higher productivity in the manufacturing sector translates directly into lower production costs and lower retail prices, keeping at the same time low the unemployment rate.
- **Target favorable interest rates**: the role of the Monetary Authority and Treasury is to keep favorable low benchmark interest rates charged to member banks which will guide rates for loans, mortgages, and bonds. Low-interest rates will also target low inflation and maintain economic

growth. The Monetary Authority and Treasury jointly will normally or ideally set the borrowing interest rates at the beginning of the year and keep them unchanged for the entire year to keep stability for all stakeholders in the borrowing market. The interest rate for the year will be decided based on a transparent process and on widespread consultation with the public, market players, large corporations, small businesses, and different stakeholder groups. Any change in interest rates during the year must be justified by the quick change in the economic situation and look at a variety of economic statistics to get the whole picture of the economy.

Unconventional monetary policy: The Monetary Authority (MA), in accordance with the Treasury, may use unconventional monetary policy such as Quantitative Easing (QE) only on certain occasions when the liquidity trap is common due to low-interest rates not being sufficient to boost spending and economic growth. The QE policies include creating money by MA and using this money to purchase different types of assets, such as government bonds and other securities, and support direct lending programs and other programs designed to improve credit conditions. QE policy aims to boost economic activity by providing liquidity to the financial system and eventually boosting bank lending to the public.

The **Treasury** will continue to issue securities for purposes other than funding itself for three main reasons: i) provide means of payment for the government of the country, ii) help the Monetary Authority (MA) in its interest-rate stabilization operations, iii) and help financial institutions meet their capital requirements posted by MA and to provide a base upon which all other securities are valued by providing a substitution for the risk-free rate. The reasons for issuing treasuries are most appropriate in a monetarily sovereign government with less self-imposed constraints where government administers both the Treasury and Monetary Authority. The need to issue treasuries will respond to a genuine requirement of the economic system, and there is wide access to Monetary Authority bank accounts for all categories of financial institutions.

The 2008 financial crisis has changed how monetary policy is done and how the central bank manages the money supply. The low inflation rate, low-interest rates, and low unemployment rates have left central banks with very few monetary policy tools and significantly reduced their independence. The proposed 'merger' of the Central Bank with the Treasury into a government sector and the creation of a monetary authority supervised by the government with specific tasks and duties are illustrated in Figure 5.4.

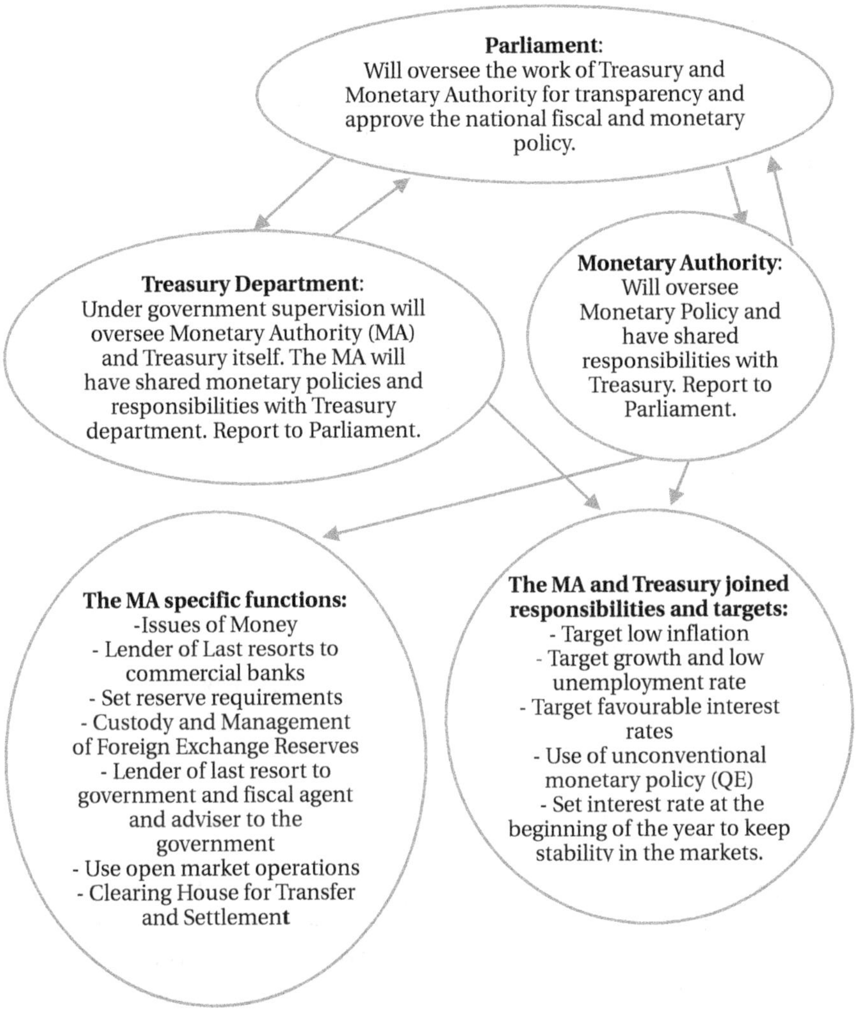

Figure 5.4 The joined role of the Treasury and Monetary Authority (MA)

The chart in Figure 5.4 reveals the joined tasks of the Treasury and Monetary Authority supervised by the government and overseen by Parliament in an economy pricing system where low inflation rate, low-interest rates, and low unemployment dominate the economic system. The newly created National Monetary Authority is focused solely on specific central banking functions and jointly with Treasury on common targets such as low inflation, low unemployment rate, and reasonable and favorable low-interest rates. Both Treasury and Monetary Authority will report quarterly to Parliament for transparency purposes on how fiscal policy, monetary policy, joint responsibilities, and targets have been managed.

The financial operations of the Treasury and Monetary Authority would be administered jointly because both are constantly in contact with each other to make fiscal and monetary policy run smoothly. The Treasury gets involved in monetary policy, and the Monetary Authority gets involved in fiscal policy. As such, the independence of the newly proposed Monetary Authority is rather limited but transparent, and it must ultimately support the Treasury in one way or another.

Conclusions

In this chapter, we have seen how monetary policy is managed in an economy pricing system dominated by low inflation, interest rates, and unemployment rates. This economy is also characterized by competition, where firms bring to market different categories of premium and non-premium products to stay competitive and control costs through global supply chain management.

We have discussed how monetary policy works when inflation, interest rates, and unemployment rates are kept low in an economy pricing system characterized by a high level of competition between firms in all sectors. The chapter, among others, has analyzed the relationship between money growth and inflation. It has also considered the Quantity Theory of Money (QTM) and the optimum quantity of money as proposed by Friedman in the 1960s and how this theory has evolved recently.

Another part of the chapter discussed the relationship between monetary policy and low-interest rates. Low inflation is the result of competitive prices, which is mostly determined by managing the supply chain, which allows companies to be able to cut excess cost and deliver products to final consumers much faster and cheaper. This is achieved by keeping tighter control of internal inventories, production, distribution, and sales costs.

Further in the chapter, we analyzed the central bank's independence. The idea of central bank independence for many economists has meant, above all, independence from direction by the short-term concerns and interference of politicians. In fact, a new monetary reality dominated by an economy pricing system with low inflation, low-interest rate, and a low unemployment rate has been suggested to have a more transparent and limited process controlled by administrative orders between the treasury department and central bank. The main idea was to reduce the independent role of the central bank and eliminate central banks' ties to large financial corporations. The new process of administrative orders between the treasury department and central banks was supposed to empower voters to exercise greater control over the political and monetary policy of the central bank by allowing the central bank to collaborate with the government and report to parliament, ensuring a transparent and democratic process.

Later in the chapter, we analyzed the central bank rules and the introduction of a new central bank rule called the *Solvency Curve,* which is based on a new concept that consists of an economy fighting recession and returning to normality by using the quantity easing (QE) and the capability of commercial banks to lend back to the public. The relationship between the central bank's rule of QE and the commercial bank-lending-to-public has the form of L shape curve while the interbank interest rates have been put close to zero.

This chapter has discussed the relationship as well between the Treasury and the Central Bank, and finally, in a separate segment was introduce the notion of a new *National Monetary Authority* intended to replace the role of the central bank, which will be supervised and administered jointly by the treasury and government. In an economy pricing system, the newly created National Monetary Authority (MA) will be focused exclusively on specific central banking functions and jointly with the Treasury on common targets such as inflation, unemployment rate, and the management of interest rates. The MA, in cooperation with Treasury and different stakeholders, will set the interest rate at the beginning of the year and maintain it for the duration of the year to keep stability in the markets. The proposed Monetary Authority's independence and monetary policy are relatively limited and more transparent to the public as it is ultimately required to support the Treasury on a more comprehensive national fiscal policy.

Chapter 6
Budget Deficit and Fiscal Policy in Economy Pricing

Introduction

The chapter will start by discussing the new era of low-interest rates and how the low-interest rate is needed to stimulate growth and investment during a recession. Low-interest rates will bring benefits to the economy. It will stimulate investments, will reduce loan mortgage rates, and help repair companies' balance sheets. There are, of course, costs associated with low-interest rates, especially in those cases where individuals and investors begin to seek out higher-yielding assets.

Monetary Policy Transmission is another topic that will be taken into consideration in this chapter. As we have seen during the initial phase of the financial crisis, an expansionary monetary policy and the lowering of interest rates are both effective methods to help eliminate uncertainty in the markets and prevent the disastrous consequences of a financial crisis. Later we'll discuss how fiscal policy is performing under low-interest rates. Both fiscal and monetary policy are the two main tools used by the government and central bank to achieve their economic objectives.

Later in the chapter, we'll have a debate about the main criticisms of the AD-AS model, which is criticized as logically inconsistent and empirically unrealistic. Another argument in the chapter will be about the standard modern macroeconomics regarding aggregate demand and aggregate supply. We will explain what the real aggregate demand and aggregate supply are in an economy pricing system. The IS-LM model will be considered in the context of an economy pricing system. More details will be given on how a monetary model with low-interest rates is represented in economy pricing, where the LM curve characterizes the money market equilibrium.

Public debt and fiscal policy are other important topics that will be discussed in this chapter. There is a valuation of whether a government is using its debt-raising capacity cautiously, which depends on the government's ability to render the borrowed money into economic growth without raising inflation. The growth in government spending and debt has been seen by some economists as a welcome policy to stimulate growth and finance infrastructures thanks to the borrowing costs that are at historic lows since the global financial crisis of 2008, except for the pandemic in 2020-23 that pushed the borrowing cost up to fight unreasonable and irrational high inflation. And lastly, we'll talk about some new theories on how Government Sovereign debt can be converted into Government Shareholder Equity to help reduce the government debt ratio more.

Benefits and Costs of Low-Interest Rates

Historically, in the last decades, slow-moving structural factors, such as lower trend productivity growth, an aging society, and global excess savings, have contributed together to a decline in the interest rate. The expected returns for various types of assets have also fallen along with the natural rate of interest. Other financial factors, such as a rise in the global demand for risk-free assets, may have contributed to the decline in interest rates.

The decline in the real interest rate has two main consequences for the management of monetary policy. The **first consequence** is that low-interest rates are needed to stimulate growth and investment during a recession and slow growth. This is because monetary policy provides stimulus if the short-term policy rate, which is adjusted for inflation, is below the equilibrium rate. The short-term policy rate could be positive or negative for monetary policy as far as it helps to put upward pressure on prices.

The **second consequence** of the monetary policy is that years of weak aggregate demand and price pressures had often forced central banks in different industrialized countries to find other monetary instruments that could provide policy accommodation when their main policy rates were approaching zero. The central banks have introduced a wide range of novel monetary policy tools in the new era of low-interest rates, such as asset purchases and negative interest rates. There is quite substantial empirical evidence suggesting that these measures were not only necessary to accomplish the price stability mandate but also to have considerable positive effects on growth and employment.

During the 2008 financial crisis and the deep recession that followed, the Federal Reserve (Fed) in the U.S. used a unique monetary policy based on a double-track response to the recession and financial crisis. The first response was to adopt for the first time large-scale unconventional monetary policies, such as the purchase of $1.25 trillion of mortgage-backed securities. The second response was through *Federal Open Market Committee* (FOMC) to reduce its interest rate target to near zero in December 2008 and then signaled its intention to security markets to preserve a low-interest rate environment for a prolonged period that could have been months or even years. Since then, the interest rates have been kept at low minimum levels creating what we call the new Era of Low-Interest Rates (except for the global pandemic and the war in Ukraine during 2021-2023).

There are benefits and costs of low-interest rates:

The **primary benefit** of low-interest rates is to stimulate growth and economic activity. Reducing interest rates at low levels can help grow business spending on capital goods and can help increase household expenditures on homes or consumer durables like automobiles, furniture, appliances, boats, etc. The effect of low interbank interest rates in the real economy is the reduction of loan mortgage rates, the result of which is the increase in home sales and, eventually, the increase in home prices.

The **secondary benefit** of low-interest rates is improving bank balance sheets and banks' capability to lend to the public. During the financial crisis, many banks of different sizes were found to be undercapitalized, which limited their ability to make loans during the financial crisis when many firms were trying to enter a recovery phase after surviving the first phase of the crisis. Central banks in different countries made the decision to keep short-term interest rates low for prolonged periods to help recapitalize the banking system by helping to raise the *Net Interest Margin* (NIM) in the banking industry, which improves retained earnings and, therefore, recapitalization.

The **third benefit** of keeping a low-interest rate for an extended period is that it can raise asset prices. Once the central bank increases the money supply, the public finds itself with more money balances than it wants to hold. Therefore, the public will use the excess money balances to increase their purchase of goods and services, as well as assets like houses, cottages, or corporate equities. Increased demand for these assets, if all else stays equal, raises their price. The first consequence of higher asset prices is that it increases the wealth of households by boosting spending and lowering the cost of financing capital purchases for the business. The second consequence of higher asset prices is that low-interest rates encourage the public to excessive borrowing and raise household debt levels.

There are also some costs associated with very low-interest rates:

First, low-interest rates provide a predominant enticement to spend rather than keep the money in the bank. In the short run, spending may not matter that much, but in the long run, low-interest rates penalize savers and those who rely deeply on interest income because of large savings. In fact, in the United States, personal interest income fell from $1.33 trillion in the third quarter of 2008 to $128 billion, or 9.6 percent, in 2010.

A **second** cost could be considered the investment in high-risk securities. In the era of low real returns, individuals and investors begin to seek out higher-yielding assets. During the 2008 financial crisis, the Fed moved to a near-zero federal funds target rate by the end of 2008, and yields on 10-year Treasury securities fell quickly on the net to less than 3 percent, while money market rates had fallen below 1 percent. The investors, given the near-zero interest rates after the financial crisis, were looking to higher nominal rates and were desirous of seeking out more speculative higher-yielding investments, increasing the risk of investments. Banks and other financial institutions were inclined to take higher risks as rates were maintained at very low levels for a lengthy period, increasing the risk of another financial crisis.

A **third** cost would be to invest in long-term assets. In fact, if short-term interest rates are low relative to long-term rates, banks and other financial institutions may be willing to overinvest in long-term assets, such as Treasury securities. If interest rates rise unexpectedly, the value of those assets will fall rapidly as bond prices and yields move in opposite directions, exposing banks to substantial losses.

A **fourth** cost associated with low-interest rates is that low short-term interest rates reduce the profitability of money market funds. The market funds for many medium and large-size corporations are normally key short-term credit providers. We have seen that in the U.S. market from early January 2009 to early August 2010, the total assets of market mutual funds declined substantially from around $3.9 trillion to about $2.8 trillion.

In a low-interest rate environment, where interest rates are close to zero, monetary policy cannot unfold its full potential. Fiscal expansion is then crucial to sustain demand and mitigate the long-term costs of the crisis. Strong complementarities reinforce the policy impact, working in both directions. There are two sides to fiscal policy in the low-interest environment. On one side, the fiscal policy will be more effective when interest rates can be expected to remain low for an extensive period. On the other side, decisive fiscal action increases the effectiveness of the monetary policy, especially in depressed areas where more investments and recovery government plans are needed.

In the last two-three decades, the central banks' main refinancing rate in industrialized countries has declined from 5% to about 0%. Consumer price inflation averaged 2.2% in 1999, down to about 1.2% during the global financial crisis in 2008, well below the inflation target of 2%, and has been since below 2%, except during the pandemic due to supply chain disruptions. In the era of a low-interest rate environment, there are strong equivalents between the fiscal and monetary policy that can help boost the economy out of the current low-growth and low-inflation trap.

Monetary Policy Transmission

Historic low-interest rates have sparked a great public debate among economists and analysts. In many advanced economies, in the last two decades, the central banks have been exposed to unadorned criticism calling into question the theory of modern independent central banking. The coincidence of low inflation and low-interest rates has led to opposing views. For some analysts and economists, the central banks are doing too little and acting too late to raise inflation, while for others, central banks are not helping savers but rather big banks and corporations.

Some market analysts and monetary economists believe that the independence of the central bank has a limited impact on the long-term trends that shape the interest rate environment in which the economy operates. The long-term trends are normally determined by the willingness of households and firms to save and invest in the future. Indeed, the central bank's objective tends to point towards a "real equilibrium" interest rate that has the capability to balance savings with investments.

In the last few decades, the change-moving structural factors such as the fast pace of technological progress, improvement of the global supply chain, lower trend productivity growth in industrialized countries and the conversion to service-oriented economies, aging society in developed countries, and global excess savings have together led to some conditions that have caused a measurable decline in the interest rates. Then the global financial crisis of 2008 caused the interest rates to drop close to zero. At these levels, the monetary policy transmission may be weak, especially when interest rates are low due to the balance-sheet recessions during and eventually after the financial crisis.

The core of monetary policy transmission is how the change in the overnight interest rate by the central bank affects the economy. The Bank's decision to set the target for the overnight interest rate influences the amount of money in the economy. The central bank policy to change the target for the overnight rate could affect the entire range of market interest rates, from the yield on 30-day treasury bills to that on 30-year government bonds, from the rate on 3-month *Guaranteed Investment Certificates* (GICs) to that on 20-year home mortgages. When a Central Bank, due to recession or slow growth, decides to lower the target for the overnight rate, the interest rates fall, and as a consequence, commercial banks increase their quantity of credit supplied to provide more loans to firms and households for their increase in demand for credit (after they repair their balance sheet).

The monetary policy transmission is fragile when interest rates are continuously low due to at least the combination of two reasons. The first reason is that the recessions feature borrowers who are not willing to borrow yet and lenders who are not ready to lend, which increases the uncertainty and misallocations among households and firms, which contribute to weakening the impact of monetary stimulus. The second reason is the economic impact that a change in interest rates has on aggregate demand and output. The lower the interest rates, the smaller the impact on aggregate demand and output. The low-interest rates may affect the net interest margins and commercial bank profitability on credit supply and bank lending. It has effects on consumption, customer savings behavior, the confidence of the customers, and expectations on investments (Borio, 2014).

During the initial phase of the financial crisis, an expansionary monetary policy and the lowering of interest rates can be effective in helping to put the confusion and uncertainty in the markets under control and prevent the disastrous outcome of the financial crisis. In a recession, the low-interest rates may help boost growth or cause positive effects on firms' profits and revenue despite the persistent adverse demand. In the aftermath of the severe period of the recession, slow demand and supply conditions may continue to weigh in on the recovery of the economy and may diminish the effects of the monetary policy.

The financial crisis and recessions have different characteristics based on different factors, which are linked to previous financial prosperity that is often characterized by unsustainable credit expansion, aggressive risk-taking, asset price increases, capital accumulation, and saving increases. After a financial crisis erupts, the low-interest rates tend to dominate the monetary policy as firms are in the middle of a balance sheet recession. Before we get to the recovery phase, there are different factors that lead to a decrease in asset value, slow growth, credit reduction, and decline in profits and revenue for many private firms and corporations.

There are several explanations for the factors contributing to recession and slow recovery:

The first explanation is that debt extension may weaken demand, especially the decrease in output, and asset prices would increase the amount of debt relative to income. Firms that have previously overestimated the revenue and income prospects will try to cut costs and lower expenditures, so they can reduce the debt burden and repair their balance sheet.

The second explanation is that a weakened financial sector would normally reduce the credit supply. In fact, losses on loans and assets during the recession will deteriorate the capability of financial institutions to lend money to the public and make it harder and costlier to raise capital. The monetary transmission is stronger when banks are weak. However, banks are under pressure from the stock markets and the government to compensate for capital losses.

The third explanation is that during a balance sheet recession, there is uncertainty about the economic prospect, and firms tend to switch from high risk-taking to less or more acceptable risk-taking, making them less responsive to government stimulus. Many firms will take advantage of the low-interest rates to pay dividends, buy back shares, finance mergers and acquisitions, etc.

The fourth explanation consists of the stimulus programs put in place by governments to fight recession which certain conditions on the supply side of the economy may weaken. During a recession, the reallocation of resources may result in certain sectors, such as manufacturing and construction, being delayed if the banking sector is recovering and not ready to lend to these sectors (Bekaert, Hoerova, and Lo Duca, 2013). In addition, low-interest rates could delay the reallocation of resources to higher productivity sectors and firms due to higher risk, which banks are not ready to take during the peak phase of the recession.

It's interesting to discuss the link between interest rates and monetary policy. There are several monetary policy transmission channels through which low-interest rates might reduce the effectiveness of the monetary policy. The list of these monetary policy channels during low-interest rates includes the positive and negative (balancing) effects on the credit supply and bank profitability, consumption and savings, resource misallocation, and uncertainty perception. Some of these monetary policy channels are explained in more detail below:

Credit supply and bank profitability:

A low-interest rate can reduce the effectiveness of the monetary policy. Therefore, a negative effect of a low-interest rate environment is that it may hinder loan supply, which depends positively on bank capitalization and profit. The profit for a commercial bank is the retained earnings in accounting terms which is the main source of capital accumulation. However, in an economy pricing system dominated by low-interest rates, as the economy recovers, the commercial banks are tempted to give more loans at an attractive low-interest rate to the public and private firms. This quickly increases the loan supply, which increases the profitability of the commercial banks balancing the negative effects of the restricted loan supply during the first phase of the recession.

On the other side, low short-term interest rates reduce a bank's net interest income. This is due to the retail bank deposits that are priced as a markdown on market rates. If the market rates go down, the markdown narrows, and the benefit from rather cheap funding reduces further, reducing the bank's net interest income. This is due to the reluctance of the banks to reduce deposit rates below zero, even when the interest rates decline to near zero. Low short-term interest rates affect the returns on the asset side as well. The negative effect of low-interest rates on net interest income is often compensated by positive effects on reduced loan loss provisions for commercial banks, as they eventually reduce borrowers' debt servicing cost and default loans and by also the increase of volume on the loan supply, which boosts profitability (Hannoun, 2015).

Consumption and savings: Low-interest rates will normally reduce returns on savings which will increase consumption through the intertemporal substitution effect. Low-interest rates also give a boost to asset prices. In fact, the asset pricing theory and standard dividend discount model suggest that changes in real interest rates would have a larger impact on asset prices when real interest rates are low. On the other side, if interest rates keep staying low, consumers may be concerned that low returns on savings will persist and render their lifetime savings insufficient to ensure an adequate standard of living after retirement. This will induce them to set up savings and reduce consumption to compensate for the pension funds or life insurance shortfall. Thus, the effect of low-interest rates on consumption may lessen and even reverse as interest rates drop to near-zero levels.

Resource misallocation: keeping low-interest rates may create disincentives for commercial banks to address delinquent debts through the channel of the banking sector. Obstinately, low-interest rates can reduce the perceived need for banks to clean up their balance sheet and reduce or charge off non-performing loans. Low-interest rates increase the expected recovery from non-preforming loans by reducing the discount factor. Hence, for given collateral values, higher discounted repayments can induce more banks to misallocate their resources by deciding to extend a financial arrangement to firms holding a larger part of their bad loans during the recession when the market for collateral is depressed (Lepetit, Strobel and Dickinson, 2011).

The big commercial banks that during the recession have benefited from quantitative easing (QE) and governments' bailouts were able to increase their overall loan supply thanks to the low-interest rates environment. But this supply was mainly focused on low and medium-quality firms that enjoyed pre-existing lending relationships with these banks. Then, these firms used the newly acquired funds and loans from banks to build up cash reserves and repair their balance sheets rather than investing or hiring new employees. However, as soon as the recession peak was gone, the firms that had cash reserves built up thanks to prior lending were able to start investing and hiring new employees.

Commercial banks normally try to keep a high level of money in their deposit accounts with the Central Bank. However, when interest rates are unusually low during a financial crisis, banks don't have a high deposit base, and the income from loans doesn't encourage taking risks, so they would loan to firms and borrowers with the highest credit ratings and substantial assets to collateralize those loans. This could change only if the commercial banks increase their deposit base due to the money they receive from the quantitative easing process. As a result, they increase the loan supply to both performing and non-performing firms as well, misallocating the resources.

Uncertainty perception: Low-interest rates could have adverse effects on perception and confidence due to monetary expansion that may create uncertainty and risk perception. Once central banks push the interest rates to remarkably low levels, the agent might start to interpret this monetary policy as a signal that the recession might last for many quarters, if not years, which might eventually offset the effects of government stimulus programs. This effect could spread to pension funds and insurance companies, which would spark the debate about their risk of underfunding the defined-benefit pension schemes and their capability to honor their previous commitments to seniors so they meet their retirement standards. Otherwise, the public will have the uncertain perception that they need to save more for old age as the pension funds and life insurance plans will be underperforming due to the low-interest rates.

It's interesting to have a look at how big commercial banks have increased their profit despite the fact that the interest rates have been persistently low, especially during the global pandemic of 2020-2022. By looking at the financial statements of the banks, it looks like their profit has surged due to, in large part, the reduction of the amount of money set aside for loans that were deemed to be bad loans (also called provisions for credit losses). This means that consumers and most businesses, including those businesses that had a high risk of going concern, were able to pay their loans during the recession and have been on top of their debt thanks in part to the government support through different subsidy programs. Box 6.1 below illustrates how some of the big commercial banks in Canada were able to see their profits climb, despite operating in the middle of the worst pandemic in a century and recording low-interest rates, thanks to new strategies for managing risk, reducing bad loans provisions, and diversifying their business in different profitable segments such as commercial, wealth and capital market businesses.

Big Commercial Banks in Canada see their profits climb despite low-interest rates

TD Bank in Canada saw its profit more than double in the first quarter of 2021, in the middle of the pandemic, compared with a year ago, as the bank recovered some of the provisions it set aside for loans that were deemed to be bad loans. TD reported a $377 million recovery of credit losses in Q1-2021 compared to a provision for credit losses of $3.2 billion a year ago. This comes because of improving economic conditions, new strategies for better-managing risk, and the strength of the bank's diversified businesses. TD Bank's revenue in Q1-2021 was $10.2 billion, compared to $10.5 billion in the same quarter in 2020. It's interesting to know that the biggest profit in TD Bank came from its Canadian retail business, which includes residential mortgages, credit cards, and commercial banking. This segment of the business earned 86 percent more in Q1-2021 than in the same quarter in 2020.

RBC (Royal Bank of Canada), Canada's biggest bank, reported a profit of about $4 billion in Q1-2021, which was up to about $1.48 billion compared to Q1-2020. This surge in profit came in part from reversed provisions. In fact, RBC reversed $96 million of its provisions for credit losses in Q2-2021 compared to the $2.83 billion it set aside in 2020 at the start of the pandemic. Revenue in Q1-2021 was $11.62 billion, up from $10.33 billion in the same quarter in 2020. Another portion of the biggest earnings gain at RBC came from its wealth management business which includes transaction accounts and investment products like mutual funds, where profits in this segment alone increased by 63 percent in Q1-2021 compared to the same quarter in 2020.

CIBC (Canadian Imperial Bank of Commerce), another big international Canadian bank, has more than tripled its Q1-2021 profit, earning $1.65 billion, compared to the profit of $392 million in Q1-2020. The increase in profit during Q1-2021 came as the money the bank set aside for bad loans in Q1-2021 fell to $32 million compared with $1.41 billion in the same quarter in 2020 at the start of the global pandemic. Meanwhile, the total revenue in Q1-2021 grew to $4.93 billion from $4.58 billion in the same quarter in 2020. The biggest income gains of CIBC came from the diversified business in the U.S., in addition to commercial, wealth, and capital market businesses.

BMO (Bank of Montreal) in Q1-2021 reported around $1.3 billion in profit, which was more than double what it reported in the same quarter in 2020. The increase came partly due to the BMO's total provision for credit losses, which fell to $60 million in Q1-2021 compared with $1.1 billion in the same quarter in 2020. In addition, revenue for Q1-2021 was nearly $6.1 billion, up from almost $5.3 billion in Q1-2020. The biggest profit gains for this bank were seen in the Canadian personal and commercial banking segment, which includes residential mortgages, commercial loans, and home equity lines of credit (HELOCs).

NBC (National Bank of Canada) for Q1-2021 reported a profit of $801 million which was more than double compared to Q1-2020. Provisions for credit losses in the first quarter of 2021 fell to $5 million compared to $504 million in the same quarter last year at the start of the pandemic and recession. Revenue was nearly $2.2 billion in Q1-2021, up from $2.0 billion in the same quarter a year earlier. The bank's personal and commercial banking division saw the biggest profit gains, earning $321 million in the first quarter of 2021 compared with $56 million a year earlier when higher provisions for credit losses hurt it due to the economic downturn. ***Source:*** Posted May 30, 2021, in Global News, a division of Corus Entertainment Inc. "Canada's big banks see their profits soar. Here's how they're making their money." By Nicole Gibillini, *The Canadian Press.*

Table 6.1 Big Commercial Banks see their profit climb despite low-interest record rates

In conclusion, we can say that there is widespread support among monetary economists that monetary transmission is less effective when interest rates are consistently low. Reduced effectiveness can arise for several different reasons, such as borrowers not being willing to borrow and lenders not being ready to lend, which increase the uncertainty and misallocations among households and firms that can contribute to weakening the impact of the monetary stimulus.

Fiscal Policy and Low-interest Rates

Fiscal policy is the use of government revenue through the collection of taxes and duties and the use of government expenditure to influence a country's economy. Current fiscal policy is based on the theories of the British economist John Maynard Keynes in the twentieth century, who theorized that government changes in the levels of taxation and government spending impact the aggregate demand and the level of economic activity in the short run. Both fiscal and monetary policy are the key strategies used by the government and central banks to achieve their economic objectives.

There is always a desired relationship between monetary and fiscal policy in different configurations of interest rates and inflation. However, after the 2008 financial crisis and the first year of the 2020-22 pandemic crisis, where interest rates dropped close to zero, and inflation was well below the target, fiscal policy was considered a leading policy tool to boost growth and, eventually, inflation. While monetary policy must support fiscal policy with forward guidance and quantity easing through asset purchases, fiscal policy must be active and contribute to cyclical stabilization to kick in growth and raise the employment rate.

The recession of 2008 exposed how monetary policy has its own limitations. In fact, the monetary policy was unable to avoid the liquidity trap when interest rate cuts were inadequate to increase demand as commercial banks were not ready to lend, and the consumers were unwilling to increase spending due to negative expectations for the economy. The fiscal policy is responsible for creating demand in the economy and providing the boost needed to get the economy out of the recession. When a deep recession emerges, both monetary and fiscal policies have their own differences and challenges; however, combining aspects of both policies to deal with an economic downturn has become a standard solution for many countries. Both policies have limited effect in time; however, while monetary policy tends to be more effective in the short term, the fiscal policy seems to have a greater impact in the long term.

During the recession, there is also the possibility of excessive fear of debt and deficit, which could lead to contractionary fiscal policies that may depress growth and inflation, making even harder the efforts of monetary policy, which may sometimes worsen rather than improve the fiscal outlook. The 2008 and 2020 recessions have changed the world so much, which has made many researchers think that fiscal policy must be reviewed. Despite low-interest rates, low inflation, and large bond, and mortgage asset purchases, the fiscal policy has been tight in general and expansionary with limited time.

Despite higher debts and deficits, interest rates have fallen, which has led to thinking that fiscal policy should start being considered as "unconventional." When inflation is below target and interest rates are already zero or negative, fiscal policy must lead with an expansionary stance, and monetary policy must cooperate as much as possible by guaranteeing low-interest rates if needed for the recovery phase. It looks that Japan, over the last two decades, has adopted this kind of monetary and fiscal policy, where the central government has adopted an expansionary policy, and the Bank of Japan has cooperated with its *Yield Curve Control.*

Regarding the *Yield Curve Control (YCC),*[1] the Bank of Japan has made a lot of efforts to keep the bond yields around a narrow range of 0% since it adopted its Yield Curve Control (YCC) policy in 2016. The objective of the Bank of Japan (BOJ) was to target yields, so it could buy fewer bonds than under its massive bond-buying program. The target was to cap the 10-year Japanese government bond (JGB) yield at zero, keeping a sustained rise in the benchmark yield. For

[1] As per definition a *Yield Curve Control* (YCC) is a monetary policy tool used by central bank to purchase government bonds or other financial assets to target interest rates at a certain level. It generally means buying bonds at a slower pace than would happen under a Quantitative Easing policy.

example, the benchmark yield was just 17 basis points in 2021 compared to the U.S. Treasury yield, which spiked at 70 points in mid-2021. The Bank of Japan was one of the most successful central banks to maintain steady control of the yield curve. For example, other central banks, such as Fed, were not able to introduce a yield cap, despite studying and testing it for years. One of the main reasons that YCC worked for the Bank of Japan was the large presence of the Bank of Japan in the bond market.

A well-planned fiscal policy can help recover the economy much faster. It also has other advantages, such as an increase in the neutral interest rates by eventually reducing public savings and limiting the constraining effect of the zero-lower bond. It helps potential growth by sustaining demand and by facilitating the return to the labor market of unemployed people during the recession phase thanks to increased public investment.

There is a strong criticism of an active fiscal policy to support demand at zero lower bonds, due to limited *fiscal space*, because of debts and deficits, which for some countries are too high. The *fiscal space* is defined as the government spending choices that give a central government more budgetary room to provide resources for public purposes without compromising fiscal sustainability. Every country has its own *fiscal space* designed and imposed by its own governing rules. For example, the *Maastricht Treaty* in the European Union imposes on its members an arbitrary 3% fiscal deficit limit and 60% debt/GDP target, which for some countries nowadays does not have any political reason to keep it. Fiscal space also gives the government the capability to adjust during a recession.

The government is often faced with the decision between reducing the fiscal deficit or reallocating the cost of adjustment between taxpayers and creditors. As debt level increases, Western governments are more predisposed to reduce the fiscal deficit by having higher primary surpluses to stabilize their debt ratios (Ostry, 2010). *Fiscal space*, like the debt/GDP ratio, is typically considered a flow concept like debt sustainability and not a stock concept. By considering *fiscal space* a flow concept, then the debt would be sustainable if gross financing needs as a percentage of GDP are kept low at about 15-20% in developed countries and even lower at about 10-12% in less developed countries. The flow concept of fiscal space becomes even more relevant in an environment where interest rates are kept low. The debt/GDP ratio can better explain the fiscal space and flow concept. The debt/GDP ratio can be expressed as a function of the debt ratio, the primary balance, and the relationship between the rate of growth and the interest rate cost of the debt. The classic function of the debt/GDP ratio is expressed below,

$$\frac{D}{Y} = \frac{(1+r)}{(1+g)} * \frac{D}{Y}(t-1) - Pf(t) \qquad (6.1)$$

where *D/Y* is the debt/GDP ratio, *r* is the interest rate cost of the debt, *g* is the rate of growth, and *Pf(t)* is the primary fiscal balance. The primary fiscal balance is the difference between Government's revenue and its non-interest expenditure (spending, not including debt payments). The primary fiscal balance is the net government borrowing, excluding interest payments on consolidated government liabilities. This difference can be measured as a percentage of GDP (Gross Domestic Product). The change in the debt can be measured as a function of primary fiscal balance and *(r-g)*, which is the difference between the interest rate cost of the debt and the GDP rate of growth. Hence, equation (6.1) can be re-written as,

$$\Delta\frac{D}{Y}=\frac{(r-g)}{(1+g)}*\frac{D}{Y}(t-1)-Pf(t) \qquad (6.2)$$

Equation (6.2) indicates that the debt path can improve if the primary fiscal balance improves, which means that the rate of GDP growth must increase or the interest cost of debt must decline (Blanchard, O. J., 1985). Therefore, on the one hand, we have government policies that increase the rate of growth through public investments in infrastructure to improve the debt path, and on the other hand, we have policies that help reduce interest rates and keep them low in the long run, such as central banks' forward guidance which can improve the debt path and increase the fiscal space.

At zero-lower bonds, where interest rates are very low and where the difference between interest rate and growth (r-g) is zero or negative, public investment finance with debt improves the debt path. Based on equation (6.2), we have that when the debt/GDP ratio increases, the progress of the debt/GDP ratio is more dependent on the difference between interest rate and growth (r-g) than on the primary balance (Reinhart and Rogoff, 2015) At high levels of debt, the monetary and fiscal policies that drive the interest rate and GDP growth rate become more important than the magnitude of the primary balance in determining the evolution of debt/GDP ratio available through fiscal space.

Naturally, bad policies can quickly harm the fiscal space, which can eventually lead to markets demanding a higher risk premium on the debt. Bad and unreliable government policies can increase the government bond yields due to the redenomination risk by the market that may fear default on the debt. On the contrary, reliable government policies can reduce government bond yields as the redenomination risk disappears. The evolution of government policies can create fiscal space that may ease a more expansionary fiscal policy. Thus, at low-interest rates, the quality is more important than the quantity of the debt and fiscal deficit to determine the fiscal space.

Fiscal space also depends on the capability of the government to control its own debt through the interaction between the supply and demand of government-issued bonds. The demand for government bonds has been very volatile, especially in recent years and during recessions. Government bonds are purchased to earn a return as a part of a portfolio, and thus their demand depends on their expected return in addition to their specific risk characteristics. A bond yield is a return that an investor can realize on a bond. The current yield is a function of the bond's price and its coupon, also called "bond's interest payment." The yield on government bonds depends mostly on two factors: the expected short-term interest rates and a risk premium that investors demand holding long-term securities.

The risk-premium can be affected by three main factors: inflation, default risk, and a shift in the relative demand for bonds versus other assets (which could affect the price of the bonds). A low-risk premium for government bonds means that the main factor of bond price is the expected short-term rates. Normally, during the recession, there is low growth which leads to a high public deficit and low-interest rates. Given that the bond price will increase when interest rates drop, it will make the government bonds a good option as a hedging investment tool in a portfolio.

A well-planned expansionary fiscal policy could reduce the bond premium, reduce long-term interest rates, and pushes the economy toward growth. The government bond premium has declined steadily in the last years for several factors, such as the inflation risk premium, default risk premium, and equity risk premium. The inflation risk premium has declined due to low inflation being below the target, and there is no need to hedge against higher inflation. The default risk premium of the bond has declined as well despite the increase in debts and fiscal deficit, which has increased the financing needs through bonds (Benjamin, Hordahl, and Xia, 2018). At the same time, the central banks' asset purchases and forward guidance policies have increased the demand for bonds and exercised downside pressure on the interest rates. The equity risk premium factor has been high due to the relative demand for equities versus bonds and has supported the demand for bonds. The demand for bonds has increased as it has been characterized by a shortage of other safe assets.

In an economy characterized by interest rates near zero levels and inflation below target, the government must design the fiscal budget in a way not to lead to a decline in the debt ratio. The primary balance gap is calculated as the current cost of debt, which in the low-interest rate environment is likely to continue to decline over coming years. Therefore, the primary fiscal balance gap, or the difference between the planned primary balance and the debt-stabilizing primary balance, must be zero or close to zero. Following this fiscal rule helps keep the fiscal policy expansionary, as inflation is below target and interest rates are close to zero. It also helps monetary policy by allowing the government to reduce the debt when the actual (*r-g*) is improving. It likewise provides incentives to improve the efficiency of fiscal policy when interest rates are low as far as the economy finds itself in periods of growth. If the economy, after the periods of growth, falls into recession, fiscal policy must be again expansionary and countercyclical. When interest rates are very low, close to zero, and inflation is too low, the monetary policy is almost ineffective, and the fiscal policy must support the efforts of monetary policy to be expansionary.

Some Criticism on Aggregate Demand and Curve Supply

IS-LM (Liquidity preference-Money supply) and AD-AS (Aggregate Demand-Aggregate Supply) models have been widely used to analyze macroeconomic issues and policies. Both the IS-LM and AD-AS models and the Aggregate Demand (AD)– Aggregate Supply (AS) framework have dominated every macroeconomics textbook that has been published worldwide since the 1980s. Despite all this, there have been significant criticisms of the AD-AS model and the concept of the aggregate demand-aggregate supply beginning in the 1990s.

There are at least two main criticisms of the AD-AS model: logically inconsistent and empirically unrealistic. The logical discrepancy between the AD curve and the short-run AS curve depends on the specific nature of the AS curve, which comprises an unrealistic short-run aggregate supply curve and a vertical long-run aggregate supply curve. The AD curve is defined by the IS-LM equilibrium income at different potential price levels. The downward-sloping AD curve is derived from the IS-LM model. The IS-LM and AD-AS models are used to illustrate the Keynesian model of the business cycle. Movements of these curves can be used to forecast the effects that various exogenous events will have on a few variables, such as real GDP, interest rates, and price level.

The basic concept of the IS-LM model was the analysis of the money market and the analysis of the goods market to determine the equilibrium levels of interest rates and output in the economy. The combination of interest rates and output (GDP) in the money market creates, in theory, the LM curve. Meanwhile, the combination of interest rates and output in the goods market creates the IS curve. The equilibrium is the combination of interest rate and output in both the IS and LM curves, as illustrated in Figure 6.1. The most typical presentation of the model IS-LM model consists of two intersecting lines. On the X-axis, we have the real gross domestic product (Y), which is the economy's output, and on the Y-axis, there are the nominal interest rates (i).

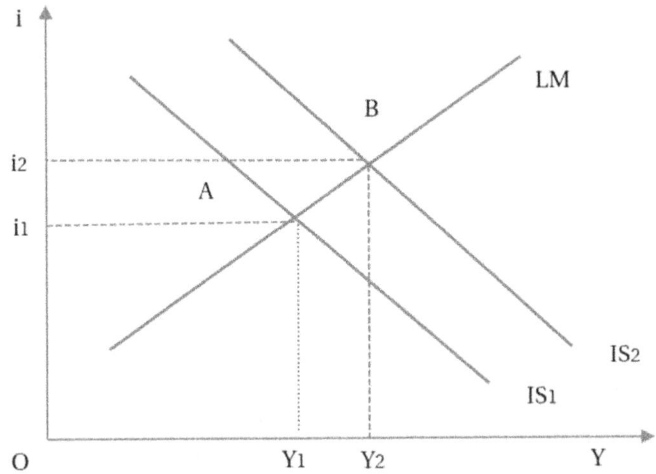

Figure 6.1 IS-LM model

The intersection of the IS and LM curves shows the equilibrium point of interest rates and output when money markets and the real economy are balanced. By moving the *IS1* curve from point A to the right at point B, where the interest rate is *i2*, the model gives us a new economic output and interest rates. The IS curve shows the locus point where total income equals total spending expressed as,

$$E = C(Y\text{-}T) + I(i\text{-}\pi) + G + NX(Y) \qquad (6.3)$$

where *C* is consumer spending as an increasing function of disposable income *(Y-T)*, output less taxes, *I* is an investment as a decreasing function of interest rates *(i-π)*, *G* is the government spending, and NX(Y) is net exports. On the other hand, the LM curve represents the money market equilibrium which is a set of points at an equilibrium between liquidity preference (demand for money) and the money supply function at a given price level given as,

$$M/P = M(r, Y) \qquad (6.4)$$

where *M* is the quantity of money and *P* is the price level, *r* is the real interest rate, and *Y* is the real income. There is a positive relationship between *Y* and *r* when *M/P* is held constant. An increase in income must be followed by an increase in the interest rate so that demand for real money increase balances equal to the supply. Money demand increases when output rises because money also serves as a medium of exchange.

The AD (aggregate demand) curve gives a relationship between the price level, *P*, and the desired real expenditure, *Y*, where both the goods and the money markets are in equilibrium. The AD curve is nothing more than an intersection of the IS and LM curves. The aggregate demand represents the total demand for goods and services at any given price level in each period. It consists of all consumer goods, capital goods (factories and equipment), exports, imports, and government spending programs. Graphically, the aggregate amount of goods and services demanded is illustrated on the horizontal X-axis, and the price level of the whole basket of goods and services is shown on the vertical Y-axis. The aggregate demand curve slopes downward from left to right and increases or decreases along the curve as prices for goods and services either increase or decrease.

On the opposite side, the aggregate supply curve (AS curve) describes the quantity of output the firms can supply for a given price level. The **classical aggregate supply curve** comprises a short-run aggregate supply curve (SRAS) which is an upward slope, and a vertical long-run aggregate supply curve (LRAS). The intersection of the short-run aggregate supply curve with the long-run aggregate supply curve and with the aggregate demand curve gives the equilibrium price level and the equilibrium output level, as illustrated in Figure 6.2.

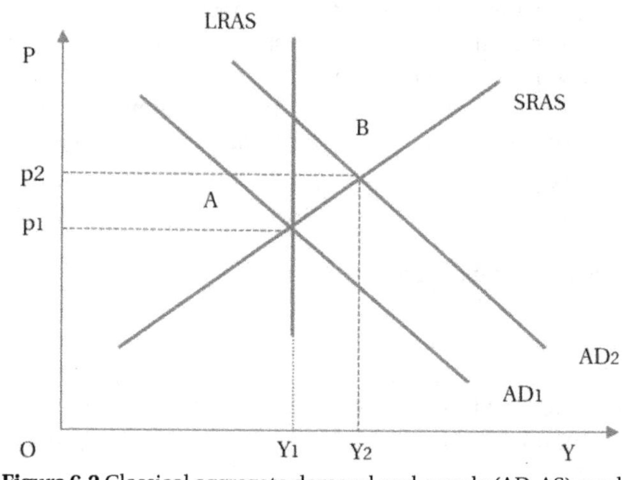

Figure 6.2 Classical aggregate demand and supply (AD-AS) model

As shown in Figure 6.2, the aggregate demand curve *AD1* will shift to the right from point A to point B when the price level increases from *p1* to *p2* and the new equilibrium is established at point B.

The AD-AS model over the last decades has been heavily criticized due to logical inconsistency and lack of empirical realism. There are few economists who have criticized the AD-AS model since the early 1990s, such as Rao, 1991, 2007; Colander, 1995; Grieve, 1996 etc.

The main criticism of the IS-LM model or theory is that it assumes firms produce goods and render services to satisfy demand, and the labor market theory of output assumes that firms produce all kinds of commodities to maximize profit as determined by wages and prices. These two different theories of output are reciprocally unreliable and logically contradictory because they envisage two different quantities of output to be produced at the same given price level, which is inconsistent with reality.

The core logical inconsistency between the AD curve and the labor market AS curve is that these two curves are based on two completely different and reciprocally inconsistent theories of output in the AD-AS model. On the one hand, the "AD" curve is basically founded on the Keynesian IS-LM theory of output, and on the other hand, the labor market "AS" curve is based on the labor market theory of output. These two theories are "blended" to determine the general equilibrium output and the price level. However, the general equilibrium in the AD-AS model is logically contradictory because these two theories of output are essentially different and lead to different conclusions about the quantity of output to be produced any time the economy is out of equilibrium.

This logical inconsistency outside of equilibrium between the two quantities of output predicted by the AD aggregate demand curve and the labor market AS aggregate supply curve can be clearly seen from the standard AD-AS curves in Figure 6.2. At the equilibrium point B, where the price is at *p2*, the AD theory concludes that firms will produce a higher output than the equilibrium output at point A - given the higher price *p2* - and the AS theory concludes that firms will produce a higher equilibrium output to reach the new equilibrium at point B. The two theories of output for the AD aggregate demand and AS aggregate supply cannot both be true at the same price level. Firms cannot produce both lower-than-equilibrium output and higher-than-equilibrium output at the same price level. Thus, at any price level other than the equilibrium price level, these two theories of output are equally contradictory.

In addition, due to logical inconsistency, the AD-AS model does not provide a comprehensive explanation of the process of adjustment from a state of disequilibrium to a state of equilibrium. In the situation just described above, where $p2 > p1$, as in Fig. 6.2, a return to equilibrium requires a reduction of price from *p2* to *p1*. However, the AD theory emphasizes that a price level reduction would cause output to increase, but the AS theory tells us that a price level reduction would cause output to decline. Output cannot both increase and decrease because of the same price decline. Hence, at any price level other than the equilibrium price level, the aggregate demand and supply demand are equally contradictory, which means that the AD-AS output model is illogical and contradictory.

Another major criticism of the AD-AS theory is that it is empirically unrealistic and unlikely to happen in a real economy. The major unrealistic characteristic of the AD-AS model is that it assumes the prices will fall under two conditions: the first condition is when there is a situation of short-run disequilibrium where *AS* is greater than AD, and the second condition is where there is a situation of short-run equilibrium, and the short-run equilibrium output is less than the full employment "natural" level of output. In addition, the AD-AS model assumes that this decline in the price level will increase the AD curve, and the economy will return to the full employment equilibrium price level and quantity of output with only minor difficulties, which is not realistic. Furthermore, even if prices were to fall, this would not increase AD and would not provide a smooth return to full employment output but would rather create a recession or a sort of financial crisis.

Aggregate Demand and Aggregate Supply in Economy Pricing

Let's go back to the concept of aggregate demand. What is the aggregate demand? As per the definition of macroeconomic textbooks, aggregate demand is an economic measurement of the total amount of demand for all finished goods and services produced in an economy for a given period. It can be expressed as the total amount of currency exchanged for those goods and services at a given price level and at a certain point in time. Aggregate demand in the long period equals the gross domestic product (GDP) because the two figures are calculated in the same way. GDP characterizes the total amount of goods and services produced in a real economy, while aggregate demand is the demand or the need to produce those goods. Therefore, because of the same calculation methods, the aggregate demand and GDP move in the same direction, increasing or decreasing together.

What is the aggregate supply? As per the textbook definition, the aggregate supply, also known as total output, is the total supply of goods and services produced within an economy at a given price at a certain period.

What is the real aggregate demand in an economy pricing system?

First, the global aggregate demand for a national economy should be split between the aggregate demand for the private, public, and import-export sectors. The aggregate demand of the private sector in an economy pricing system is measured as the total demand of all finished goods and services, both premium and non-premium, generated in all sectors of the economy. The aggregate demand for the private sector is expressed as the total amount of money exchanged for the combination of premium and non-premium goods and services offered at different prices with a price range that goes from a low-price floor given by discounted prices to a high-price ceiling given by regular prices, at any given period.

Instead, the aggregate supply of the private sector is given by the aggregate production capacity utilization of all firms offering premium and non-premium products in an economy at a given period. The aggregate demand and aggregate supply of the private sector, including premium and non-premium finished goods, are illustrated in Figure 6.3.

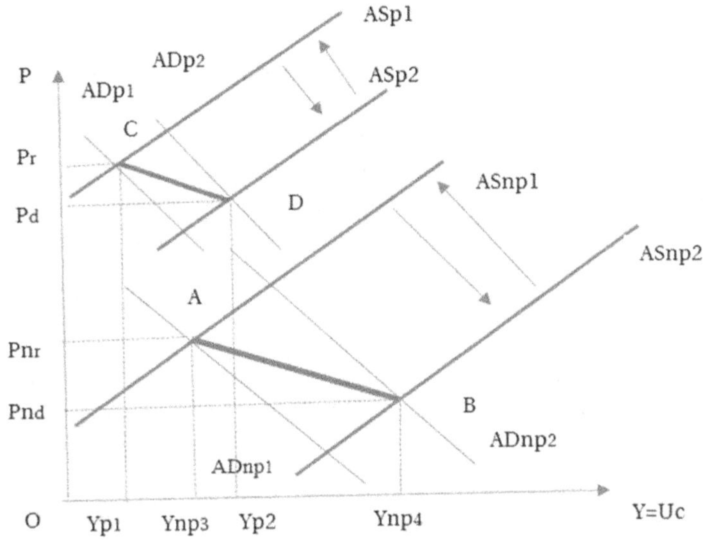

Figure 6.3 Aggregate demand and aggregate supply (AD-AS) model for the private sector of the combined premium and non-premium products

Figure 6.3 illustrates the aggregate demand and supply curves for premium and non-premium products indicated as a relationship between output and two different sets of price ranges: *(Pd-Pr)* for discounted and regular premium prices and (*Pnd-Pnr*) for discounted and regular non-premium prices. The AD-AS model follows a different logic in an economy pricing where firms work in a very competitive environment. It works mostly from the supply side by using push marketing strategies onto customers to lure them into buying a variety of products offered at competitive prices. A substantial number of firms operating in the same industry will offer sales incentives, mostly for non-premium products and occasionally for premium products, to the department stores to push their products onto customers. In fact, these competitive firms use the tactic of attracting customers by continuously promoting sales events and "pushing" them to buy their products. This "push" marketing strategy on the supply side is illustrated in the aggregate demand and supply model for the private sector in Figure 6.3.

Figure 6.3 illustrates how private firms selling mass-produced non-premium products offer sales incentives by lowering the regular price *Pnr* to the discounted price *Pnd* to push the supply curve from point A to B where it intersects the aggregate demand *ADnp2* at an increased output from *Ynp3* to *Ynp4* to meet the production utilization capacity target. We can use the same logic for firms in the private sector that offer premium products. The price of premium products will move from the regular price *Pr* to the discounted price *Pd*, shifting the supply curve from *ASp1* to *ASp2* or from equilibrium point C to D to intersect the aggregate curve *ADp2*.

The logic of the Aggregate demand and supply (AD-AS) model for the private sector in Fig. 6.3 is to show how same firms that sell both premium and non-premium products combined in a certain order need to reach the desired production capacity utilization of around 70-80% and meet the forecasted sales target to have a positive cash flow and maximize the current ratio in a given fiscal period. Because of this, the supply side and output produced in the private sector are limited to the production capacity utilization, *Uc*, required to produce the combination of premium and non-premium products to meet the sales target.

The private aggregate supply will switch between *ASp2* and *ASp1* curves or between points A and B depending on the price offered in the price range of *Pnr-Pnd* for non-premium products and between points C and D for the price range of *Pr-Pd* for premium products. In traditional macroeconomics terminology, the general equilibrium is achieved when *ADnp* intersects *ASnp* for non-premium products at points A and B, and *ADp* intersects *ASp* for premium products at points C and D. In economy pricing; instead, the general equilibrium of aggregate and supply curves in the private sector is a moving target based on the sales events indicated by the bold line between point A and B for non-premium products and by the bold line between point C and D for premium products. The desired total income in the private sector could be written as,

$$Y = C[Y_p - T(Y_p)] + C[Y_{np} - T(Y_{np})] = U_c = Sales\ Target \quad (6.5)$$

Where *C* is consumer spending as an increasing function of disposable income *(Y-T)* for premium *(Yp)* and non-premium *(Ynp)* products outputs less taxes *T(Yp)* and *T(Ynp)*, and *Uc* is the production capacity utilization required to meet the sales target. The desired total output Y equals the desired production capacity utilization (60-70%) to meet the sales target required to make a desired profit and is given as,

$$dY = [C_{yp-1}(1 - T_{yp})dy] + [C_{ynp-t}(1 - T_{ynp})dy] = U_c \quad (6.6)$$

After rearranging (6.6), we have that the desired output dY takes the form as,

$$dY = \frac{1}{[[(1-C_{yp-t}(1-T_{yp})]+[1-C_{ynp-t}(1-T_{ynp})]]} \quad (6.7)$$

The increasing disposable income will come if households decide to spend more on cheaper non-premium products than on more expensive premium products, which could help them save more money, especially during the financial crisis and recession. If we add investment *Ir* and government spending *G*, we have that the total output for the aggregate spending in equation (6.6) can be written as,

$$dY = [C_{yp-t}(1 - T_{yp})dy] + [C_{ynp-t}(1 - (T_{ynp})dy] + I_r + G \quad (6.8)$$

where *Ir* is an investment as a function of the interest rate *r*, and *G* is government spending. For the investment *Ir*, we have that a higher rate of interest has a higher cost of capital, leading entrepreneurs to lower the level of investment, and vice versa, a low-interest rate will lower the cost of capital, leading the entrepreneurs to increase the level of investments. After rearranging (6.8), we have the output given as follows,

$$dY = \frac{I_r dR + dG}{[[(1-C_{yp-t}(1-T_{yp})]+[1-C_{ynp-t}(1-T_{ynp})]]} \quad (6.9)$$

Increasing government spending stimulates the output for a given level of interest rate, especially if the interest rate is low, as often happens in an economy pricing system.

What about the IS-LM Model in an Economy Pricing System?

The LM curve represents the combination of output and interest rate that leads to the equilibrium in the money market for a given price level. The money market is represented by the equation below as,

$$M/P = L(i,Y) \quad Li<0 \text{ and } Ly>0 \quad (6.10)$$

where *M* is the quantity of money, *P* is the price level, and *L* is the liquidity preference for the public of holding money. The equation (6.10) equates the total money supply, M/P, to the real demand for money L. Since L(d) is decreasing in interest rate, *i*, and increasing in output *Y*, the set of combinations of *i* and *Y* that satisfies the LM curve is upward sloping. The standard Keynesian LM curve represents all combinations of output **Y** and rate of interest *R* for which the money market is in equilibrium. From (6.10), we have that the LM curve can be expressed using the implicit function as,

$$d\left(\frac{M}{P}\right) = l_Y dY + l_R dR \Rightarrow dR = \frac{d\left(\frac{M}{P}\right) - l_Y dY}{l_Y} \quad (6.11)$$

where the slope of the curve *LM* is $-ly/lr \geq 0$ and the effect of the total money supply on the rate of interest is equal to $1/lr \leq 0$. The *LM* curve basically slopes upwards and shifts to the right if real money balances expand. As per the standard LM curve, a higher interest rate lowers money demand, so national income must be higher to boost money demand back to the unchanged level of the money supply. In addition, a higher money supply or a lower price level pushes up bond prices and thus lowers the interest rate. The LM curve is vertical for high rates of interest and horizontal for low rates of interest (if we accept Keynes' liquidity). However, at low levels of interest rates, the LM curve tends to be flat. Graphically the flat or quasi-flat LM curve is derived in Figure 6.4.

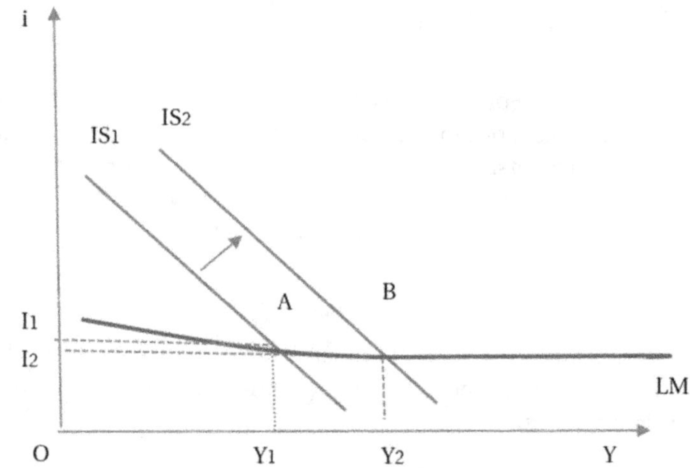

Figure 6.4 Flat LM curve at low-interest rates

The intersection of the IS and LM curves shows the equilibrium point of interest rates and output when money markets and the real economy are balanced in a low-interest rate environment. By moving the IS1 curve from point A to the right at point B (IS2), where the interest rate moves from *i1* to an even lower interest rate at *i2*, the model gives us a new economic output and interest rate equilibrium at point B. At point B, the output is much higher than at point A, thanks to the cheaper cost of borrowing money at a lower interest rate *I2*. The LM curve is flat and almost horizontal due to the availability of cheap money borrowed at a very low-interest rate.

In general, cheap money is very good for borrowers but, unfortunately, not so good for investors who will eventually see the same low-interest rates yielding low returns on their investments, such as savings accounts, money market funds, bonds, and other securities. Another unpleasant outcome of cheap money is to have damaging economic consequences in those cases where a certain number of borrowers take on excessive leverage and are eventually unable to pay loans back on time. However, cheap money is a good deal for most borrowers who can repay all the loans on time. As a matter of fact, cheap money is supposed to enhance the performance of struggling economies by making it more affordable for consumers and businesses to borrow money. In fact, the cheaper the loans are, the more people will borrow to buy homes and vehicles, start new businesses, and undertake new ventures that will help boost economic growth.

However, cheap money has another side effect as it puts more money into circulation, which can contribute to inflation because it drives up prices creating an upward monetary inflation effect. Fortunately, this inflationary effect has not occurred in an economy pricing system due to low commodity prices except for the real estate market. The commodity prices have been kept low, which has resulted in keeping inflation low in recent years, thanks to the competitive factors and increased variety of non-premium products, improved supply chain management, technological progress, and increased “push” marketing strategies and sales events on the supply side. All these factors have contributed to keeping inflation at low record levels (except during the global pandemic years of 2020-2022 due to the disruption of the global supply chain and the sharp increase in online purchasing).

During the 2008 financial crisis, it was believed that a large infusion of money through Quantity Easing (QE) operation would create inflation or, even worse, hyperinflation and, eventually, the collapse of the domestic currency. However, QE did not create hyperinflation or even much in the way of any inflation. The first reason that QE did not lead to high inflation was that the state of the economy was already deflationary when the financial crisis began in 2008. The second major reason was that banks and financial institutions hoarded enough money to repair their balance sheets due to bad loans and stay afloat by regaining profitability. Therefore, the money that was injected into the system by QE increased the M0 monetary base and was principally retained by the financial sector rather than by the public.

In a Keynesian economy, the money market equilibrium consists of the liquidity preference function based on the desire to hold cash. As per the Keynesian theory, there are at least two main elements that determine the holding of money balances: The first one is the transaction demand for money which includes the willingness to hold cash for daily transactions and for emergency cases. The second element is the speculative demand for money, that is, the willingness to hold cash instead of securities for investment purposes. In this case, the speculative demand is inversely related to the interest rate. As the interest rate rises, the speculative demand for holding cash money falls.

There is also a third element for holding cash money if we consider the economy pricing system as a part of disposable income that will be quickly used in economy pricing. Economy pricing includes many components, such as a large variety of cheap non-premium products, price discounts, bundle products, a high frequency of sales events, online sales, etc., that lure customers into spending more money and using more of their disposable income even without planning to do so. This is normally known as the "economy pricing portion of the disposable income."

As soon as employees receive cash money in their paychecks every two weeks or so (after paying or planning to pay the monthly bills), they will be lured by massive and aggressive advertising to start spending on any premium or non-premium product that offers discounts. The cash is gone even without knowing it. This drag of cash in an economy pricing system creates a fluctuation in demand for money.

Hence, the demand for real money balances is an increasing function of disposable income for premium and non-premium products during seasonal sales events and a decreasing function of disposable income during regular off-season sales events. Big sales events, such as Thanksgiving, Black Friday, Christmas, boxing day, New Year sales, Labor Day, etc., will increase the real demand for money from the public and reduce savings. Regular off-season purchases will reduce the demand for money and increase savings, as people tend to buy less if there are no promotions or discounts available. Graphically the LM curve takes the form of a snake as it fluctuates based on the demand for money during seasonal and off-seasonal sales, as illustrated in Figure 6.5.

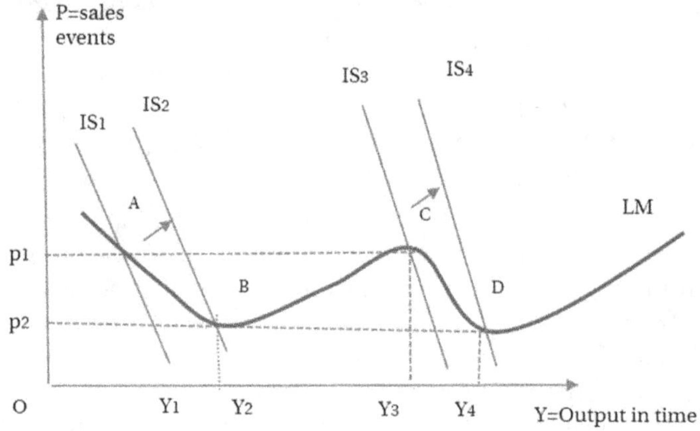

Figure 6.5 Sales events and IS-LM curves in time

The intersection of the IS and LM curves shows the equilibrium of sales prices and non-sales prices during sales events and non-sales events and the output when money markets and the real economy are balanced in a low-interest rate environment. The interest rate in this model does not affect the demand for money (given the low-interest environment). The only parameter that affects the demand for money is the discounted price offered for the sales of non-premium and premium products during the seasonal and off-seasonal sales. Price *p1* represents the regular price during the off-sales season period, and *p2* represents the discounted price during the sales season, where massive sales are expected to happen due to aggressive advertising. By moving the *IS1* curve from point A to the right at point B (IS2), the price will move from regular price *p1* to sales price *p2,* and the model will give us a new combination of economic output and price sales at point B.

When the sales season is over, the demand for money is reduced as fewer sales are expected to happen, then the economy moves to point C (IS3) and then back to point D (IS4) as soon as the sales events restart and the demand for money increases again. Figure 6.5 indicates the output-in-time Y during the second massive sales event reaching the equilibrium of IS-LM curves in points B and D, where the volume of output and demand for money reach again the highest levels. Because of this, the LM curve fluctuation has the form of a 'snake shape' based on the demand for money during seasonal and off-seasonal sales events.

In economy pricing, a money model with low-interest rates can be characterized by the LM curve, which represents the money market equilibrium as a set of points in equilibrium between liquidity preference (demand for money) and the money supply function at a given low-interest rate and can be written as,

$$M/RL=M(Ps,Y) \qquad (6.12)$$

where *M* is the quantity of money, *Ps* is the price level for seasonal and non-seasonal sales events, *RL* is the real interest rate, and *Y* is the real income. The LM curve above can be expressed using the implicit function as,

$$d\left(\frac{M}{R_L}\right) = l_Y dY + l_P dP_s \Rightarrow dP_s = \frac{d\left(\frac{M}{R_L}\right) - l_Y dY}{l_p} \qquad (6.13)$$

where the slope of the curve LM is $-ly/lp \geq 0$ and the effect of the total money supply on the price during seasonal events is equal to $1/lp \leq 0$. Here, the LM curve slopes downwards and shifts to the right if real money balances expand during massive sales events. Therefore, if there are no sales events, the demand for money goes down. The national income must increase to boost the aggregate demand and the demand for money at a higher level. This could be reached by the re-start of sales events and by offering discounts on a variety of non-premium products, so consumers will be lured to spend more and more of their disposable income.

Public Debt and Fiscal Policy

The growth in government spending and debt has been seen by some analysts as a welcome policy to stimulate growth and finance infrastructures such as roads, bridges, hospitals, and schools, vital for job growth thanks to the borrowing costs that were at historic lows since 2008 after the first global financial crisis of the twenty-first century. The valuation of whether a government is using its debt-raising capacity cautiously depends on the government's ability to translate the borrowed money into economic growth without raising inflation and keeping at a stable level the household's standard of living at.

The definition of public debt is that it represents the total amount of debt, including total liabilities, borrowed by the government of a country to meet its development budget. The term public debt can also be used to indicate the overall liabilities of the central government. The main goal of debt management consists of raising low-cost funding to meet the financial requirements of the government and facilitate the capital market conditions for government-issued securities.

Government deficit spending is the difference between how much money the government takes in through taxes and how much it spends during the year. Public debt is the accumulation of all the deficit plus any other money the government spent that wasn't part of the budget. For example, the United States' public debt in August 2021 was around $28.43 trillion USD dollars. In 2020 alone, the U.S. Government spent about 371 billion U.S. dollars of taxpayers' money on interest for debt held by the public.

The total public debt of the United States of America is divided into two main categories: the **debt held by the public** and **intragovernmental holdings.** It is interesting to see how the U.S. government raises money through federal government auctions of treasury securities such as U.S. Savings Bonds, Treasury Bills (T-Bills), and other security notes from domestic and foreign investors. During the auction process held by the U.S. government, investors bid for securities in two different options: **competitive** or **non-competitive bids**. In the first option of a competitive bid, investors state the interest rate at which they're willing to buy the securities. In the second option of non-competitive bid, investors agree to purchase the securities at the average interest rate of all bids.

In addition to debt held by the public, there are also intragovernmental holdings which are treasury securities purchased by the U.S. government to strengthen federal savings programs like social security and health care. Sometimes the federal savings programs are also called *Unfunded Liabilities* as these unfunded liabilities are larger than the conventional stock of government debt. A better indicator of a nation's indebtedness is the ratio of its public debt to its GDP or total national income. The more debt a country holds, the less money it's able to put away in savings and reinvest in the nation's economy. The debt-to-GDP ratio is one of the main vital indicators of the sustainability of government finance. Public debt is basically calculated as the sum of the liability categories such as debt securities, currency and deposits, loans, insurance, pensions, and other accounts payable. Changes in government debt principally show the accumulated public debt over time and reflect the impact of past government deficits.

Technically speaking, a government can sustain the same level of debt by running small deficits forever (for years and even decades) if GDP is increasing because GDP is a close substitution for the tax base. The higher the GDP, the higher the tax base of the government, and the higher the level of economic growth, the more additional debt the government can take on each year. There are, of course, some negative effects of government debt. Government bonds compete with corporate bonds for investors' money, which pushes up interest rates for everyone. And if the government is absorbing a larger proportion of the capital available, there is less capital left for the private sector. The positive effects of government debt are that the government, with the borrowed money, can invest in productive investments destined to grow the tax base, such as roads, bridges, schools, ports, hospitals, universities, school loans, basic research, and other expenditures like government-run programs, etc.

It is a well-known fact that government debt as a fraction of GDP has been increasing in advanced countries in the last five decades. The government debt theories can explain the increase in the level of debt in certain periods during a response to macroeconomic shocks; however, they cannot explain the trend of debt accumulation in any advanced countries. The fiscal policy tries to create a trade-off between the commitment to keep under control spending in normal periods and having the flexibility to react quickly during economic shocks and financial crises. This trade-off is reached using different optimal fiscal rules, such as escape clauses, information dependence, cross-country coordination, etc. (Yared, 2019).

The political economy theories have the capability to explain the long-run trend deriving from an aging population in advanced countries, political polarization, and certain electoral uncertainty. These theories highlight the time inconsistency in government regarding political decisions and, consequently, the necessity for a fiscal policy that limits policymakers. The main three problems that are caused by national debt are, first, lower national savings and, eventually, lower income in certain cases. Second, large amounts of interest payments for debt could lead to large tax hikes and unreasonable government spending cuts. Third, decreased ability to respond quickly to economic shocks and a greater risk of a fiscal crisis and, ultimately, financial crisis.

The primary drivers of the future public debt in advanced countries such as the U.S., E.U. countries, U.K., Canada, Japan, Australia, etc., are the mandatory spending programs that every government needs to comply with. For example, in the U.S., the main drivers of the public debt continue to be the mandatory spending programs, also called the social programs or Social Security programs such as Medicare and Medicaid. Their total cost, as predicted, in recent years has counted for approximately half of all federal spending in the U.S. This cost is expected to increase as a percentage of GDP because of the aging population in the U.S., which requires more health expenses. Figure 6.6 below illustrates the U.S. Federal Budget spending for 2021.

Mandatory spending	**Mandatory spending**	**Mandatory spending**	**Mandatory spending**	**Discretionary spending**	**Discretionary spending**	**Interest Payment**	**Total**
23%	**15 %**	**9%**	**15%**	**15%**	**14%**	**9%**	**100%**
Social Security (retirement insurance, disability insurance, hospital insurance for the aged, drug benefits)	**Medicare** (hospital coverage, medical coverage, prescription drug coverage)	**Medicaid** (family planning care, prescription drug cost, hospital services, pediatric services, mental and dental health care)	**Other** (employment benefits, food and income support, federal pension, antipoverty tax credits, crop insurance)	**Defense**	**Non-defense** (transportation, infrastructure, health, housing, education, social services, veteran's benefit, etc.)	Servicing public debt	
$1 trillion	$644 billion	$409 billion	$642 billion	$676 billion	$661 billion	$375 billion	$4.407 Trillion

Figure 6.6 U.S. Federal Budget Spending for 2021
Source: *U.S. Congressional Budget Office (2021)*

As illustrated in Figure (6.6), most of the federal budget goes toward privileged or entitlement programs, also called *Mandatory spending,* such as Social Security, Medicare, Medicaid, etc., which counts for more than 50-60% of the U.S. federal annual budget. Meanwhile, under *Discretionary Spending,* there are other programs such as defense and non-defense (transportation, infrastructure, education, housing, etc.). Differently from Discretionary Spending, which is approved by U.S. Congress each year through the appropriation process, mandatory spending is automatic unless legislation for these underlying programs is changed.

The U.S. government is expecting that the corresponding tax revenues are projected to remain stagnant, therefore not able to cover the increasing social security program expenses. Meanwhile, the interest payment on the public debt has normally reached around 8-10% of the annual budget and eventually might rise as spending continues to have a slow but steady rise. Another option to balance the budget was to cut taxes through a new tax bill, as happened during the Donald Trump administration (Tax Cuts and Jobs Act [TCJA]), which became law on December 22, 2017, to help boost economic growth and increase government revenue. The main idea of the *Tax Cuts Act* was to enhance growth and the annual GDP by 1 percent over the next ten years but also to increase the annual budget shortfalls and eventually add about $1.8 trillion to the public debt over the same 10-year period. The U.S. has the highest debt-to-GDP ratio compared to other advanced countries.

Despite this, the U.S. is still the world's largest economy, with no chance of defaulting on its debt. After WWII, the U.S. dollar has been the world's reserve-currency country and still nowadays is considered the world currency and used as a reserve currency for many central banks around the world. Therefore, there has always been a a high demand for the U.S. dollar, which has helped the U.S. finance its own debt with no risk of default. In fact, many investors consider putting a premium on holding low-risk dollar-denominated assets such as U.S. Treasury bills, notes, and bonds. The high demand for U.S. dollars from foreign creditors has helped the Government of the United States to borrow at relatively low-interest rates. Domestic and foreign investors, different national governments, and private funds hold the U.S. Treasury securities. Foreign investors and governments hold more than 40 percent of the U.S. public debt. The biggest holders of the U.S. Treasury bills are China and Japan, holding more than $1 trillion, and then the U.K.

There are at least two political views regarding the debt: the first view is that the United States will become stuck in a "debt trap" like under-developed countries with high debt limiting growth, which itself leads to more debt. The second view is that the U.S. government can handle debt as far as the country can afford to print more money. The U.S. dollar is considered a world reserve currency as far as the U.S. economy grows every year.

There is a worry from some economists that a large accumulation of government debts can drag the economy into recession. In this case, the investors could lose confidence in the U.S. Government's ability to control large amounts of debt and could be asking for higher interest rates for the U.S. Treasury securities. As a result, this could increase further the public deficit, and the increased borrowing could turn into a debt spiral, which could require a sudden change in fiscal policy by eventually applying government spending cuts or tax increases. Another conspiracy theory about the U.S. dollar is that if the U.S. dollar continues to weaken, it could lead to a significant decrease in demand for the U.S. dollar and U.S. dollar-backed securities. This means that the United States won't be able to sell off its debts to foreign countries. However, this scenario is unlikely to happen.

Economists and policymaker experts have tried to put different strategies to balance the federal budget of the United States of America and reduce debt. Most of these strategies include a combination of deep spending cuts and tax increases for healthy and rich and other categories to bend the debt curve. The most optimistic policymakers believe that the U.S. Federal Government could continue to expand public debt for many years into the future with very few consequences, thanks to the trust the investors have and have had in the U.S. economy since the end of WWII. On the other side, the less optimistic politicians and economists believe the reservoir of trust the U.S. economy has accumulated might be reduced year over year, which could increase the risk of a debt crisis.

From Government Sovereign Debt to Government Shareholder's Equity

Governments in both developed and developing countries have at least two options to reduce the debt-to-GDP ratio: first, they need to run fiscal surpluses large enough to repay the debt, and second, raise nominal GDP growth. The growth of the debt-to-GDP ratio is given by a simple equation that describes the relationship between a country's primary balance, the interest rate it pays on debt, and the growth rate of nominal GDP. A country's primary balance or fiscal balance normally excludes the interest payment, and the growth rate of nominal GDP depends on the inflation rate and real GDP growth rate. Therefore, the debt-to-GDP ratio is written as,

$$D_t = \left(\left[\frac{1+i_t}{1+g_t}\right] D_{t-1}\right) - Prim_t \qquad (6.14)$$

where *Dt* is the projected government debt-to-GDP ratio for the next period, *(1+i)t* is the interest rate on a government bond, *(1+g)t* is the nominal GDP growth forecast, *Dt-1* is the current government debt-to-GDP ratio, and *Prim*t is the primary balance of the government. The importance of the equation above is that it highlights the role of interest rates in controlling government debt. Fortuitously, the governments in different countries have profited from very low-interest rates since the 2008 financial crisis until the start of the pandemic waves in 2020-2023. Therefore, despite the fact that the government debt has increased relatively, interest payments have consistently decreased, which has given many national governments a powerful tool to use cheap capital to finance government spending.

A simple definition of a budget deficit is that the budget deficit is the rate of change of the stock of debt. The rate of change in the stock of real debt is given as,

$$D'(t) = [G(t)-T(t)] + r(t)\, D(t) \qquad (6.15)$$

where *D(t)* is the debt outstanding at period t, *G(t)* denotes the government purchases and *T(t)* is the taxes at time *t*, and *r(t)* is the real interest rate at period *t*. The above equation implies that the rate of change in the stock of real debt equals the difference between the government's spending and revenues plus the real interest on its debt. The term in square brackets on the right side of the equation (6.15) indicates the primary deficit (Romer, 2001). The primary deficit is often a better way to show how fiscal policy at a given period is contributing to the government's budget constraint. The government must run primary surpluses large enough to offset the primary deficit.

Governments face budget constraints, which means that the present value of government purchases and services must be less than or equal to the government's initial wealth. The budget constraint can be expressed as the value of a unit of output at time *t* discounted back to period 0. By denoting *G(t)* the government's real spending, *T(t)* the government's revenue through taxes at time *t*, and *D(0)* the initial real debt outstanding, we have that the government's budget constraint is given as,

$$\int_{t=0}^{\infty} a^{-R(t)}\, G(t)dt \leq -D(0) + \int_{t=0}^{\infty} a^{-R(t)} \mathrm{T(t)dt} \qquad (6.16)$$

where *R(t)* is the real interest rate at time *t*, and $a^{-R(t)}$ is the value of a unit of output at time *t* discounted back to time 0, and *D(0)* is the debt entered as negative into the budget constraint. By introducing the primary deficit from (6.15), we can rewrite the government budget constraint above in the following form,

$$\int_{t=0}^{\infty} a^{-R(t)}\, [T(t) - G(t)]dt \geq -D(0) \qquad (6.17)$$

The above equation of government budget constraint means that government must run primary surpluses in the present value to offset the initial debt at period 0. There are at least four possible paths to reduce government debt ratios: 1) make fiscal adjustments to reduce fiscal deficits, 2) increase GDP growth through productivity improvements, 3) raise inflation targets and 4) restructure sovereign debt (Stiglitz, 2014).

The first path consists of making fiscal adjustments to repay the debt, which requires the government to maintain significant fiscal surpluses to cover debt service in the long run. This path is not easy to achieve. For example, a country moving from a fiscal deficit of 3.0 percent of GDP to a surplus of at least 2.0 percent of GDP would require a shift of 5.0 percent of GDP. This achievement would require tough, unpopular choices about increasing taxes and cutting government spending.

The second path of reducing the government debt ratio consists of increasing the real GDP growth through productivity improvements and structural reforms. Based on this path, countries are required to generate more growth than projected to see government debt ratios reduced, especially in the most indebted countries. For example, in an indebted country, the GDP must grow by 2.0-2.5 percent points faster than the planned growth of 1.5 percent to reach at least a growth rate of 4.0 percent per year to start seeing a reduction in the government debt ratio.

The third path of reducing the government debt ratio consists of raising the inflation target to boost nominal GDP growth, which is part of the denominator of equation (6.14) to reduce the debt ratio. If the government debt is held in local currency, rising inflation will reduce the amount government has to pay back to investors. In recent years inflation has remained at low levels despite interest rates being at a record low which has not helped reduce the debt ratio (the exception is the year 2022, with the war in Ukraine and inflation skyrocketing).

The fourth path to reduce the government debt ratio consists of restructuring the sovereign debt. Sovereign debt restructuring comes with a high price, including austerity policies such as government spending cuts and increasing taxes. However, if nothing is done to restructure sovereign debt, it may generate a financial crisis and, consequently, deep recession; therefore, a default is considered a last resort. For some countries with increased government debt in recent years, the absence of political will to continue with austerity and the inability to recover from crisis and pick up a growth path have left these countries with no options but to try new tools to restructure the sovereign debt.

The International Monetary Fund (IMF) suggests several reforms to enable sovereign debt restructuring to progress more proficiently (IMF staff report, 2014, 1-48). The IMF recognizes contractual reforms intended to address collective action problems through *Collective Agreement Clauses (CAC)* in a few countries facing a sovereign debt restructuring. Most of the contractual provisions are made by the sovereign issuer and its creditors. Therefore, the role of the IMF is to facilitate agreements on the design and use of the provisions.

After over two centuries of government debt in the early modern era, it has come time to discuss another path based on a completely different logic for reducing government debt. This logic emphasizes a different way of raising money using the capital market, which is normally used by public and private corporations. This is not a new concept, but rather a different perspective and a different logic to develop this concept.

The question is: Can a Sovereign government debt become a Government Shareholder's equity? Can a government issue securities in equity?

In public finance, government debt, also known as sovereign debt, is the total amount of all debt owed at a point in time by a government to domestic lenders or to foreign lenders. How does the capital market work?

There is a large amount of literature in finance regarding capital markets and how companies use them to raise funds. As per definition, capital markets are financial markets in which securities are issued to raise medium to long-term financing and where market participants trade those securities. Securities are financial assets that are traded and represent either an ownership position in a corporation (a share) or a creditor relationship with a government body or a corporation (a bond).

Capital markets serve two purposes. First, they work as a channel for the demand and supply of debt and equity capital. This means that they channel the money provided by savers and depository institutions to borrowers and investees through the sale and purchase of securities (bonds and shares). Second, they provide a secondary market where holders of these securities can exchange them with one another at market prices. Capital markets are widely regulated. Financial regulators, such as the U.K.'s Bank of England, the U.S. Securities and Exchange Commission (SEC), or the Ontario Securities Commission in Canada, oversee the capital markets in their respective jurisdictions, among other things, to protect investors against fraud.

Companies use the capital markets to raise funds needed to finance activities such as buying manufacturing facilities, warehouses, equipment, and inventories, conducting research and development, and supporting essential corporate activities. Much of the money comes from major institutions such as pension funds, insurance companies, investment funds, banks, foundations, government grants, colleges, and universities. In addition, there are also individual investors wishing to earn interest or dividends on their savings and use capital markets to buy positions in securities they consider attractive. The capital market has two components: the stock market and the bond market. The stock market is where shares of publicly traded companies are issued, bought, and sold. This market allows companies to access capital in return for giving the investor proportionate ownership in the company. Investors can then buy and sell these shares. The bond market is where bonds are issued by corporations and governments. A bond is a debt instrument that has a fixed interest rate and maturity date.

Shareholder's equity, per definition, is how much owners of a company have invested in the business, either by investing money in shares and receiving dividends or by retaining earnings over time. On the balance sheet, shareholders' equity is broken down into three categories: common shares, preferred shares, and retained earnings.

Issuing securities: from finance, we know that the sale of new securities is affected by general market conditions. Corporations, in general, try to sell new shares during a rising market where the demand for new shares is particularly strong so they can realize the highest prices for their shares. There are a few steps to issue new securities in a corporation as follows:

1-) The Board of Directors must approve the issuance of securities. The next important decision is whether to sell the securities through a private placement or a public offering. To be listed on a stock exchange, the listing requirements must be met. Companies must meet a threshold of revenues or assets to qualify for listing, which can vary by the stock exchange.

2-) The next step is to hire an investment bank to act as the company's underwriter. An underwriter assists with the issuing process by advising on the offer price and helping to market and sell the new securities.

3-) If a private placement is to be completed, the investment bank will prepare an offering memorandum and help sell the issue to interested private investors.

4-) For a public offering, the company must decide on the method of a public issue to be used based on two types: a cash offer and an a-rights offer. In a cash offer, the securities are offered to the public as part of the public offering. In a-rights offer, the securities are offered to existing shareholders in proportion to their current holdings.

5-) If a cash offer is being made, the company must decide on the type of underwriting arrangement: a bought deal, a firm commitment, a best-effort arrangement, or a Dutch auction.

6-) The next step is to prepare, finalize, and file the necessary documents, including the prospectus. The underwriter will use this prospectus for marketing the shares. A prospectus is a written document prepared by the issuer outlining the number of funds to be raised in the offering, the nature and terms of the securities to be issued, the use of the funds, a description of the issuer's business and strategy, and historical financial statements.

7-) The last step is for the underwriter to advise on the final offer price. Once this is known, the prospectus is finalized, the regulators give their final approval, and the shares can start to trade on the primary market for the first offering.

Investors buy these newly issued shares, and the issuing company receives in exchange the cash on sale. Later, shares and bonds are sold subsequently in the secondary market, where investors buy securities from other investors. The buying and selling of securities in the secondary market allow investors to liquidate their holdings when necessary. In the secondary market, it is the selling investor who receives the cash on sale and the buying investor who pays the cash to receive ownership of the security. Transactions in the secondary market create the ability to freely trade security which in finance is known as *liquidity*. Liquidity is the ability in which assets can be converted into cash. The creation of liquidity through the existence of a secondary market increases the inclination of investors to invest in the primary market, as they rely on the secondary market to liquidate their position in case they need cash to invest elsewhere. Prices in the secondary market are influenced by past and new information.

How can a sovereign government issue government securities in equity like a public corporation?

Based on the steps to issue new securities in a corporation, we think that a sovereign government can follow similar steps to issue government securities:

1-) The government does not have a board of directors like a private or public company; however, it can have an agency or finance department that decides how the securities can be issued. Government securities are different from government bonds as they do not represent debt but rather "ownership" of the underlying government's projects, such as highways, ports, airports, power-generating corporations, etc.

2-) The second step is when government creates a legal document that outlines the conditions under which the securities can be issued and underlies the projects that government needs to accomplish with the money received from securities, such as building roads, ports, hospitals, schools, airports, factories, etc. Government officials must also decide how the securities will be sold in the primary market. Like the issuance of government bonds for government securities as well, the government can offer security auctions and invites multiple underwriters to attend and participate in the bidding process.

3-) The third step is to prepare a preliminary official statement or disclosure document to deliver to potential buyers. This document is very important as it tells investors what projects the government is going to undertake with the money raised from public offerings. In addition, this document should specify how the government is going to pay dividends to investors like a profitable public corporation. The government should pay dividends to the holders of government securities when the national economy is doing well and growing so the securities can be more liquid and tradeable in the secondary market. If the economy is not doing well during a fiscal year - as in a normal profitable company - the dividends are retained by the government and reinvested in different projects to help the economy grow. This document should also state how long the security is going to trade in the secondary market: one year, two years, five years, ten years, or more. Differently from the shares of a public corporation that do not expire, government securities should have a time limit after which they should expire. At the expiration date, the government should pay back the original issued amount to all investors holding them. Investors typically examine the price, risk, trade value in the secondary market, and expected dividends of each government security offering before deciding to place a bid.

4-) The fourth step is the legal requirement for government securities to hold a public meeting after a reasonable marketing period. During this marketing period, usually lasting one, two, or a few weeks, potential purchasers go thoroughly review and evaluate the disclosure document. When the government holds a government securities auction, each group of investors submits its purchase bid during public meetings. The auction continues until all the government securities are consequently distributed.

5-) The fifth and last step is when the underwriters pay the purchase price of government-issued securities to the paying agent, who pays the cost of issuance to the government agency in charge of issuing the securities. The role of the agent is to make sure that raised funds are accordantly distributed based on the intended purpose of the securities issue. After the closure of the distribution, a complete set of closing documents are distributed to each investor participating in the auction. Then the government securities can start to trade on the primary market for the first offering. Individual investors working with a financial institution or brokers can buy and sell previously issued government securities in the secondary market.

Those governments deciding to get financed through government-issued securities have a duty to investors to ensure that the issues are liquid, marketable, and of a size enough to guarantee a tradable market. These factors guarantee the marketability of the government's securities issue and make it more attractive to potential domestic and international investors. A few months before the end of the securities life (2, 3, 5, or 10 years), the government announced that the government securities are going to retire on a certain date (retirement date) at the original issue value, or they will be renewed for another term. If the government is not able to pay the original face value of the securities to the investors, then the investors have the right to claim shares in government-owned entities such as government-run-companies, ports, airports, highways, power generation facilities, government-owned lands, mining rights, etc.

Representatives of the investors or holders of the government issued-securities must participate in the government meetings opened to investors to discuss the government infrastructure spending and ongoing projects that are financed by government issued-securities. These meetings have the purpose of helping recall government responsibilities in front of investors for cost overruns and other problems associated with these projects.

The difference between Government issued-bonds and Government issued-securities

Government Bonds	Government Securities
Issued by Government used to raise capital for various projects such as infrastructure and other spendings. The bond issue is for both, Mandatory Spending and Discretionary Spending.	Issued by the Government for various projects such as infrastructure spending, government projects, etc. The government-issued securities are only for Discretionary Spending.
Government bonds are also used by Central Bank to control the nation's money supply.	Government-issued securities are used by Government to finance specific large-scale projects in infrastructure, such as roads, bridges, ports, airports, subways, hospitals, power generation companies, etc. No involvement from the central bank.
Pay fixed rate interest every 3 months, 6 months, or 12 months.	Pay dividends if economy is doing well and growing. Otherwise, no dividends.
Not marketable in the secondary market	Marketable in the secondary market.
Face value stays the same throughout the bond duration	Fair value of the securities is based on the market. Goes up or down based on the performance of the national economy, using parameters such as employment rate, inflation, interest rate, tax revenue, GDP growth rate, etc.
Yields change daily	No yields
The expiration date has been determined since the beginning of the bond issue.	The expiration date could change based on the market value, and government needs to issue new securities and retire the old ones.
Government bonds have a high cost for some governments, such as those in developing countries where government bonds are not so liquid, so they would pay high fixed interest rates to attract investors.	Government securities do not have high costs as they do not pay interest but rather dividends. However, the government is not required to pay dividends if the economy is not performing well.
Government bonds are used for both developed and developing countries.	Government-issued securities are used by both developed and developing countries as an easy and cheap way to raise funds, mainly for infrastructure projects.
Governments that are unable to pay interest (cash payments) on bonds go into default.	Governments unable to pay the original face value of the securities will have to transfer government-owned company shares to the holders of the government securities at the retired date. Government has another option to convert them into Government-bonds.
Public debt or sovereign government debt increases year over year if not checked and may not be manageable in the long run.	Public debt remains stable or decreases as Shareholder's equity increases, however manageable in the long run.
	Holders of government-issued securities can participate in government meetings opened to investors regarding the projects financed by the sale of these securities. This increases the responsibility of the government on ongoing public projects, so the money is spent accordingly.

The scope of government-issued-securities is to help heavily indebted developing countries to reduce the debt-to-GDP ratio by converting the debt-raising capacity to a hybrid debt-securities-raising capacity to translate the borrowed money into economic growth, keeping inflation stable and trying to raise the level of the household's standard of living. The securities-raising method regarding government spending should be used mostly for *Discretionary Spending*, such as transportation, infrastructure, roads, ports, airports, hospitals, generation power facilities, etc., that help grow the national economy, and not for *Mandatory Spending*, such as social security, education, retirement insurance, disability insurance, hospital insurance for the aged, drug benefit, etc. which instead should be covered by a combination of government-issued bonds and tax revenue.

Before the end of the government-issued-securities life government can have a general meeting with the representatives of the holders of government securities to decide how to proceed with security retirement and renewal. This meeting will announce the date securities will be "frozen" and pulled out of the secondary market for retirement. Here as well, the government has at least three options based on the market value of the government-issued securities on the retirement date:

Options for the retirement of government-issued securities

Option 1	**Option 2**	**Option 3**
Market Value < Original issued value	Market Value > Original issued value	Market Value > Original issued value
The government pays the original-issued value of securities to investors as lump-sum payout or as deferred payments. This has a higher cost for the government if the economy is not performing well and the fair value of securities is lower than the book value.	The government pays the original-issued value and, in addition, converts the portion of the difference between market value and original-issued value to government bonds with fixed interests.	If Government is unable to pay the original-issued value, it has the option to transfer a portion (less than 50%) of the ownership of the government-owned companies to the government securities holders.
Or government securities are renewed for another term and kept trading in the secondary market, and the government continues to pay dividends.	Or government securities are renewed for another term and kept trading in the secondary market, and the government continues to pay dividends.	Or government securities are renewed for another term and kept trading in the secondary market, and the government continues to pay dividends.

There are advantages and disadvantages to each method of raising funds for government spending.

Government Debt-raising Method:

Advantages:

- There is a steady interest income return
- Low risk of default for the bonds issued by the government of developed countries.
- There is a liquid market for reselling
- Government bonds are assessable through mutual funds and Exchange Trade Funds (ETF).

Disadvantages:

- Government bonds offer low rates of return
- In some countries, fixed income from bonds falls behind with rising inflation
- There is a carry risk when market interest rates increase
- There is a default and other risks on foreign bonds issued from developing countries
- In many jurisdictions, interest income from Treasury securities is subject to federal/government income tax

Government-issued-securities-raising method:

Advantages:

- There is no risk of default
- There is a liquid market for reselling them in the secondary market
- Steady dividend payments when the national economy performs well
- Market value increase in the secondary market when the national economy performs well. Investors could buy and resell government securities for a capital gain or a quick rate of return.
- Convertible in government-owned companies' shares or government bonds.

Disadvantages:

- If the national economy goes into recession, there are no dividend payments
- There is a risk for government securities to underperform if parameters such as employment rate, inflation, interest rate, tax revenue, and GDP growth rate are not performing well as forecasted.
- Capital gains are taxable when government securities are sold at a profit.

As illustrated below, the government-issued-securities strategy can also be used to save big banks and other financial intuitions on the brink of collapse.

Government Shareholder's equity strategy to save big Banks

The government-issued securities can be used to save large public corporations and big banks on the brink of bankruptcy, which are important and too big to fail for an economy. Rather than using a bailout strategy, as happened in 2008 when President George W. Bush and U.S. Congress decided to purchase with the taxpayer's money failing assets of big banks and other financial institutions in the U.S. ahead of the Great Recession, the government could have the option of using a different and more effective strategy to rescue big banks.

The government's first step is to nationalize the big banks by buying their shares at the market value, using taxpayers' money, so they don't fail and collapse with huge repercussions in capital markets. The second step is to issue new government securities (with a security life of 2, 3, 5, or 10 years) on the primary market for the first offering, which are correlated to the 'ownership' of underlying government projects which, in this case, are the big banks to save. By acting in this way, the government can cash in the money from the primary market offering and use a portion of it to recover the taxpayers' money used in the bailout and purchase of shares of the failing banks and another portion to inject money into the failing banks, so they can start repairing their balance sheets. At the end of the government-issued-securities life, the government will have a general meeting with the investors and representatives of the holders of government securities used to save big banks from deciding how to proceed with the retirement of these securities. Based on the market value of the government-issued-securities, the government can opt to transfer the ownership of the 'repaired' big banks to investors and owners of the government-issued-securities or renew for another term and keep trading in the secondary market and continue to pay dividends. The government-issued-securities strategy is a more efficient approach to saving the failing assets of big banks and other large corporations, as it quickly recovers the taxpayer's money.

The budget deficit can now be expressed in a hybrid form using both the rate of change of the stock of debt $D(t)$ and the government issued-securities stock $S(t)$. The rate of change of the combination of the stock of real debt $D'(t)$ and government equity $S'(T)$ can be rewritten from equation (6.15) into a hybrid form as,

$$D'(t)+ S'(t) = [\, G(t)-T(t)] +r\,(t)\, D(t)+d(t)S(t) \qquad (6.18)$$

where $D(t)$ is the government debt outstanding at period t, $G(t)$ denotes the government purchases, $T(t)$ is the taxes at time t, and $r(t)$ is the real interest rate at period t, $S(t)$ is the government issued-securities outstanding, and $d(t)$ is the dividend payable at period *t*. The above equation implies that the rate of change in the stock of real debt and government equity equals the difference between the government's spending and revenues plus the real interest on its debt and eventual dividends payable on outstanding equity. The term in square brackets on the right side of (6.18) indicates the primary deficit. The government must run primary surpluses in the present value to offset the initial debt at period 0 and the primary deficits. However, the budget deficit and real stock of debt can be reduced if government incurs more often spending (discretionary spending) using government issued-securities which reduces the real interest payments on debt, given that dividends payable on government securities are not consistent and often are subject to changes. As per equation (6.18), we have that a change in the trend of the stock of real debt and government equity is shown as,

$$D'(t)\downarrow + S'(t)\uparrow = [\,G(t)-T(t)] + r\,(t)\,D(t)\downarrow + d(t)S(t) \qquad (6.19)$$

where debt outstanding D'(t)↓ is decreasing, government-equity S'(t)↑ is increasing, total interest payments on debt r (t) D(t)↓ is decreasing, and dividend payments on equity d(t)S(t) stay the same or decreases during the economic downturn and increases during economic growth. Consequently, the government must increase the government-issued-securities program to reduce the stock of real debt and offset the primary deficit even without running large primary surpluses.

Conclusions

In this chapter, we have seen that in a low-interest rate environment, monetary policy cannot fulfill its mission. Therefore fiscal expansion is then vital to sustain demand and mitigate the long-term costs of the crisis. So far, we have seen that monetary policy transmission is less effective when interest rates are consistently low. The low-interest rate could reduce the effectiveness because borrowers may not be willing to borrow, and lenders may not be ready to lend, which increases the uncertainty among households and firms and could contribute to the deterioration of the impact of monetary stimulus.

It also discussed how fiscal policy operates under a low-interest environment. And we have seen how a well-planned fiscal policy can help recover the economy much faster. An increase in the neutral interest rates will reduce public savings and limit the constraining effect of the zero-lower bond. Increased public investments help growth by sustaining demand and by facilitating the return to the labor market of unemployed people during the recession.

In this chapter, we have also talked about the two main criticisms of the AD-AS model, which is considered logically inconsistent and empirically unrealistic. Based on the AD-AS model debate, we uncovered that the logical discrepancy between the "AD" curve and the short-run "AS" curve depends on the specific nature of the "AS" curve, which comprises an unrealistic short-run aggregate supply curve and a vertical long-run aggregate supply curve. In addition, the main logical inconsistency between the "AD" curve and the labor market AS curve was that these two curves are based on two completely different and reciprocally inconsistent theories of output in the AD-AS model. On the one hand, the "AD" curve was basically founded on the Keynesian IS-LM theory of output, and on the other hand, the labor market "AS" curve was based on a labor market theory of output, which increases the inconsistency and seems to be unrealistic in practice.

Later in the chapter, we discussed what the real aggregate demand in an economy pricing system is. We explained that the global aggregate demand for an economy should be split between the aggregate demand for the private sector, public sector, and import-export sector. The aggregate demand of the private sector in an economy pricing system is measured as the total demand of all finished goods, premium and non-premium, produced in different sectors of the economy. For the aggregate supply, we described that the aggregate supply of the private sector was given by the aggregate production capacity utilization of all firms offering premium and non-premium products within an economy at a given period.

In this chapter, we have also seen how in economy pricing, a money-model with low-interest rates has an LM curve representing the money market equilibrium which is a set of points in equilibrium between liquidity preference (demand for money) and the money supply function at a given low-interest rate. The intersection of the IS and LM curves shows the equilibrium of sales prices and non-sales prices during sales and non-sales-events and output when money markets and the real economy are in equilibrium in a low-interest environment. This equilibrium explains how the low-interest rate does not affect the demand for money, given that it operates in a low-interest environment. In fact, in economy pricing, the only parameter that affects the demand for money is the discounted price offered for the sales of non-premium and premium products during seasonal and off-seasonal sales. The higher the discount price offered for multi-products, the higher the demand for cash money and disposable income from the public.

We have also perceived how public debt and fiscal policy affect the real economy. A government can sustain the same level of debt by running small deficits forever for years and even decades if GDP is increasing because GDP is a close substitution for the tax base. There is a positive impact on public debt when GDP is growing. The higher the GDP, the higher the tax base of the government, and the higher the level of economic growth, which can result in more additional debt the government can take on each period. However, there is also the risk that a large accumulation of government debts can drag the economy into recession. If this happens, the investors could lose confidence in the Government's ability to control large amounts of debt and could be asking for higher interest rates for government bonds. As a result, this could further increase the public deficit and increase borrowing, turning into a debt spiral, which could require a sudden change in fiscal policy, such as government spending cuts or tax increases which could hurt a large portion of the population. The fiscal policy has tried to create a trade-off between the commitment to keep under control spending in prosperous periods and having the flexibility to react quickly during economic shocks and financial crises using some optimal fiscal rules, such as escape clauses, etc.

The last segment of the chapter talked about a new theory of how Government Sovereign debt could be converted to Government Shareholder's Equity. The scope of government issued-securities was to help heavily indebted developing countries to reduce the debt-to-GDP ratio by converting the debt-raising capacity to a hybrid debt-securities-raising capacity to translate the borrowed money into economic growth, keeping inflation stable and, at the same time, trying to raise large funds to invest in infrastructure and elevate the level of the household's standard of living. The government-issued-securities raising method, regarding government spending, is advised to be used for *Discretionary Spending*, such as transportation and infrastructure, and not much for *Mandatory Spendings*, such as social security programs and education, which should be covered by a combination of government-issued bonds and tax revenue.

Bibliography

Adobe Analytics' Digital Economy Index 2021. March 15, 2022.

Amitabh R, S., and Evans J, R. 2005. *Principles of Operations Management.* Mason, OH: Thomson/South-Western.

Bankruptcy and Insolvency Act (RSC, 1985, c. B-3). www://laws-lois.Justice.qc. Ca >acts.

Barthwal, R. R. 2007. *Industrial Economics: An Introductory Textbook.* p. 31.

Basuroy, S., Chatterjee, S., and Ravid, S. A. 2003. "How critical are critical reviews? The box office effects of film critics, star power, and budgets." *Journal of Marketing,* 67(4), pp. 103–117.

Bekaert, G., Hoerova, M., and Lo Duca, M. 2013. "Risk, Uncertainty and Monetary Policy." *Journal of Monetary Economics,* 60(7), pp. 771-788.

Benjamin, H. C., Hordahl, P., and Xia, D. 2018. "Term Premia: Model and some Stylized Facts." BIS, *Quarterly Review,* pp. 70-91.

Bernard, A. B., Jensen, J. B., Redding, S. J., and Schott, P. K., 2007. "Firms in International Trade." *Journal of Economic Perspectives,* 21(3), pp. 105-130.

Bernard, A. B., Jensen, J. B., Redding, S. J., and Schott, P.K., 2010. "Multi-Product Firms and Product Switching." *American Economic Review,* 100(1), pp. 70-97.

Bernard, A. B., Jensen, J. B., Redding, S. J., and Schott, P. K., 2011. "Multiproduct Firms and the Trade Liberalization." *Quarterly Journal of Economics,* 126(3), pp. 1271-1318

Berndt, E., and Morrison, J., 1981. "Capacity utilization measures: Underlying Economic Theory and an Alternative Approach." *American Economic Review,* 71, pp. 48–52.

Bindseil, U. 2004. "The Operational Target of Monetary Policy and the Rise and Fall of Reserves Doctrine Position." *ECB Working Paper,* no. 372.

Blix, M. 2015. *The Economy and Digitalization—Opportunities and Challenges.* Research Institute of Industrial Economics, pp. 1-203

Blanchard, O. J. 1985. "Debt, Deficits, and Finite Horizons." *Journal of Political Economy,* 93(2), pp. 223–47.

Borio, C. 2014. "The Financial Cycle and Macroeconomics: What have we learnt?" *Journal of Banking and Finance,* vol. 45, pp. 182-198.

Brancaccio, E., and Fontana, G. 2011. *The Global Economic Crisis: New Perspectives on the Critique of Economic Theory and Policy.* Oxon, UK: Routledge.

Brancaccio, E. and Fontana, G. 2015. "Solvency Rule and Capital Centralization in a Monetary Union." *Cambridge Journal of Economics,* advance access online, DOI: 10.1093/cje/bev068.

Bureau of Labor Statistics (BLS). Year published, 2020, Labor Department www.usinflationcalculator.com/inflation/historical-inflation-rates.

Cochrane, J. H. 2014. "Monetary policy with interest on reserves." *Journal* of *Economic Dynamics* and *Control,* Elsevier, vol. 49(C), pages 74-108.

Colander, D. 1995. "The stories we tell: A reconsideration of ASAD analysis." *Journal of Economic Perspectives,* 9(3), pp. 169–188.

Congressional Research Service. 2021. "Unemployment Rate during Covid-19 Pandemic", *CRS report, R46554,* August 2021.

Corrado, C., and Mattey, J. 1997. "Capacity Utilization." *Journal of Economic Perspectives,* 11(1), pp. 151-167.

CPI, 2023 (*Consumer Price Index, Province of British Columbia*), published in: www2.gov.bc.ca>data>statistics>economy, January 17, 2023.

Friedman, M., and Schwartz A. J. 2008. *A Monetary History of the United States, 1867-1960.* Princeton University Press.

FRED. 2019. *Economic Data: Economic Research, Federal Reserve Bank of St.* Louis, St Louis, Fed 2019.

Fullwiler, S. T. 2006. "Setting Interest Rates in the Modern Money Era." *Journal of Post Keynesian Economics,* 28(3), pp. 495-525.

Gali, J. 2015. *Monetary Policy, Inflation, and the Business Cycle: An Introduction to the New Keynesian Framework and Its Applications.* Second Edition. Princeton: Princeton University Press.

Garcia-Schmidt, M., and Woodford, M. 2015. "Are low-interest rates deflationary? A paradox of perfect foresight analysis." *Conference on Deflation, Sveriges Riksbank,* 2015, pp 1-93.

Geoffrey, A. J., and Philip, J. R. 2011. "Advanced Microeconomic Theory", Third Edition, Pearson, Harlow, England.

Gibillini, N. 2021. "Canada's big Banks are Seeing their Profits Soar. Here's How they're Making their Money." *The Canadian Press. Global News,* a division of Corus Entertainment Inc. Posted in May 30, 2021.

Gordon, R. J. 2011. "The History of the Phillips Curve: Consensus and Bifurcation." *Economica,* 78(309), pp. 10-50.

Gordon, R. J. 2018. "Why Has Economic Growth Slowed When Innovation Appears to be Accelerating?" *NBER Working Paper Series, Working Paper 24554,* Cambridge, MA 02138, pp. 1-27.

Gray, S. 2011. "Central Bank Balances and Reserve Requirements." IMF, Working Paper WP/11/36, pp.1-55.

Grieve, R. 1996. "Aggregate demand, aggregate supply, a Trojan Horse and a Cheshire Cat." *Journal of Economic Studies,* No.23, pp. 64-82.

Hallowell, B. C., and Williamson, K. M. 1961. "Debt Management's Contribution to Monetary Policy." *Review of Economics and Statistics,* 43(1), pp. 81-84.

Hannoun, H. 2015. "Ultra-low or Negative Interest Rates: What They Mean for Financial Stability and Growth." *Bank for International Settlements,* Eurofi High-Level Seminar, Riga, April 22, 2015.

Heijdra, B. J. 2017. *Foundations of Modern Macroeconomics.* Third Edition. Oxford University Press: Oxford, UK.

Hilton, R., Maher, M., and Selto, F. 2004. *Cost Management: Strategies for Business Decisions.* Fourth edition. McGraw-Hill Irwin.

Hornstein, A., and Kudlyak, M. 2020. "Why Is Current Unemployment So Low?" *Federal Reserve Bank of San Francisco, Working Paper Series 2020-05,* pp. 1-23.

Hutchison, T. W. 1953. *A review of economic doctrines, 1870–1929.* Oxford: Oxford University Press.

Hutchison, T. W. 1978. *On revolutions and progress in economic knowledge.* Cambridge: Cambridge University Press.

IMF staff report. 2014. *Strengthening the Contractual Framework to Address Collective Action Problems in Sovereign Debt Restructuring.* Staff paper, Sept. 2014, pp. 1.48.

Jaffe, W. 1975. "Menger, Jevons and Walras dehomogenized." *Economic Inquiry,* 14, pp. 511–524.

Johnson, J. 2023. "What Is ERP Software, and How Can It Increase Efficiency?" *Business.com.,* Contributing Writer, Updated. January 23, 2023.

Kass, D. I. 1998. "Economies of Scope and Home Healthcare." *Health Services Research* 33(4).

Kirmani, A., and Rao, A. R. 2000. "No pain, no gain: A critical review of the literature on signaling unobservable product quality." *Journal of Marketing,* 64(2), 66–79.

Koo, C. R. 2014. "The Escape from Balance Sheet Recession and the QE Trap: A Hazardous Road for the World Economy." *John Wiley & Sons Singapore Pte Ltd, 1st edition.*

Laurence, M. B., and Mazumder S. 2011. "*Inflation Dynamics and the Great Recession.*" NBER, Working Paper no. 17044, May 2011, pp. 337-405.

Lavoie, M. 2013. "The Monetary and Fiscal Nexus of Neo-Chartalism: A Friendly Critique." *Journal of Economic Issues,* 47(1), pp. 1-31.

Leeper, E. M., and Leith. C. 2016. "Understanding Inflation as a Joint Monetary-Fiscal Phenomenon." NBER Working Paper No. 21867, pp. 1-125.

Lepetit, L., Strobel, F., and Dickinson, D. 2011. "Does Uncertainty Matter for Loan Charge-offs." *Journal of International Financial Markets, Institutions and Money,* vol. 22, pp. 264-277.

Levinson, J. and Petrin, A. 2003. "Estimating production function using inputs to control unobservables." *Review of Economic Studies,* 70, pp. 317-341.

Maas, H. 2005. *William Stanley Jevons and the making of modern economics.* Cambridge: Cambridge University Press.

Masse M., and Beaudry, P. 2016. *The State of Competition in Canada's Telecommunications Industry-2016.* Montreal Economic Institute, pp. 1-48.

Menger, C. 1871. *Principles of Economics.* Translated by J. Dingwall and B. F. Hoselitz, with an introduction by Friedrich A. Hayek. New York: New York University Press.

Meulendyke, A. M. 1998. *U.S. Monetary Policy and Financial Markets,* New York: Federal Reserve Bank of New York.

Milgrom, P. and Ilya, S. 2002. "Envelope Theorems for Arbitrary Choice Sets." *Econometrica,* vol. 70(2): 583–601.

Milgrom, P., and Roberts, J. 1986. "Price and advertising signals of product quality." *Journal of Political Economy,* 94(4), pp. 796–821.

Nicholson, W. 2005. *Microeconomic Theory: Basic Principles and Extensions.* Thomson/South-western, pp. 339–345.

Ostry, J. D., Ghosh, A. R., Kim, J. I., and Quereshi M. S. 2010. *Fiscal Space.* IMF Staff Position, Note 10/11, pp. 1-25.

Perloff, M. J. 2013. *Microeconomic: Theory and Applications with Calculus.* Third Edition. Pearson Addison Wesley: Boston.

Rao, B. B. 1991. "What is the matter with aggregate demand and supply?" *Australian Economic Papers,* 30(57), pp. 264-77.

Rao, B. B. 2007. "The nature of the ADAS model based on the ISLM model." *Cambridge Journal of Economics,* No. 31, pp. 413-22.

Reinhart, C. M., Reinhart, V., and Rogoff, K. 2015. "Dealing with Debt." *Journal of International Economics,* 96(1), pp. S43–S55.

Roberts, J. M. 1995. "New Keynesian economics and the Phillips curve." *Journal of Money,* Credit, and Banking, 27, pp. 975–984.

Romer, D. 2001. *Advanced Macroeconomics.* Second Edition. McGraw-Hill Irwin.

Rusticelli, E. 2015. "Rescuing the Phillips Curve: Making Use of Long-term Unemployment in the Measurement of the NAIRU." *OECD Journal: Economic Studies,* 2014(1), pp. 109-127.

Stiglitz J. E. 2014. "The World Needs a Sovereign Debt Restructuring Mechanism." *Emerging Markets.Org,* December 10, 2014.

Summers L. 2014. "U.S. Economic Prospects: Secular Stagnation, Hysteresis, and the Zero Lower Bound." *Business Economics,* 49(2), pp. 65-73.

Taussig, F. W. 1919. "Price-Fixing as Seen by a Price-Fixer." *Quarterly Journal of Economics* 33, pp. 205–241.

Taylor, J. B. 1993. "Discretion versus Policy Rules in Practice." *Carnegie-Rochester Conference Series in Public Policy,* 39 (December), pp. 195-214.

Tymoigne, E. 2014. "Modern Money Theory and Interrelations between the Treasury and the Central Bank: The Case of the United States." *Levy Economics Institute of Bard College.*

U.S. Congressional Budget Office. *The Congressional Budget Office projects ballooning U.S. debt in its 2021 long-term budget outlook. Source,* www.cbo.gov/publication/56970.

U.S. Inflation Rates. Historical data (BLS, 2020, 2022), https://data.bls.gov>timeseries.

Vickrey, W. 2008. "Marginal and Average Cost Pricing." In *The New Palgrave Dictionary of Economics.* Palgrave Macmillan, London.

Walras, L. 1969. *Elements of Pure Economics; or The Theory of Social Wealth.* Translated by William Jaffé. New York: A. M. Kelly, p. 204.

Williamson, S. D. 2014, *Macroeconomics.* Fifth edition. Pearson: Washington University, St. Louis.

Williamson, S. 2016. "Scarce Collateral, the Term Premium, and Quantitative Easing." *Journal of Economic Theory,* Vol. 164, pp. 136-65.

Woodford, M. 1995. "Price-Level Determinacy Without Control of a Monetary Aggregate." Carnegie-Rochester Conference Series on Public Policy, vol. 43, pp. 1–46.

Wray, L. R. 2012. *Modern Money Theory: A Primer on Macroeconomics for Sovereign Monetary Systems.* First Edition. New York: Palgrave Macmillan.

Yared, P. 2019. "Rising Government Debt: Causes and Solutions for a Decades-Old Trend." *Journal of Economic Perspectives,* 33(2), pp. 115–140.

Zervas, G., Proserpio, D, and Byers, J. W. 2017. "The Rise of the Sharing Economy: Estimating the Impact of Airbnb on the Hotel Industry." *Journal of Marketing Research,* 54(5), pp. 687-705.

Index

A

B

C

D

E

F

G

H

I

K

L

M

N

O

P

R

S

T

V

W

Y

Z

www.ingramcontent.com/pod-product-compliance
Lightning Source LLC
LaVergne TN
LVHW010721210926
848485LV00007B/1413/J
* 9 7 8 1 6 4 8 8 9 6 7 0 5 *